ANCIENT EGYPT

Pyramids and Hieroglyphs
Enduring Symbols of a Great Civilization

AIDAN DODSON

NEW HOLLAND

First published in 2006 by New Holland Publishers (UK) Ltd
London • Cape Town • Sydney • Auckland

2 4 6 8 10 9 7 5 3 1

www.newhollandpublishers.com

Garfield House, 86–88 Edgware Road, London W2 2EA, UK

80 McKenzie Street, Cape Town 8001, South Africa

14 Aquatic Drive, Frenchs Forest, NSW 2086, Australia

218 Lake Road, Northcote, Auckland, New Zealand

ISBN 10: 1 84537 590 4
ISBN 13: 978 1 84537 590 4

Editorial Director: Jo Hemmings
Senior Editor: Kate Michell
Assistant Editors: Kate Parker, Rose Hudson, Jo Cleere
Design & cover design: Alan Marshall and Casebourne Rose
Design Associates
Production: Joan Woodroffe
Cartography: William Smuts
Index: Richard Bird and Ingrid Lock

Reproduction by Pica Digital Pte Ltd, Singapore
Printed and bound in Singapore by Star Standard Industries (Pte) Ltd

Front cover: New Kingdom papyrus of Amenemsaf; back cover (left):
Rameses II's entrance to the temple of Luxor; back cover (middle):
'Fecundity figure' in the temple of Rameses II at Abydos; back cover
(right): Khaefre's pyramid and the tomb at Amenemonet; spine: Funerary
mask of Tjuiu, 'Royal Ornament' (lady in waiting) at the court of
Amenhotep III; half title page: King Menkauhor, as shown in an
Eighteenth Dynasty relief from the tomb of Amenemonet at Saqqara;
title page: Khaefre's pyramid and the Sphinx at Giza; page 4: Statue of
Khaefre; page 5 (top): The Step Pyramid at Saqqara, (middle) The Bent
Pyramid at Dahshur, (bottom) The pyramid of Senwosret II at Lahun.

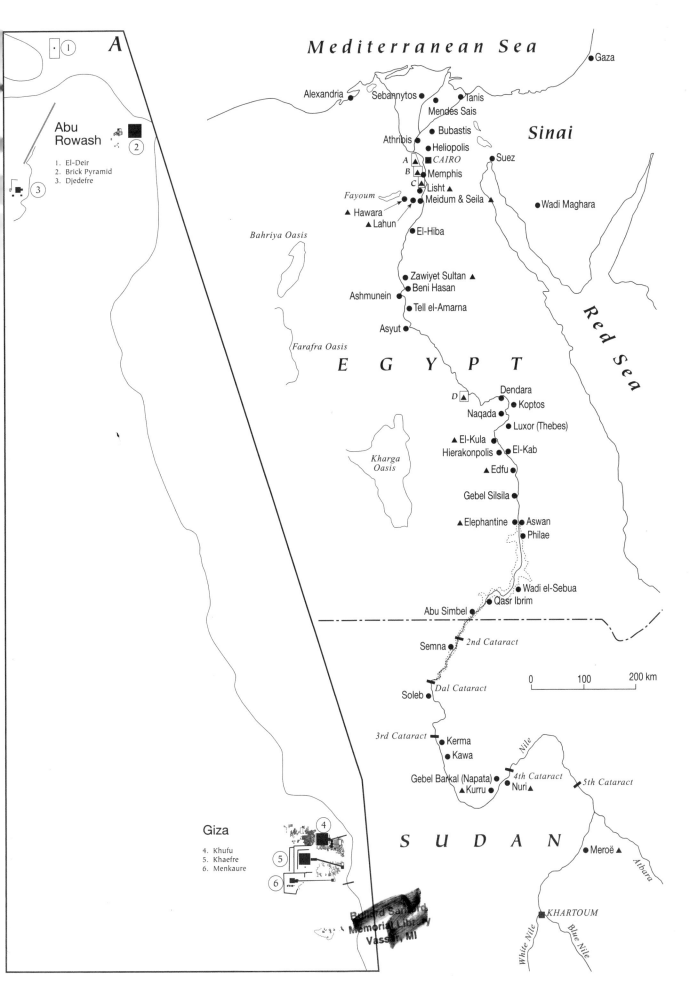

Mediterranean Sea

Gaza

Alexandria
Sebannytos
Tanis
Mendes Sais
Bubastis

Sinai

Athribis
Heliopolis
A CAIRO
B Memphis
C Lisht
Meidum & Seila

Fayoum
Hawara
Lahun
El-Hiba

Wadi Maghara

Suez

Bahriya Oasis

Zawiyet Sultan
Beni Hasan
Ashmunein
Tell el-Amarna

Asyut

Farafra Oasis

E G Y P T

Red Sea

D Dendara
Koptos
Naqada
Luxor (Thebes)
El-Kula
Hierakonpolis El-Kab
Edfu

Gebel Silsila

Kharga Oasis

Elephantine Aswan
Philae

Wadi el-Sebua
Qasr Ibrim
Abu Simbel

Semna
2nd Cataract

Soleb
Dal Cataract

0   100   200 km

3rd Cataract
Kerma
Kawa

Nile

Gebel Barkal (Napata)
Kurru
4th Cataract
Nuri
5th Cataract

S U D A N

Meroë

Atbara

KHARTOUM

White Nile
Blue Nile

A

□ ①

Abu
Rowash
■ ②
1. El-Deir
2. Brick Pyramid
3. Djedefre
③

Giza
4. Khufu
5. Khaefre
6. Menkaure
④
⑤
⑥

CONTENTS

PREFACE

If one mentions the term 'ancient Egypt', the immediate image conjured up in most minds is that of the Giza pyramids, apparently standing isolated in the desert – although in reality but a stone's throw from Cairo's western suburbs. Not far behind are the apparently mysterious, tiny pictures that make up the ancient hieroglyphic script. This volume therefore provides what are intended to be accessible illustrated guides to both the pyramids of the kings of Egypt as a whole, and to the hieroglyphs and what the Egyptian used them for.

The book also recounts how modern Egyptologists have derived our knowledge of the pyramids and the hieroglyphs. What we now know about both is the current result of some two centuries of scientific work. However, such researches are never finished and every year brings forth new facts and understandings, whether a brand-new pyramid or the comprehension of some hitherto-obscure aspect of Egyptian grammar.

However, the flow of new knowledge does not mean that the wisdom received from one's Egyptological forebears is any less valuable, and certainly not that all 'new' ideas will come to replace the 'old': what matters is what best fits all the evidence, from whatever direction it comes. It is this failure to comprehend the whole of the wide body of evidence that now exists that damns to failure a large body of literature that has appeared in recent years and has often distinctly tenuous links with reality.

These tomes include those concerned with weaving gossamer-thin theories that the pyramids – or at least the best-known ones at Giza – were built or inspired by a very ancient lost civilization (usually Atlanteans or extra-terrestrials, although you can insert your group of choice and someone will have thought of it). As to the pyramids' purpose (or at least that of the biggest one at Giza), navigation beacons for space-ships, initiation centres (Masonic or otherwise), energy-generation devices, observatories and repositories for encoded knowledge (whether or not crystal-encoded) are a random selection of 'suggestions'. They often attempt to back up their 'evidence' with misreadings of ancient texts, usually based on translations made in the 19th century, when our understanding of Egyptian vocabulary and syntax was far inferior to that of today. But rarely will such theorists actually try and learn to read the language themselves!

While this book does not aim to teach one how to read hieroglyphs, it is intended to reveal what hieroglyphs meant to the ancient inhabitants of the Nile valley. Beginning with an overview of the Egyptian language itself, we then look at the kinds of material that were committed to writing, and then the labours of the early scholars who struggled to understand them.

It is thus hoped that the reader of this book — whether planning a trip to the land of the Nile, to a museum or if simply an armchair voyager — will be brought a little closer to understanding these two manifestations of this ancient north African civilisation. To an ancient Egyptian, to speak the name of a dead person was to make them live: as we gaze on the pyramids and read the hieroglyphs in and around them, the ancient desire for eternity is fulfilled.

Aidan Dodson
Department of Archaeology
and Anthropology,
University of Bristol

Explanatory Notes

This book is intended to cover all pyramids built by the kings and queens of Egypt, but not the large number subsequently erected by private individuals, after royalty had abandoned pyramid burials at the beginning of the New Kingdom. In addition, a number of related monuments that fit into the developmental sequence of the pyramid complex, although without a truly pyramidal central feature, are included. Thus, every known king's tomb from the Third Dynasty to the opening of the Eighteenth Dynasty is covered.

For each monument the same basic data is provided, insofar as it is available. This comprises the ancient and modern designation(s) of the monument; its date; its owner; the evidence upon which this attribution is based; and the designed dimensions of the pyramid itself, insofar as they can be reconstructed from its current state. The text describes the salient features of the pyramid and its complex, highlighting the explorations of the monument in the modern era.

It may be noted that many pyramids and tombs have been given numbers or letters; royal examples are set out on pages 257–62. A large number were catalogued by Carl Richard Lepsius in the 1840s — these are the Roman numerals prefixed with the letter 'L.'. Other prefixes are used for other tombs, and the less obvious ones are included in the glossary..

INTRODUCTION

During the three millennia of Egypt's ancient history, pyramids were used for the burial of kings and queens for just over a thousand years. They varied widely in size and detail, but otherwise fitted into a basic concept for the Egyptian tomb that can be traced from the earliest times.

So what is this ancient and fascinating land that has produced such breathtaking monumental architecture?

Below: The River Nile has been the key to the life of Egypt since time immemorial. From Aswan, the southernmost city of Egypt, the river winds 800 miles (500km) to the sea.

The modern Arab Republic of Egypt (ARE) occupies nearly a million square kilometres of the north-east corner of the African continent. However, only a tiny proportion – four per cent – of the territory is inhabited. A small part of the population lives in the oases of the Western Desert, but the overwhelming majority live in a narrow strip bordering the River Nile. Indeed, the Egypt of old was defined as this strip of land. As the river flows northwards, to travel south is to go up-river: thus southern Egypt is 'Upper' Egypt, while 'Lower' Egypt comprises the Nile delta and the adjoining area around modern Cairo.

Above: Cairo – the largest city in Africa – sprawls for mile upon mile. From the ancient citadel, look through the smog and across Cairene rooftops to glimpse the pyramids of Giza on the opposite side of the city

Upper and Lower Egypt

Upper and Lower Egypt are very different. In the south, the cultivable area varies in width from nothing to a number of miles, beyond which it gives way to low desert that rapidly rises up to the arid plateaux of the Eastern (Arabian) and Western (Libyan) deserts. In contrast, the delta spreads out in a great triangle towards the Mediterranean, with mile upon mile of flat, fertile land, criss-crossed by canals and wholly dissimilar to the southern Nile valley in both appearance and ethos.

Traditionally, the ancient Egyptian state was held to have extended from the shores of the Mediterranean to Aswan; however, at many points in its history it reached much further south into Nubia, encompassing the southern part of the present ARE and the northern part of what is now the Democratic Republic of the Sudan. The lands bordering this section of the Nile, which since the building of the High Dam at Aswan in the 1960s have been swallowed up by the waters of Lake Nasser, were far more barren than those further north, and mainly of interest as a source of raw materials and a trade route to the far south. River-borne communication south of Aswan was hindered by a series of cataracts or rapids, the first just above that city, the sixth and last just below modern Khartoum.

The Gift of the Nile

It has become the ultimate cliché to describe Egypt as the 'gift of the Nile': a phrase coined by the Greek writer Hecetaeus, and almost universally misattributed to his grandson, the famous traveller Herodotus, who visited Egypt around 450 BC. By 'gift of the Nile' Hecetaeus meant that without the river, the country and its civilization would not – could not – have existed in anything like the form that is so well known. For, outside the margins of the river and the handful of oases, the country is desert.

Today, agriculture in Egypt is dependent upon year-round irrigation, made possible by a series of dams built across the river since the beginning of the 20th century. In all the preceding centuries, however, the growing of crops depended on the annual natural inundation of the Nile. In summer, rains in the Ethiopian highlands swell the river's tributaries, the Atbara and Blue Nile; today, this inundation merely restocks Lake Nasser, but in the past it led to the flooding of the entire Nile valley and delta, an inundation given divine personification as Hapy. The waters spread to cover all the agricultural land, and on receding in October–November they left behind a rich layer of fertile silt on the fields. Crops planted in these fields were ready for harvesting in March–April, with little or no watering required in the interim.

Below: Just north of Cairo and many of the pyramids, the Nile valley opens out into the delta. Looking from Abu Rowash towards Cairo, the pyramids of Giza and the green fields of the southern tip of the delta itself are visible on the right and left respectively.

Throughout these centuries, agriculture was the principal occupation of the Egyptian population, based upon small villages dotted up and down the river. The inundation cycle made for a very irregular distribution of work across the year. After the rising of the flood, dykes would have to be maintained to prevent the water from leaving the fields too early, or flooding the villages, and then the crops would have to be sown and, later, harvested. In between these high-points of activity, work was rather easier than under perennial cultivation methods. One consequence of this was that men could more easily be diverted to labour on public works. The fairly low ancient population, ranging from only two million in the New Kingdom (16th–11th centuries BC) to perhaps five million in Roman times (compared with well over 60 million today), meant that agriculture did not need to be particularly intensive to provide for adequate sustenance plus the surplus from which taxes were levied to support the many activities of the state.

The people of Egypt

The population of Egypt has always been racially mixed, its inhabitants ranging in appearance from the light skin-tones of the north to the dark brown of the far south. Further variety and mixing resulted from successive waves of immigration, both peaceful and hostile, particularly into the north-east delta – as witnessed by

the Bible stories of Abraham and Joseph. Thus, by the time of the New Kingdom, Egypt was a cosmopolitan society, with foreign gods worshipped and men of foreign extraction holding senior government and military positions.

Human habitation of the area now called Egypt goes back to Palaeolithic (Old Stone Age) times, when the territory bore little resemblance to its later form: what is now desert was covered in forests and fed by numerous watercourses. Plentiful stone tools survive, particularly from the Middle Palaeolithic era (*c.*100,000–50,000 BC) and later, relating to a hunting, fishing and gathering society.

The dawning of the Neolithic era (New Stone Age), with its adoption of agriculture, seems to have followed on from climatic changes around 7000 BC, producing what are referred to as the Fayoum A and B cultures in Lower Egypt. Separate material cultures flourished in Upper (i.e. southern) Egypt; the first known grouping, the Badarian, appears just before 5000 BC and then develops into the Naqada I (or Amratian: *c.* 4000–3500 BC), Naqada II (or Gerzean: *c.* 3500–3150 BC) and Naqada III (*c.* 3150–3000 BC) cultures, each distinguishable by its forms of pottery and other items. Collectively, they are usually known as the Predynastic Period, although it is now common to spin off Naqada III as the Protodynastic. These cultures are named after the sites where they were first identified – Badari, El-Amra, Gerza and Naqada; Naqada I and II are simply alternative, more modern, terms for the Amratian and Gerzean.

Above: South of Cairo, in the valley, the desert sometimes constricts cultivation to a narrow strip on one or both banks of the Nile. Here, at Beni Hasan, the far (west) bank is by far the more fertile.

Above: The obelisk of Senwosret I is the last surviving standing monument of the city of Heliopolis, the focus of the sun-cult that was so important to the pyramid builders. Pyramids themselves were symbols of the sun's rays striking through the clouds.

By around 3300 BC, the polities of southern Egypt seem to have begun to coalesce into a more substantial grouping, centred on the town of Hierakonpolis. It is here that we find the first known traces of large-scale ritual architecture – a temple, in effect – founded perhaps as early as 3500 BC, and used for two centuries or more. While details remain obscure, it seems that the next century or so saw further expansion of the southern state northwards and the earliest manifestations of the hieroglyphic script. Finally, around 3000 BC, the north of the country was absorbed, creating the state we know as Egypt.

Kingdoms, Periods and Dynasties

Egyptian history is divided into a series of 'Kingdoms' and 'Periods', and then sub-divided into 'Dynasties'. The latter are based upon a scheme drawn up by an Egyptian priest, Manetho, around 300 BC. He divided Egypt's kings into a series of numbered dynasties, corresponding to Europe's idea of royal 'houses' (e.g. Plantagenet, Habsburg, etc.). These broadly fit in with known changes in the ruling family, but in some cases the reason for a shift is unclear.

Ancient dating was by means of regnal years – that is, years within each monarch's reign – rather than the kind of 'era' dating used today (e.g. BC/AD or AH). Thus absolute dates, in terms of years BC, have to be established through various indirect methods. Some reigns can be fixed by links to events in better-dated cultures, while others can be placed by reference to mentions of various astronomical phenomena. Dates of other reigns can then be calculated from these fixed points. Nevertheless, there remain many areas of uncertainty and, while dating is solid back to 663 BC, margins of error before then may run in excess of a century.

Broadly speaking, the 'Kingdoms' denote eras of unity and power, the 'Periods', ones of disunity and/or foreign domination. The Archaic (also known as Early Dynastic) Period (First and Second Dynasties) is a formative time, which saw the consolidation of technology and literacy, but also civil war; this conflict may, however, ultimately have led to the establishment of the absolute royal power that underpinned the Old Kingdom (Third to Sixth Dynasties, *c.* 2700–2195 BC).

Land of the Pharaohs

It was the Old Kingdom that saw the building of the first – and greatest – pyramids, as well as many other architectural and artistic masterpieces; foreign trade flourished, too. The following First Intermediate Period witnessed a splintering of power, possibly the result of a failure of the Nile flood and consequent famine and disorder. At length, civil war brought unity under the Eleventh Dynasty, the first of the three houses that comprise the Middle Kingdom (*c.* 2000–1650 BC).

The dynasties of the Middle Kingdom recommenced major public works and trade, but royal power once again decayed under the Thirteenth Dynasty. Palestinian rulers appeared in the north-east delta, and eventually obtained control of the north of Egypt and, briefly, of the whole country. Ultimately, however, the Palestinians were driven out by the kings of Thebes (the main centre in the south), who then founded the Eighteenth Dynasty and the New Kingdom (*c.* 1550–1100 BC).

The New Kingdom was Egypt's imperial age, during which it obtained overlordship over much of Syria, Palestine and the northern part of Sudan. A brief official experiment with monotheism under Akhenaten was rapidly ended under his successor Tutankhamun; then, during the Nineteenth Dynasty, wealth and power began gradually to seep away. By the end of the Twentieth Dynasty, economic problems and civil strife had set in, and the succeeding Third Intermediate Period (21st to 25th Dynasties) saw a split in the country just south of the Fayoum. The senior king ruled from Tanis in the delta, while the south was ruled by a series of soldier-priests based on Thebes, some of whom were proclaimed pharaohs in their own right. Reunification came under the Sudanese Twenty-fifth Dynasty, but was followed by Assyrian invasion, and it was nearly a century more before central power was definitively re-established in the form of the Twenty-sixth Dynasty (also known as the Saite Period, 664–525 BC).

The Late Period (525–332 BC) was dominated by a struggle for independence from the Persian Empire. Three native dynasties in turn wrested control, but all were finally defeated by the Persians – who were then themselves overthrown by Alexander the Great. With the dissolution of Alexander's empire, Egypt came under the rule of the Macedonian Ptolemaic Dynasty for some three centuries, until the defeat of Kleopatra VII in 30 BC brought the country into the Roman Empire.

Above: A pharaoh in characteristic pose on the Seventh Pylon of the Greater Temple of Amun at Karnak: Thutmose III of the Eighteenth Dynasty smites his enemies.

EGYPTIAN TOMBS AND THE AFTERLIFE

The continued existence of the body on earth formed a key part of the ancient Egyptian view of the afterlife – visualized as a bigger and better Egypt. Consequently, provision of eternal accommodation for the body was granted high priority. For much of Egyptian history, the realm of the dead was envisaged as being ruled by the god Osiris, once an earthly divine king who was killed unjustly and then resurrected, as the first mummy, to rule the world of the dead.

The earliest set of texts dealing with the next world are the Pyramid Texts, inscribed inside the royal tombs of the late Fifth and Sixth Dynasties, although on internal evidence apparently composed generations before then. They deal specifically with the posthumous destiny of the king, which differed greatly from that of the mass of humanity: as a divine being he would dwell with his fellow gods in the entourage of the sun-god, Re. These texts are a miscellaneous compilation of spells of various kinds and lengths, with no two pyramids having precisely the same sets of spells; indeed, some are unique to a single tomb. They include instructions for ceremonies, hymns and spells to aid the progress and transformation of the spirit, possibly arranged in sets radiating out from the kernel of the pyramid, the sarcophagus.

Spirits of the dead

The spiritual part of the dead person was believed to have a number of aspects, including the *ka*, the *ba*, the *akh* and the 'shadow'. The *ba* was depicted as a human-headed bird, which was the

Right: Anubis, god of embalming; from the
Nineteenth Dynasty temple of Sethy I at Abydos.

Below: The Giza necropolis, showing the mixture of
rock-cut tombs and mastabas south-east of Khaefre's
Pyramid. In the foreground is the tomb of Queen
Khentkaues I (see page 123).

form in which the spirit travelled within and
beyond the vicinity of the tomb. it would fly
around or sit before the grave, taking its
repose in the 'cool sweet breeze'. The concept
of the *akh* was somewhat more esoteric, being
the aspect of the dead in which he or she had
ceased to be dead, having been transfigured
into a living being. Viewed as a light in contrast to the darkness of death, the *akh*
was often associated with the stars. The notion of the *ka* was even more complex,
being an aspect of the person created at the same time as the body and surviving
as its companion. It was the part of the deceased that was the immediate recipient of offerings, but had other functions, some of which remain obscure.
However, whatever ethereal form the deceased took, it required sustenance for
eternity, and it was from this fact that the fundamental facets of the tomb derived.

The Egyptian tomb comprised a number of basic components that are
generally present in all of the myriad types of sepulchre known. Their appearance
may vary considerably, but without an understanding of how each fits into the
underlying scheme it is impossible to relate one monument to another.

Above: The kernel of the Egyptian tomb: the burial chamber. This chamber belongs to the Fourth Dynasty sepulchre of the courtier Debhen (LG90) at Giza, part of the rock-cut cemetery near the pyramid of Khaefre (see previous page).

Elements of the tomb

At its most fundamental level, a tomb is divided into two, and frequently three. At the core is the burial place itself (the substructure), containing the body. The physical corpse seems to have been the dead person's link with earth, the conduit of the sustenance received from the world of the living. It thus had to be kept incorrupt, and so the practice of mummification came into being: a technique of preserving the body by drying it out and wrapping it in bandages. Protection – both physical and magical – was ideally provided by one or more decorated coffins and, perhaps, a sarcophagus. To ensure security, the entrance to the burial chamber was blocked, and the approach shaft, corridor or stairway filled in. Safety might be further enhanced by the addition of plug-blocks or portcullis-slabs of hard stones, or by other architectural innovations which might make penetration by the omnipresent tomb-robber more difficult. Of course, this ideal state of protection for the dead was reached by the rich few only: most substructures were no more than holes in the desert.

The next element is the offering place, acting as the interface between this world and the hereafter in which the deceased dwelled. This was where offerings would be left by relatives and priests, or be generated by inscriptions and painted or carved tableaux. The latter concept was based on the Egyptian view that the writing or depiction of a thing could make it exist by means of magic – hence, many offering places featured images of food production to ensure that the dead person would go on being fed long after the last priest or relative had visited.

Offering places varied greatly in size and form. At the lowliest level, it would simply have been the place on the east side of the grave where a jar of beer and a loaf of bread might be left on feast days. At the other extreme, huge, elaborate temples with dozens of rooms would provide for the cult of the deceased. In between were many smaller chapels, which might be cut out of a cliff-face, erected against or within a built superstructure, or simply free-standing on the desert surface.

Many tombs added a third element: the superstructure. This could take a number of forms, the most characteristic being the mastaba – a low, bench-shaped building (the Arabic word 'mastaba' means 'bench') – and the pyramid. Both the mastaba and the pyramid can be solid, although mastabas often had chapels built within them, and the burial apartments of some pyramids penetrate into them. There are many tombs where the offering place and superstructure are so intimately entangled that it is not easy to analyze them separately.

These two or three elements could share the same site, being fully integrated with one another, or they could be separated, sometimes by distances of several miles. For example, during the New Kingdom, the substructure of a king's tomb was a set of corridors and chambers cut in the rock of a desert valley – the place known today as the Valley of the Kings – while the offering place was one of a

row of free-standing temples on the other side of a mountain, on the very edge of the desert and looking over the fields. The 'superstructure' was perhaps felt to be the mountain peak that overlooked the whole necropolis.

The offering place, or probably the courtyard in front of it, was the setting for the elaborate ceremonies that accompanied the funeral. Prior to this, the body would have been prepared by the embalmers. At its most perfect, attained during the New Kingdom, the process involved the removal from the body of all the internal organs — except the heart and kidneys — and its desiccation using a dry powder known as 'natron'. This is a mixture of salts, in particular sodium chloride — common salt — plus sodium bicarbonate, sodium carbonate and sodium sulphate, which was piled upon a stone slab; the corpse was laid on the salts, and then covered with a further layer of natron. After a number of weeks, the body was extracted and wrapped in bandages, as were the also-dessicated internal organs. The body was then placed in the coffin and the organs in the so-called 'canopic' containers: four jars and/or a chest. The details of the coffin (or nest of coffins) and the canopic containers varied over time: the former was rectangular until the Second Intermediate Period (c. 1650 BC), when mummy-shaped coffins began to replace the old design. Depending on the period and the status of the deceased, the coffin(s), of whatever shape, might be placed in a rectangular sarcophagus of stone or wood; the canopic chest generally matched the style of the sarcophagus.

Above: The offering place varied in size and form, but ideally contained depictions of the creation of food offerings and the deceased carrying out his or her daily life. This one belonged to the mayor Khnumhotep iii of the Twelfth Dynasty, at Beni Hasan (BH3).

Mummification

In the Old Kingdom, mummification had taken a rather different form. Although natron seems to have been coming into use, the main aspect of the process was the

'We took our copper tools and forced a way into the pyramid of this king through its innermost part. We found the substructure, and we took our lighted candles in our hands and went down. Then we broke through the blocking that we found at the entrance to his crypt, and found this god lying at the back of his burial place.'

EXTRACT FROM THE CONFESSION OF THE ROBBERS
OF THE PYRAMID OF SOBKEMSAF I, *c.* 1100 BC

Below: Napoleon Bonaparte's scientific team measuring the Great Sphinx in Giza in 1798.

tight wrapping of the individual limbs with linen, and then the application of a layer of plaster in which the individual's features were modelled. This contrasts with later mummies, where the limbs were lost from view amid the swathes of bandages and an all-enveloping outer shroud.

Throughout Egyptian history, the prepared mummy would be taken in procession to the tomb with the items to be placed with it in the burial chamber. The cortège would be accompanied by the mourning family and friends of the deceased, priests, and perhaps a host of professional mourners. The ceremonies of interment culminated in the ceremony of 'opening the mouth', in which the dead body was reanimated, involving implements that recalled those used at birth, including that which cut the umbilical cord.

The pyramids' enemies

After the completion of the ceremonies, the burial chamber was sealed and the spirit of the deceased set out on its journey to eternity. As envisioned in the New Kingdom and later (from 1550 BC), this involved overcoming the obstacles placed in its way by the guardians of the various gates that lay between it and its goal, the 'Hall of Judgment'. Here, Osiris, King of the Dead, presided over the weighing of the deceased's heart — regarded as the seat of intelligence and knowledge — against the feather of *maat*, the personification of truth, order and justice. If the pans of the scale balanced, the dead person would come before Osiris and pass into life eternal. If the heart proved heavier, it would be fed to a monster named 'the Devourer', and the spirit cast into the darkness. However,

the magical 'guidebooks' supplied for the deceased – the best known being the 'Book of the Dead', introduced in the New Kingdom – contained spells guaranteeing the spirit success in its great journey.

Although magic could guarantee that the spirit's journey to 'the West' was as effortless as possible, the main threat to its well-being was on earth: the tomb-robber. From the earliest times, tempted by the rich grave-goods placed in high-status tombs, robbers would penetrate sepulchres and strip them of their contents. Indeed, tombs have been found still sealed, but wrecked: evidence that those charged with the burial had ransacked the body and its equipment, probably before the mourners had even got back home. In spite of harsh penalties – the preferred penalty for tomb-robbers seems to have been impalement – at certain periods tomb-robbery became endemic. Records survive of the trials of those accused of robbing royal tombs in the time of Rameses IX (*c.* 1100 BC), including the pyramid of Sobkemsaf I.

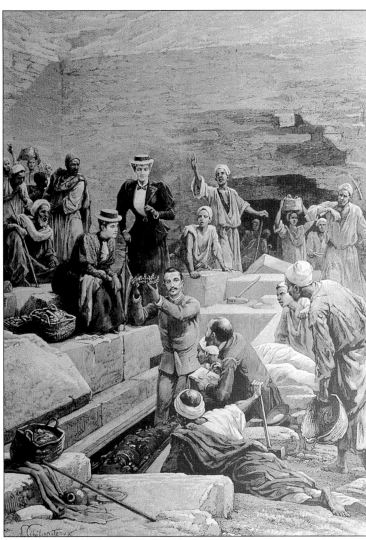

Above: Jacques de Morgan holds aloft the circlet of Princess Khnemet, having just removed it from her mummy in the funerary complex of her father, Amenemhat II, at Dahshur.

Following the final collapse of the ancient Egyptian civilization and religion in the face of the forces of Christianity and Islam, the old cities of the dead lost their last remaining shreds of sanctity and physical protection, and many tombs fell victim to the monotheistic iconoclasts and treasure-seekers. Medieval Arabic accounts tell, often with wondrous embellishments, of ventures into the pyramids and tombs to recover their riches. However, by the 16th century AD, the first real signs of European interest in ancient Egypt were becoming apparent, beginning the process that would culminate in the scientific resurrection of its monuments from the 19th century.

The first manifestation of this enthusiasm for reclamation was a horrifying free-for-all in the early 19th century, in which monuments were disfigured or even destroyed to garner objects for Western museums and private collections. Matters improved with the foundation of the national Egyptian Antiquities Service in 1858 and the consequent licensing of excavations. Today, all fieldwork in Egypt is tightly regulated; all discoveries are recorded, and very few objects are allowed to leave the country. Vast amounts of new information are published every year, with fresh data leading to frequent revisions of the interpretation of even long-known monuments.

THE EGYPTIAN PYRAMID COMPLEX

It is important to recognize that in spite of their monumental size, the royal pyramids of the Old and Middle Kingdoms conform precisely to the 'generic' tomb structure described in the previous chapter. They do, however, add further elements to produce what is known as the 'Pyramid Complex'. While there are of course deviations from the norm – particularly during the earliest and latest phases of pyramid building – the basic components are constant.

Below: The key to the whole purpose of the pyramid was the burial chamber. In most cases this had a pointed roof, and this typical construction is shown clearly in the ruined pyramid of Queen Neferhetepes at Saqqara (see page 124).

The Substructure

Usually, the burial chamber lies below the approximate centre of the superstructure, oriented east–west, with a stone sarcophagus at the western end. A square stone chest – the canopic chest for the embalmed internal organs – is frequently sunk in the paving to the south-east. Outside the burial chamber may be an antechamber and perhaps a store-room, from which a passage leads towards the exterior. Until the middle of the Twelfth Dynasty, the entrance was placed in the middle of the north face of the pyramid. The entrance passageway was normally interrupted by up to three portcullis slabs of granite, lowered to block the corridor after the funeral. The sloping outer part of the entrance – the descending passage – was generally filled with rubble, or large plug-blocks of stone, slid in from the outside. The actual entrance lay either on the face of the pyramid or just in front of it. In both cases the entrance was sealed with stone blocks – supposedly for eternity.

The substructure was usually built in a cutting in the bedrock, which was then concealed under the pyramid. A few examples exist of the substructure being tunnelled out of rock, but the 'cut and cover' approach was far more common. It had the great advantage of allowing heavy items like sarcophagi and portcullis slabs to be installed by being lowered in from above, rather than manhandled through the low and narrow passages of the substructure.

The Offering Place(s)

On the east side of the pyramid is the mortuary temple. The focus of this is against the face of the pyramid, where there is generally found a false door stela – a slab of stone carved as a stylized doorway, representing the physical interface between the earthly world and the next. Alternatively, or in addition, there may be an offering table to perform a similar role of taking offerings and passing them to the dead king.

The temples of the earliest pyramids had a pair of stelae flanking the offering table, but very little outside this enclosed sanctuary area. However, as time went by, additional elements were added. Typically, a room with five niches for statues lay just outside the sanctuary, as did various corridors and store-rooms. This inner complex was fronted by a courtyard, surrounded by a pillar-supported porch – the peristyle court. In front of the courtyard stood a solid walled entrance hall as the gateway to the temple, decorated, like much of the building, with scenes showing the king in the presence of the gods and offerings being brought for the benefit of his spirit.

In addition to the mortuary temple, a small chapel is often found in the middle of the north face, over or adjacent to the entrance of the pyramid. Like the mortuary temple, the chapel would have been built of limestone, with details and paving in harder stones, including columns of granite from Aswan, far up the Nile.

'May heaven rain with fresh myrrh, may it drip with incense upon the roof of the temple of King Seneferu.'

AKHEPERKARESONBE, C. 1475 BC

The Pyramid

Except in the earliest stages of its development, a royal pyramid of the Old and Middle Kingdoms is a straight-sided structure rising at an angle of around 52 degrees. Its size varies greatly with time; while the majority are around 80 metres square, the largest examples run up to well over 200 metres square. Heights range up to 146 metres, although around 50 metres is most common. The overall aspect was a dazzling white, derived from the fine-quality Tura limestone that was used for the outer layers of the monument. Tura limestone was taken from the eponymous quarries on the east bank of the Nile opposite many of the pyramid sites.

Left: *Until the appearance of the Pyramid Texts, substructures were generally unadorned, with the exception of such items as the panelling found in this vestibule in the Third Pyramid at Giza (see pages 62–3).*

The cores of most pyramids were built from lower-quality limestone quarried adjacent to the building site. The size of the blocks varied with time: the largest and best squared are found early in the pyramid sequence. Some of the later pyramids had cores of sun-dried mud brick, the principal building material of Ancient Egypt. All pyramids depended heavily on their Tura limestone casings for long-term stability. This stone was coveted by later builders, and nearly all pyramids were stripped of their casings during ancient and medieval times. The result is that many pyramids are now little better than mounds of rubble, with only the earlier, better-built examples retaining something of their original form.

The Subsidiary Pyramid

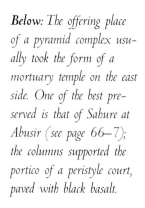

Below: The offering place of a pyramid complex usually took the form of a mortuary temple on the east side. One of the best preserved is that of Sahure at Abusir (see page 66–7); the columns supported the portico of a peristyle court, paved with black basalt.

A feature of all but the very latest pyramid complexes was a dummy tomb, usually in the form of a small, steeply angled pyramid. This initially lay opposite the centre of the south face of the main pyramid, but came ultimately to be placed south of the sanctuary of the mortuary temple.

The purpose of this dummy tomb is unknown, although many suggestions have been made. It can best be characterized as 'ritual' – archaeological shorthand for 'of unknown purpose, but clearly important'!

The Causeway and Valley Building

A royal pyramid could lie anywhere up to 1,500 metres west of the desert edge, east of which lay fields, canal networks and the Nile. This gap was bridged by a stone causeway that terminated in the entrance hall of the mortuary temple. The causeway was decorated in the same way as the temple, and generally had a roof. A surviving causeway (at Unas' pyramid) was lit by a slot down the centre of the ceiling.

Access to the causeway was via the valley building, so called as it was on the desert edge nearest the river. The valley building usually had one or more quays

where boats could dock, either on a canal or when the flood waters covered everything up to the desert edge. Centred on a pillared hall, the valley building also played a role in the royal cult; in at least one case it became the principal place where offerings were left after the mortuary temple itself fell out of use.

Other elements

A king's pyramid complex was generally a focus for other high-status burials. In particular, the king's wives were interred nearby. Most had small pyramids, but others had mastabas or even rock-cut tombs. Although locations vary, it is common to find queens' tombs on the east side of the king's pyramid, particularly in the north-east quadrant.

The tombs of the nobility and lesser members of the royal family were initially kept well away from the king's tomb complex, but during the Fourth Dynasty this tendency was radically reversed, with huge cemeteries purposely built close to the Great Pyramid at Giza. This strictly planned approach did not last, but in future the standing of an individual could be measured by the proximity of his tomb to that of his king.

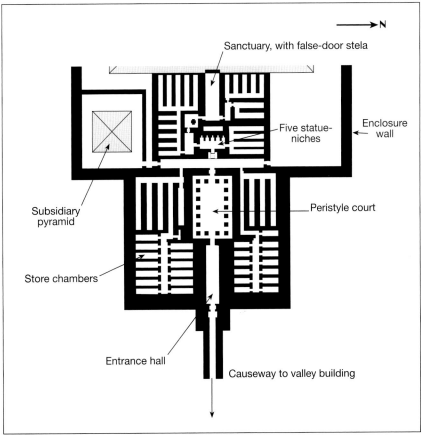

Above: Plan of a typical Fifth/Sixth Dynasty mortuary temple.

Left: The causeway ultimately evolved into a covered corridor leading from the edge of the desert to the mortuary temple. This causeway connects the elements of Unas' complex (see pages 72–3).

EXPLORING THE PYRAMIDS

The pyramids have always attracted attention. They were tourist destinations as early as the Eighteenth Dynasty, as we know from graffiti at Saqqara, Dahshur and Meidum. Early in the next dynasty, Prince Khaemwaset, High Priest of Ptah and son of Rameses II, was undertaking antiquarian investigations and carving the name of the pyramid's founder on the casings of a number of pyramids.

Below: The English traveller, George Sandys (1578–1644) approaches the pyramids of Giza in 1611.

The Twenty-fifth and Twenty-sixth dynasties saw a revival in ancient art styles, and a number of pyramids were entered. In Menkaure's pyramid, the king's broken body was provided with a new coffin, while a new entrance gallery was pushed under the Step Pyramid of Djoser. Here, copies were made of the reliefs in the underground chambers, as shown by the grids drawn over them in ink.

The ancient Greeks and Romans also flocked to the pyramid field. The fifth-century BC historian Herodotus records the tall tales told to him by his guides at Giza, which compare well with some of those told today. However, with the absorption of Egypt into the Islamic world in AD 640, Western travellers largely disappeared. Knowledge of the pyramids' true purpose had become hazy with the collapse of paganism in the fourth and fifth centuries, and they came frequently to be called the 'Granaries of Joseph', allegedly built by the patriarch in the years of plenty.

Others, however, did realize that the pyramids were tombs, and thus also potential treasure-houses. Many pyramids show signs of mediaeval investigations, most famously the Great Pyramid of Giza. Contemporary writers recorded the Caliph Maamun cutting or enlarging a tunnel in the north face of the pyramid and penetrating the interior. What he found is not totally clear, but it seems to have included human remains. Whether or not these belonged to the pyramid's founder, Khufu, remains a moot point.

Other investigators were more interested in the pyramids as sources of raw materials. The fine limestone

'Full West of the City, close upon those desarts, a-loft on a rocky level adjoyoning to the valley, stand those three Pyramides (the barbarous monuments of prodicgality and vain-glory) so universally celebrated.'

GEORGE SANDYS, 1610

casings were stripped off almost all pyramids that still had them – many had gone in pharaonic times – and the same stone was also ripped from interiors, leaving many Fifth and Sixth dynasty pyramids in a sorry condition.

The Europeans

European travellers began to reappear in the 17th century AD, with the first 'scientific' survey at Giza being made by John Greaves in 1639–40. Useful work was done over the next century by a variety of individuals, but real advances came only with the French military campaign of 1798, which also included a large contingent of scholars. Their research sparked a resurgence of interest in Ancient Egypt and the creation of national collections of its antiquities. The resulting market was supplied in part by the various European consuls in Egypt who, on a purely freelance basis, collected material and also hired others to do so on their behalf. The British Consul Henry Salt (1780–1827) employed the Italian archaeologist Giovanni Belzoni, while later Colonel Patrick Campbell (1779–1857) sponsored Richard Vyse's work at Giza.

Nationally sponsored scientific expeditions were sent to Egypt by France and Prussia in 1828 and 1842–5, respectively; the latter, under Carl Lepsius, was responsible for the first comprehensive cataloguing and mapping of the pyramids. They were, however, little considered by the new Egyptian Antiquities Service, founded by the Viceroy in 1858, and whose first director was the French Egyptologist François Mariette. Apparently devoid of inscriptions, the pyramids were deemed unlikely to repay the effort needed to open the large number that remained unexplored.

Just how wrong this assumption was became apparent with the discovery of the Pyramid Texts by the German Brugsch brothers in 1881 – a breakthrough that was rapidly followed by the opening of a large number of pyramids by Maspero during the early 1880s. At the same time, William Petrie undertook an elaborate survey of the Giza plateau, beginning a career that included the excavation of a whole range of pyramids by him and his associates, based at University College London.

Among the pyramids investigated by Petrie were particular examples from the Middle Kingdom, knowledge of which was further enhanced in the 1890s by work undertaken by de Morgan, Gautier and Jéquier for the Antiquities Service. This pattern of work, conducted in parallel by both the Egyptian authorities and foreign teams, has continued to the present day.

A Plan of the Pyramids of Saccara, and Dashour.

Above: *Richard Pococke's 1739 map of the pyramid fields of Saqqara and Dahshur.*

Below: *Gaston Maspero, successor to Mariette, seen here inside the pyramid of Unas. Maspero undertook the full study of the Pyramid Texts, and in the 1880s he opened most of those pyramids that had, until then, remained closed.*

Particular examples of Egyptian work have been at the pyramid complexes of Djoser, Isesi, Unas, Userkaf, Sekhemkhet, Pepy II, Khendjer and Seneferu (the Bent Pyramid), while foreign teams have contributed to the investigation of such sites as Giza, Saqqara-South, Dahshur, Mazghuna, Lisht, Meidum, Lahun and Hawara.

Recent activity

In recent years much work has been devoted to revisiting sites excavated in the past, to check data and search for what may have been missed. Perhaps the most important of all such investigations have been the surveys made by Maragioglio and Rinaldi in the 1960s and 1970s, which recorded in great detail everything that was then visible or could be accessed from earlier publications. Unfortunately, only seven of the projected 14 volumes of their report appeared prior to the researchers' deaths.

Above: John Perring, whose solo survey of the pyramid sites in 1838–39, and his work with Richard Howard Vyse at Giza in 1837, make him perhaps the greatest of all pyramid explorers.

Others have undertaken new excavations and, today, years may be devoted to one pyramid. Back in 1894–95, de Morgan excavated three Dahshur monuments in an aggregate of only half a year's work; now, Arnold's seven and 16 (so far) years' work, respectively, in the pyramid complexes of Amenemhat III and Senwosret III at Dahshur has found not only new details, but whole new galleries and chambers! Painstaking work has allowed the shattered chamber walls of Pepy I and Nemtyemsaf I to be restored, while even the intensively dug site of Giza still springs surprises. In 1991, Hawass discovered the remains of Khufu's subsidiary pyramid, and he also continued with the excavation of the village occupied by the men who built the pyramids there. The exploration of the pyramids is by no means over.

Right: Excavations continue today; here, a Czech expedition to Abusir clears the ruined substructure of Neferefre in December 1997. The roofing of the chambers was removed centuries ago, but the bottom of the entrance corridor can be seen at the far end of the excavation.

Pyramid Explorers

Giovanni Belzoni: pioneer excavator and the first European to enter the Second Pyramid at Giza.

ALY, Mohammed A.
Egyptian archaeologist; Inspector of Antiquities at Edfu in 1980.

AMÉLINEAU, Émile
(1850–1915) French Egyptologist. Professor of History of Religions at the École des Hautes Études, Paris. Excavated at Abydos, 1894–8.

ARNOLD, Dieter
German Egyptologist. Excavated for German Archaeological Institute, Cairo, and now a Curator in the Metropolitan Museum of Art, New York.

AYRTON, Edward Russell
(1882–1914) English archaeologist. Excavated for the Egypt Exploration Fund 1902–1905, and then in the Valley of the Kings. He subsequently worked in Ceylon, where he drowned while hunting.

BALLERINI, Francesco
(1877–1910) Italian Egyptologist, on the staff of the Egyptian Museum, Turin.

BARSANTI, Alessandro
(1858–1917) Italian archaeologist and conservator. Worked for the Egyptian Antiquities Service throughout Egypt.

BÁRTA, Miroslav
Czech Egyptologist.

BELZONI, Giovanni Battista
(1778–1823) Italian archaeologist and explorer. Employed by the British Consul to collect antiquities, 1816–18, and made a number of major discoveries. Died of dysentery while exploring in West Africa.

BORCHARDT, Ludwig
(1863–1938) German Egyptologist. Director of German Archaeological Institute in Cairo; excavated at Abusir and Amarna.

BRUGSCH, Émile
(1842–1930) German Egyptologist. Assistant Conservator of Egyptian Museum, 1870–1914. First European to enter a pyramid containing Pyramid Texts, and also discovered the cache of royal mummies at Deir el-Bahari, all in 1880–81.

BRUGSCH, Heinrich Ferdinand Karl
(1827–1894) German Egyptologist and brother of Émile. Professor of Egyptology at Göttingen; worked on the Pyramid Texts.

BRUNTON, Guy
(1878–1948) English Egyptologist. Assistant Keeper of Cairo Museum 1931–48. Previously had excavated widely in Egypt.

CAILLIAUD, Frédéric
(1787–1869) French mineralogist. Travelled extensively in Egypt and Nubia both professionally and on his own account, 1815–22.

CAPART, Jean
(1877–1947) Belgian Egyptologist. Professor of Egyptology at University of Liège.

CARTER, Howard
(1874–1939) English archaeologist and artist. Chief Inspector for Upper Egypt 1899–1904; later excavated for the Earl of Carnarvon, discovering the tomb of Tutankhamun in 1922.

CAVIGLIA, Giovanni Battista
(1770–1845) Genoese mariner. Excavated at Giza, 1816–36, ultimately for Vyse.

CHASSINAT, Émile Gaston
(1868–1948) French Egyptologist. Director of French Institute for Oriental Archaeology, Cairo, 1898–1911; worked at a number of sites in Egypt and published many religious texts from major temples.

CURRELLY, Charles Trick
(1876–1957) Canadian Egyptologist. Excavated with the Egypt Exploration Fund from 1902; Director of the Royal Ontario Museum, Toronto, 1914–46.

DARESSY, Georges Émile Jules
(1864–1938) French Egyptologist. Assistant Keeper of Cairo Museum 1887–1923.

DAVISON, Nathaniel
(d. 1809) British diplomat. Travelled in the Levant from 1763 and excavated and explored in Egypt; Consul-General at Algiers 1780–83.

DE MAILLET, Benoît
(1656–1738) French Consul-General in Egypt 1692–1708.

DE MORGAN, Jacques Jean Marie
(1857–1924) French archaeologist. Director of the Egyptian Antiquities Service 1892–7; excavated at Susa in Iran.

Jacques De Morgan supervises excavations in the pyramid complex of Senwosret III; the shaft leads to the tombs of the king's family.

DREYER, Günter
German Egyptologist. Director of the German Archaeological Institute, Cairo.

DUFFERIN and AVA, Frederick Temple Hamilton-Temple Blackwood, Marquess of
(1826–1902) Irish statesman. Travelled in Egypt 1858–9.

EL-KHOULI, Ali
Egyptian Egyptologist.

EL-MALLAKH, Kamal
Egyptian architect and archaeologist.

ENGELBACH, Reginald (Rex)
(1888–1946) English Egyptologist. Worked with Petrie from 1910 and then as Chief Inspector for Upper Egypt 1920; Assistant and then Chief Keeper of Cairo Museum 1924–41.

Rex Engelbach worked with Petrie for a number of years and was responsible for exploring the pyramids of Mazghuna.

FARAG, Naguib
Egyptian archaeologist. Inspector of Antiquities at Medinet el-Fayoum in the mid-1950s.

FAKHRY, Ahmed
(1905–1973) Egyptian archaeologist; held various Inspectorates of Antiquities from 1932 onwards until he became Professor of Ancient History at Cairo in 1952.

FIRTH, Cecil Mallaby
(1878–1931) English archaeologist. Inspector of Antiquities at Saqqara from 1923.

FISHER, Clarence Stanley
(1876–1941) American archaeologist. Excavated widely in the Near East.

GABRA, Sami
(1892–1979) Egyptian Egyptologist. Professor of Ancient History, Cairo University, 1930–52; best known for excavations at Tuna el-Gebel.

GAUTIER, Joseph Étienne
(1861–1924) French archaeologist. Excavated widely in Egypt and the Middle East.

GONEIM, Mohammed Zakaria
(1911–59) Egyptian archaeologist. Inspector, then Keeper, of the Theban Necropolis 1939–51; Keeper of Saqqara from 1951. Found dead in Nile in 1959.

GREAVES, John
(1602–52) English mathematician and astronomer. Professor of Astronomy at Oxford 1640–48.

HABACHI, Labib
(1906–84) Egyptian Egyptologist. Chief Inspector of a number of areas 1944–58; wrote extensively on historical and archaeological matters.

HARVEY, Stephen P.
American Egyptologist. Assistant Professor of Egyptian Art and Archaeology, University of Chicago.

HASSAN, Selim
(1886–1961) Egyptian Egyptologist. Professor of Egyptology, Cairo University, from 1931.

HAWASS, Zahi
Egyptian Egyptologist. For many years in charge of the Memphite necropolis, and head of the Supreme Council for Antiquities from 2002.

HÖLSCHER, Uvo
(1878–1963) German archaeologist. Professor at the Technical High School in Hanover.

HUSSEIN, Abdelsalam Mohammed
(d. 1949) Egyptian archaeologist. Director of the Pyramids Study Project from 1945 until the end of his life. He worked successively on the pyramid of Isesi, the Red Pyramid and the Bent Pyramid until his death in the USA. Unfortunately his excavation notes have never been located.

ISKANDER, Zaki
(1916–79) Egyptian conservator. Principal scientist of the Antiquities Service for many years, finishing his career as Director General of Egyptian Antiquities Organization, and holding a number of university chairs.

JÉQUIER, Gustave
(1868–1946) Swiss Egyptologist. Excavated widely for the Institut Français d'Archéologie Orientale and the Egyptian Antiquities Service.

KAMAL, Ahmed
(1849–1923) The first Egyptian Egyptologist. Assistant Curator of the Cairo Museum; dug widely in Egypt.

LABROUSSE, Audran
French archaeologist. Director of the French Archaeological Mission of Saqqara.

LACAU, Pierre Lucien
(1873–1963) French Egyptologist. Director of the Antiquities Service 1914–36, and Professor of Egyptology at the Collège de France from 1938.

LANSING, Ambrose
(1891–1959) American Egyptologist. Curator of Egyptian Department of Metropolitan Museum of Art, New York.

LAUER, Jean-Philippe
(1902–2001) French architect

and archaeologist. Excavated at Saqqara from 1926 onwards.

LECLANT, Jean
French Egyptologist. Professor of Egyptology at the Collège de France, Paris.

LEPSIUS, Carl Richard
(1810–84) German Egyptologist. Keeper of the Egyptian Museum, Berlin.

Carl Lepsius, leader of the great Prussian expedition of the 1840s and inveterate cataloguer of pyramids. His numbering system remains in use today.

LORET, Victor Clément Georges Philippe
(1859–1946) French Egyptologist. Director of Egyptian Antiquities Service 1897–9.

LYTHGOE, Albert Morton
(1868–1934) American Egyptologist. Curator of Egyptian Art at Metropolitan Museum of Art, New York.

MACE, Arthur Cruttenden
(1874–1928) English archaeologist. Associate Curator of Egyptian Art at Metropolitan Museum of Art, New York.

MACKAY, Ernest John Henry
(1880–1943) English archaeologist. Worked with Petrie from 1907, and then in Mesopotamia and India from 1919.

MAKRAMALLAH, Rizkallah
(1903–49) Egyptian archaeologist. Assistant Director of Works at Saqqara 1931–7; Chief Inspector for Upper

Egypt 1937–9, later Lecturer at Cairo and Alexandria Universities.

MARAGIOGLIO, Vita Giuseppe
(1915–76) Italian army officer and archaeologist. Undertook extensive survey of pyramid sites with Rinaldi from the 1950s onwards.

MARIETTE, François Auguste Ferdinand
(1821–81) French Egyptologist. Employed at Louvre from 1849; in 1858 founded Egyptian Antiquities Service, of which he remained Director until his death.

Auguste Mariette, founder of the Egyptian Antiquities Service. He undertook relatively little work on pyramids, believing them to be 'mute', or devoid of inscriptions. It was only on his deathbed that he learned of the existence of the Pyramid Texts.

MASPERO, Gaston Camille Charles
(1846–1916) French Egyptologist. Director of Egyptian Antiquities Service 1881–6 and 1899–1914.

MATHIEU, Bernard
French Egyptologist. Director of Institut Français d'Archéologie Orientale.

MELTON, Edward
(c. 1635–after 1677) English traveller; travelled extensively in the Levant and West Indies between 1660 and 1677.

MILLET, Nicholas
American Egyptologist. Curator responsible for the Egyptian collections at the

Royal Ontario Museum, Toronto.

MINUTOLI, Johann Heinrich Benjamin Menu, Freiherr von
(1772–1846) Prussian soldier. Travelled in Egypt 1820–21.

MOND, Sir Robert
(1867–1938) British chemist and excavator. Sponsored numerous excavations; President of Egypt Exploration Society from 1929.

MOUSSA, Ahmed
Egyptian archaeologist. Chief Inspector at Saqqara.

MUSES, Charles Arthur
(1919–2000) American mathematician and scientist. Excavated at Heliopolis and Dahshur in 1957.

NAVILLE, Henri Édouard
(1844–1926) Swiss Egyptologist. Professor of Egyptology at the University of Geneva; excavated widely for Egypt Exploration Fund.

PALANQUE, Charles
(1865–1910) French Egyptologist. Excavated at a number of sites for the Institut Français d'Archéologie Orientale.

PERRING, John Shae
(1813–69) English civil engineer. Worked in Egypt 1836–40.

PETRIE, Sir William Matthew Flinders
(1853–1942) English Egyptologist. Professor of Egyptology at University College London 1892–1933.

POCOCKE, Richard
(1704–65) English clergyman. Travelled in Near East 1737–40.

POLZ, Daniel
German Egyptologist. Deputy Director of German Institute from 1998.

QUIBELL, James Edward
(1867–1935) English archaeologist. Chief Inspector of

Flinders Petrie began his long career surveying at Giza in 1880. Here, he is outside the rock-cut tomb-chapel that he (and previous visitors) used for lodgings.

Antiquities 1898–1913, and then Keeper of Cairo Museum until 1923.

REISNER, George Andrew
(1867–1942) American Egyptologist. Curator of the Egyptian Department, Museum of Fine Arts, Boston.

RIFAUD, Jean Jacques
(1786–1852) French excavator. Worked on behalf of the French Consul, Bernardino Drovetti, 1816–26.

RINALDI, Celeste
(1902–77) Italian civil engineer. Undertook extensive survey of pyramid sites with Maragioglio from the 1950s onwards.

ROWE, Alan
(1891–1968) English archaeologist. Excavated for Pennsylvania University Museum and Harvard–Boston expedition to Giza; Curator of Graeco-Roman Museum, Alexandria, 1940–49, and subsequently taught at Manchester University.

SAAD, Zaki Youssef
(1901–82) Egyptian Egyptologist. Excavated at various sites in Lower Egypt; Director of Inspectorates of the Antiquities Service 1954–60.

SAINTE FARE GARNOT, Jean (1908–63) French Egyptologist. Director of

Institut Français d'Archéologie Orientale, 1953–59, and then Professor of Egyptology at the Sorbonne, Paris.

SANDYS, George
(1578–1644) English traveller. Made extensive foreign tour from 1610.

SCHIAPARELLI, Ernesto
(1856–1928) Italian Egyptologist. Director of the Egyptian Museum, Turin, 1894–1927.

SEGATO, Girolamo
(1792–1836) Italian explorer. Excavated and explored in Egypt, 1818–22.

SHAHIN, Mohammed
(fl. 1880) Chief Workman for Egyptian Antiquities Service.

STADELMANN, Rainer
(b. 1933) German Egyptologist; joined German Archaeological Institute, Cairo, in 1968; Director 1989–98.

SWELIM, Nabil M. A.
Egyptian Egyptologist and naval officer; retired as Commodore. Received his PhD. from Eötvös Loránd University, Budapest in 1982.

VALLOGGIA, Michel
Swiss Egyptologist.

VARILLE, Alexandre
(1909–51) French Egyptologist. Excavated for Institut Français

d'Archéologie Orientale and Egyptian Antiquities Service.

VERNER, Miroslav
Czech Egyptologist. Professor of Egyptology at Charles University, Prague.

VYSE, Richard William Howard
(1784–1853) English army officer. Excavated in Egypt 1835–7.

WAINWRIGHT, Gerald Avery
(1879–1964) English archaeologist. Excavated for Petrie and the Egypt Exploration Society; Chief Inspector for the Antiquities Service in Middle Egypt 1921–24.

WEIGALL, Arthur Edward Pearse Brome
(1880–1934) English Egyptologist. Excavated with Petrie from 1901; Inspector-General of Antiquities for Upper Egypt 1905–14. Subsequently author, journalist and theatre designer.

WEILL, Raymond
(1874–1950) French Egyptologist. Excavated at various sites in Egypt.

WILBOUR, Charles Edwin
(1833–96) American traveller and copyist. Spent the last two decades of his life travelling in Egypt.

WILKINSON, (Sir) John Gardner Wilkinson
(1797–1875) English Egyptologist. Lived in Egypt 1821–33 and visited in 1843 and 1848–9, studying and copying the monuments.

WINLOCK, Herbert Eustis
(1884–1950) American Egyptologist. Excavated for Metropolitan Museum of Art from 1906 until 1931, when he became the museum's Director.

WOOD, Robert
(c. 1717–71) British traveller. Travelled in Egypt in 1743 and 1750–51.

VISITING THE PYRAMIDS

With the exceptions of Seneferu's miniature pyramids, which are spread along the length of Egypt, all the royal pyramids lie within reach of a day trip from Egypt's capital, Cairo. Almost all are situated close to the north–south Agricultural Road, and to the main route to Upper Egypt, which runs closer to the west bank of the Nile. Anyone intending to make more than one excursion to pyramid sites during their stay in Cairo would be well advised to stay in a hotel in Giza, the portion of Greater Cairo on the west of the river.

Below: Visitors descend from the Red Pyramid at Dahshur after the arduous but rewarding trip to the spectacular corbelled chambers inside.

Although the new ring road has greatly improved matters, it can still be a long haul through traffic-clogged streets from the centre of Cairo to the west. This said, there is far more to do and see 'downtown' than out in Giza, so the visitor must prioritize!

Many tour companies run trips to pyramid sites. The most common formula is to visit Giza and Saqqara, often as a single day's outing, though some simply do Giza, paired with the Egyptian Museum. Specialist operators, on the other hand, target enthusiasts and run week-long excursions that aim to cover as many monuments as humanly possible. It is perfectly feasible to 'do' most sites as an independent traveller, generally by hiring a taxi for the day: car hire is not recommended, given the nature of Egyptian traffic. For the budget traveller, there is plenty of local transport, although this will require plenty of planning – and probably plenty of walking as well!

It must be noted that access to sites and monuments changes regularly in accordance with the demands of restoration, staffing and other issues. It is, therefore, important to check the latest situation before setting off on a long trip. Access usually requires the purchase of a ticket. Photography within tombs and pyramids is no longer allowed. Tipping of *gaffirs* (guardians) is optional, but any particular act of kindness certainly deserves recognition.

Above: Two intact boat-pits have been found along the south side of the Great Pyramid at Giza. The huge cedar boat from one of the pits has been reassembled in the Solar Boat Museum above, which has been built directly over the pit. The other boat remains sealed in its pit, awaiting further investigations.

Giza and beyond

The most straightforward visit is to the Giza pyramids that lie at the end of Sharia el-Ahram (Pyramids Street), where modern houses, shops, offices and hotels extend right to the edge of the desert. They are within a short taxi ride of local hotels, and can be reached from elsewhere in the city by air-conditioned bus, ordinary bus or taxi. As of 2006, the authorities are planning to implement a major change in the access arrangements to the plateau, which will see the vehicular entrance moved to the Desert Road on the far west side. There is an entry ticket for the plateau as a whole, but you will also need separate tickets for some of the individual monuments. Tickets for the Great Pyramid, for example, are strictly limited in number each day to reduce the damage caused by visitors.

The mountain of Abu Rowash, with Djedefre's pyramid on top, can be seen clearly from Giza, and also from the elevated ring road. As of 2006, it is not routinely open to visitors, although, as with all 'closed' sites, permission to visit can be obtained from the site director's office near the Great

Above: The central atrium of the Cairo Museum houses the largest objects of the museum's collection, among which are the cap-stones of the pyramids of Amenhemhat III and Khendjer, both in the centre foreground.

Pyramid. The most straightforward access is from the Cairo–Alexandria Desert Road, from which a track leads towards the pyramid. The Brick Pyramid lies within the area of Abu Rowash village, close to the Agricultural Road and the area in which local children now play soccer.

Zawiyet el-Aryan is largely taken up by a military base, which completely encloses the Unfinished Pyramid and whose perimeter wall runs close to the Layer Pyramid. Access to the Unfinished Pyramid is impossible, and the latter should not be approached without the company of an Antiquities Inspector.

Abusir is not officially open and for the time being can only be visited 'unofficially'. The site can be reached either via a right turn alongside a canal on the road from Memphis to Saqqara (see below), or from the north, by a road that branches off the main road a little south of Giza. This 'scenic' route allows a clear, distant, view of the Layer Pyramid.

Saqqara and beyond

Saqqara, reached via the villages of Bedashrein and Mit Rahina (the site of ancient Memphis), is well organized for the visitor. The site entrance ticket covers most of the monuments. Of the pyramids of Saqqara, only one interior is normally accessible – either that of Teti or that of Unas. Additionally, the enclosure of the Step Pyramid may be visited, but not its interior.

The pyramids of Saqqara-South are not formally 'open', and are difficult to reach without four-wheel-drive transport. An ordinary car could reach the foot of Isesi's causeway, from where it is a long desert walk to the other monuments. The largely vanished Thirteenth Dynasty pyramids are cut off from the site by a railway line.

Access to Dahshur is via the main north–south road, with a right turn through the village of Minshat Dahshur. A paved road leads to the Red Pyramid, whose interior is open and lit, while a dirt road leads on to the Bent Pyramid, which may be opened in due course. The Middle Kingdom pyramids along the front of the necropolis are more problematic. It is possible to follow the line of the Bent Pyramid's causeway down to its valley building, from where a stiff walk brings one to the Black Pyramid – this can also be reached via a track alongside the canal outside the entrance to the site proper. The almost vanished White Pyramid requires a scramble up a steep bank of soft sand. The pyramid of Senwosret III lies beyond the gas works to the right of the site entrance but at the time of writing was under excavation.

The pyramids of Dahshur-South and Mazghuna are very difficult to reach. Moreover, they are in such a state of ruin that they are almost impossible to locate! In contrast, the Lisht monuments are easily visible from the road; the usual means of access is through the village at the south end of the site, which brings one out at the modern cemetery behind Senwosret I's pyramid. Neither this pyramid, nor that of Amenemhat I, which can be reached via a track to the north of the village, can be entered, although many elements of the pyramid complexes can still be recognized.

Above: The dramatic shape of the pyramid of Meidum is visible from far away across the green fields that approach to within 100 metres of the base of the monument.

Hawara, Lahun and Meidum

Hawara, Lahun and Meidum lie on the margins of the Fayoum. The Hawara monument is visible from the main road: various fragments of stone sculpture and architectural elements lie around the area of the Labyrinth, and it is possible to enter the pyramid, albeit only for a short distance, after which point the corridor is filled with water. Continuing along the road beyond Amenemhat III's pyramid and crossing a bridge, one arrives at the ruined pyramid of Neferuptah, just to the right of the road. Lahun is difficult to get to; access is either via the narrow streets of the nearby village, or from the area of its valley building, with a bone-shaking ride up to the pyramid itself. It cannot be entered, but the tombs of the royal family are clearly visible.

As one approaches Meidum, there are many spectacular vistas from both main directions of approach. The interior and mortuary temple are both open, and it is also possible to view the interior of the large mastaba that lies adjacent to the pyramid. A large cluster of ruined mastabas lies some distance to the north. Of the small pyramids attributed to Seneferu, few are visitable without specialist knowledge and an escort from the Supreme Council of Antiquities. The principal exception is that at Zawiyet Sultan, which lies just inside the entrance to the antiquities site, directly on the road along the eastern bank of the Nile, 8.5 kilometres south of Minya. The Elephantine pyramid may be seen from a distance along the usual tour route around the island of Elephantine and its museums.

THE PREHISTORY OF THE PYRAMID

What may well be the oldest surviving Egyptian royal burial is Tomb 100 at Hierakonpolis. Among the large tombs found at this site, which seems to have been the capital of the first rulers of southern Egypt, there is one whose main room, a brick-lined cutting in the desert surface, was adorned with scenes of boats and hunting. This earliest known decorated tomb may have been made for a 'proto-pharaoh' of prehistoric times, *c.* 3300 BC.

Above: The earliest burials in Egypt were simple pits in the desert, the body interred in a crouched position. The dry conditions have sometimes dried out the corpses to produce natural mummies, as seen here.

From just a little later, shortly before Egypt was unified around 3000 BC, comes the first sepulchre that we know to be that of a king — at Abydos, later to become one of the most sacred of all Egyptian cities of the dead. Here lay the ancient cemetery of Umm el-Qaab, at the mouth of a valley leading up into the Western Desert; its early choice as a burial place may have resulted from its being regarded as a gateway to the West, the home of the dead. The largest of the earliest tombs, known as U-j, is identical in construction to Tomb 100, but now has a dozen rooms. It is the direct ancestor of a whole series of similar tombs built there by the kings of the First Dynasty, the first rulers of the whole country.

First Dynasty Developments

As the dynasty continued, the substructures at Umm el-Qaab became more elaborate, the most important innovation being the introduction of a stairway entrance during the reign of King Den. Previously, the tomb-chamber had had to be left unroofed until after the burial, thus postponing the construction of the

PREDYNASTIC PERIOD
BADARIAN CULTURE
(5000–4000)

NAQADA I (AMRATIAN) CULTURE
(4000–3500)

NAQADA II (GERZIAN) CULTURE
(3500–3150)

PROTODYNASTIC PERIOD
NAQADA III CULTURE
(3150–3000)

BLACK TOPPED RED
POT FROM ABYDOS
TOMB, 1730

RED-LINED
POT

CARVED
MACE HEAD
FROM REIGN
OF KING
SCORPION

superstructure. Now, this element could be built in advance. Although virtually no Umm el-Qaab superstructure has survived, a key element was a pair of stelae that marked out an offering place, apparently on the east side of the tomb. There may also have been a low mound directly over the burial chamber; however, this may not have projected above ground level.

This modest installation was only one part of the

arrangements for the sustenance of the royal spirit. A wadi (dried-up watercourse) leads from Umm el-Qaab towards the edge of the desert and the ancient town of Abydos, and on its margins, nearly two kilometres from the royal tombs, a series of huge brick enclosures was constructed, each partnering a tomb at Umm el-Qaab. Although almost all have been destroyed, it seems that they each contained a chapel, and perhaps temporary wooden buildings as well. At least one was

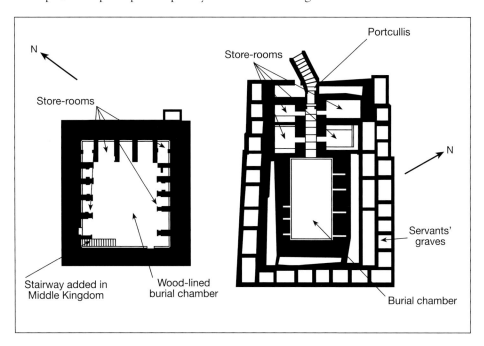

Above: The First Dynasty royal cemetery was at Umm el-Qaab, a low mound at Abydos that lies at the mouth of a wadi — dried-up watercourse — leading west into the High Desert. This may have been regarded as a gateway to the realm of the dead, and therefore an appropriate place to be buried.

Left: The substructures of the tombs at Umm el-Qaab comprised brick-lined cuttings in the desert gravel. That of Djer (O) had no means of access other than through its ceiling; the later tomb of Qaa (Q) has, in contrast, a stairway from outside the perimeter.

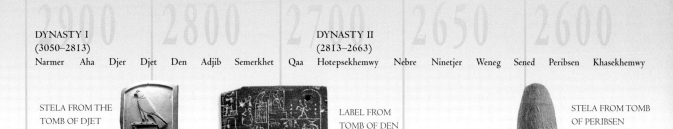

DYNASTY I (3050–2813)							DYNASTY II (2813–2663)							
Narmer	Aha	Djer	Djet	Den	Adjib	Semerkhet	Qaa	Hotepsekhemwy	Nebre	Ninetjer	Weneg	Sened	Peribsen	Khasekhemwy

STELA FROM THE TOMB OF DJET

LABEL FROM TOMB OF DEN

STELA FROM TOMB OF PERIBSEN

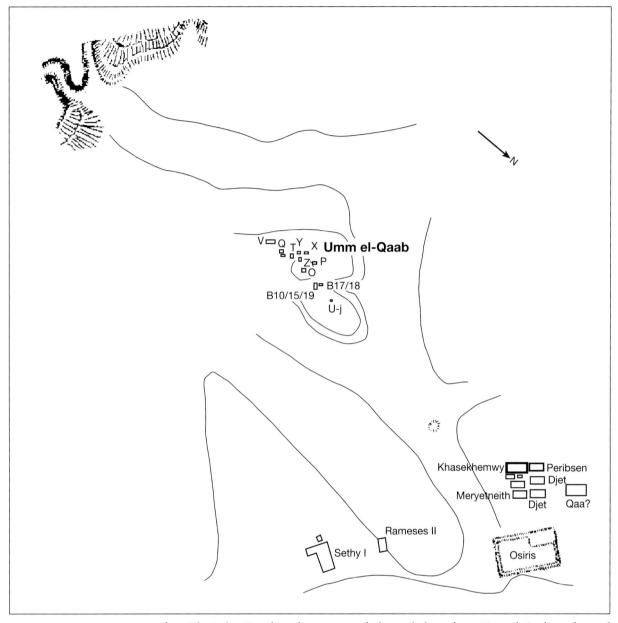

Above: The Archaic Period royal cemetery at Abydos, with the tombs at Umm el-Qaab supplemented by the funerary enclosures near the edge of the desert and the temple of Osiris. The Umm el-Qaab tombs are as follows: O, Djer; P, Peribsen; Q, Qaa; T, Den; U, Semerkhet; V, Khasekhemwy; X, Anedjib; Y, Meryetneith; Z, Djet; B10/15/19, Hor-Aha; B17/18, Narmer; U-j, 'Scorpion'.

equipped with a fleet of real wooden boats, while most were surrounded – like the Umm el-Qaab tombs – with the graves of members of the royal household. At least some of these seem to have been filled at the same time as that of the king, indicating a custom of human sacrifice that was to die out before the building of the first pyramid. It is possible that these enclosures were dismantled relatively soon after a king's death, when the structure to honour the next monarch was begun. This may explain why the only example still standing is that of the last king to be buried in the area, the Second Dynasty's last monarch, Khasekhemwy.

The Second Dynasty

The advent of the Second Dynasty around 2800 BC led to an important change in royal burial arrangements, with its founder, Hotepsekhemwy, abandoning Umm el-Qaab in favour of Saqqara, over 300 kilometres to the north. This site, on a ridge overlooking the city of Memphis, was the principal cemetery of Egypt's capital, founded at the beginning of the First Dynasty, and already housed the tombs of many of the nobility of the

time. The location chosen by the king was some 1,500 metres to the south of these sepulchres, reflecting the 'cordon sanitaire' that separated the ruler and the ruled in death for the first four centuries of Egypt's united history. The substructure of the tomb is of a wholly new type, tunnelled out of the bedrock and many times larger than anything that had come before, with around 80 chambers and a series of portcullis slabs blocking the entrance corridor.

The whole area above Hotepsekhemwy's tomb was destroyed when the pyramid of Unas (see pages 72–3) was built nearly 500 years later, but the slightly more recent example of Ninetjer shows a superstructure in two distinct parts. The northern element seems to have been an area some 19 or 20 metres deep, intended for funerary ceremonies; floored with a layer of clay, it lay above the outer passages and chambers of the tomb. Beyond this, to the south, was a rock

Above: The monumental part of the Abydos royal tombs lay closer to the edge of the desert, the only preserved example being the Second Dynasty example of Khasekhemwy.

Below: This detailed view of Khasekhemwy's monument shows the massive panelled enclosure wall.

Right: The brick tombs of the First Dynasty nobility lie along the ridge at Saqqara, overlooking the site of the capital, Memphis. In the distance the pyramids of Abusir and Giza are visible.

'step', apparently marking the spot where the substantial part of the superstructure may have begun.

Like the royal tombs of Abydos, Hotepsekhemwy's tomb also included a rectangular enclosure, although in this case it lay in the desert beyond the burial place, at the end of a wadi that seems to have been the ancient ceremonial route to the new royal necropolis (see 'D' on aerial image below). The enclosure that seems to have belonged to the king had been constructed by piling up desert gravel to delineate an area considerably bigger than any of the brick enclosures at Abydos. Another enclosure, known as the Gisr el-Mudir, and perhaps belonging to Ninetjer, lies a little to the southwest, and had stone walls – a candidate for the earliest major stone-building work in the world.

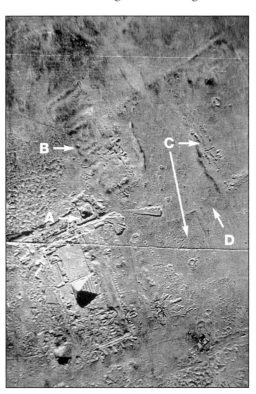

Right: The early Second Dynasty royal tombs lay about a kilometre to the south. The tombs themselves were situated near the later pyramid of Unas (A), while the monumental enclosures were further out into the desert (C). In between lies the pyramid of Sekhemkhet (B), as yet unexcavated in this 1940s aerial photograph. In ancient times these tombs would have been approached along a wadi from the north (D).

At least three other Second Dynasty kings appear to have been buried at Saqqara, but Peribsen opted to move back to Abydos, with a tomb that closely reflects First Dynasty norms in both size and construction. Civil war appears to have followed Peribsen's tenure of the throne, and the only further royal tomb known from the dynasty is that of the war's victor, Khasekhemwy, at Abydos.

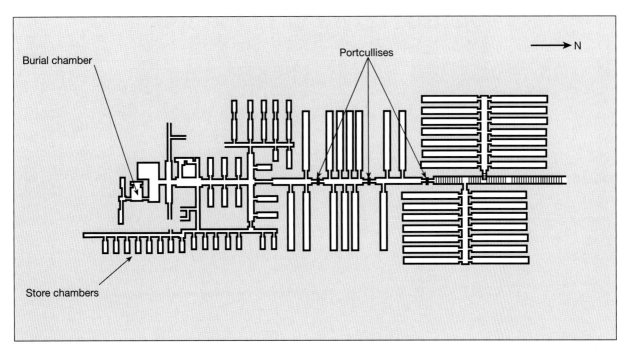

Burial chamber

Portcullises

N

Store chambers

Khasekhemwy's substructure appears to represent an attempt to marry the labyrinthine design of Hotepsekhemwy's tomb with the conditions at Umm el-Qaab, where tunnelling was impracticable causing the chambers to be built in a cutting. Khasekhemwy's enclosure, situated alongside those of his predecessors near the desert edge, is by far the best preserved. Most of the exterior wall still survives, as do traces of buildings within, including a Late Period basin, apparently for breeding sacred ibises. Its traces were initially misinterpreted as those of a brick-sheathed mound.

In Egyptian cosmology, creation took place on a mound that rose above the waters of creation – in the same way as newly fertile land appeared as the annual Nile inundation subsided. Thus the 'primaeval' mound could play a role in the essential act of creation that was the rebirth of the soul after death. Such a mound had been placed above the burial apartments of royal and private tombs of the First Dynasty, and it is not improbable that this motif would provide the point of origin for the development of the pyramid at the beginning of the Third Dynasty.

At the end of the Second Dynasty, the basic form of the royal tomb had been set for some four centuries as a burial complex of chambers topped by a monument, along with an associated rectangular enclosure for ritual structures situated some distance away.

Above: The actual tombs of the Second Dynasty kings were far more elaborate than earlier examples. This is the tomb of Hotepsekhemwy.

Left: Two kings of the Second Dynasty were buried at Umm el-Qaab; the first was Peribsen, one of whose stelae is shown here. The largely erased figure at the top is the god Seth, to whom the king seems to have been devoted, rather than the traditional royal god, Horus.

THE EVOLUTION OF THE PYRAMID: THE OLD KINGDOM

Below: The Step Pyramid complex of Djoser in Saqqara was the first royal funerary monument to be built entirely from stone.

The beginning of the Third Dynasty marked a major conceptual and technological leap forward, compared with the previous dynasty. This included the erection of the first known pyramid, the precursor of a series that would not come to an end until nearly 3,000 years later.

CHRONOLOGY OF THE OLD KINGDOM

DYNASTY III						DYNASTY IV				
Djoser	Sanakhte	Sekhemkhet	Khaba	Huni	Seneferu	Khufu	Djedefre	Khaefre	Menkaure	Shepseskaf

STEP PYRAMID OF DJOSER

STATUETTE OF KHUFU

STATUE OF KHAEFRE

MENKAURE, GODDESS HATHOR AND GOD OF THEBES

The Third Dynasty

Khasekhemwy was succeeded by the founder of the Third Dynasty, a ruler known to history as Djoser. This king was long remembered, and his importance was signalled by his name being written uniquely in red in a later list of monarchs. Millennia later, the fourth-century BC Egyptian historian Manetho recorded that his reign saw the 'invent[ion] of the art of building in hewn stone'. Although this is not strictly true,

Above: The Step Pyramid enclosure in essence turns the earlier brick enclosure into stone; this is its entrance.

in view of the known stone monuments of the Second Dynasty, it is clear that the reign witnessed an extraordinary advance in building technology.

Sadly, our knowledge of the rest of the Third Dynasty is very sketchy, with even the royal succession uncertain. Much of what has been reconstructed is based on the unfinished tombs that have been identified around the Memphite necropolis.

DJOSER'S PYRAMID (STEP PYRAMID)

The Step Pyramid dominates the site of Saqqara, dwarfing the surrounding monuments, and rising in six levels to a summit some 60 metres above its foundations. Built entirely of quarried blocks of stone, it is generally regarded as the first large stone building in the world. It was begun as a low, square structure, which was then enlarged into a four-stepped pyramid, and then into the final six-stepped rectangular structure. It lay in the centre of an extraordinary complex of stone buildings, enclosed by a panelled stone wall, the western part of which incorporated a probable royal tomb of the Second Dynasty. The building material apart, the wall has much in common with the brick examples at Abydos. Like them, it was entered from a gateway at the southern end of the east side, leading into an open courtyard containing elements associated with the ritual race that formed part of the royal jubilee (*Heb-sed*) ceremonies. A complex of shrines in the adjacent 'Heb-sed Court' were also associated with these activities, and many of the other structures within the pyramid enclosure also seem to be related to either jubilee or coronation ceremonies. A temple on the north side of the pyramid follows a plan known (in private tombs) since the First Dynasty, and included a statue of the king enclosed in a windowless room known as a *serdab*. A

MODERN DESIGNATION: L.XXXII; el-Haram el-Mudarrag; the Step Pyramid

LOCATION: Saqqara

DATE: *c.* 2663–2643 BC

OWNER: Netjerkhet Djoser

BASIS OF ATTRIBUTION: Inscriptions within substructure and complex

DIMENSIONS: Base 121 x 109 metres; height 60 metres

A SCRIBE OF DYNASTY V

RELIEF OF MENKAUHOR

SARCOPHAGUS OF QUEEN ANKHENESPEPY IV

Above: Elaborate chapel buildings lie within the Step Pyramid, all based on temporary wooden structures that were here transformed into limestone buildings.

Below: Plan of the Step Pyramid enclosure, showing the key elements.

mastaba was built into the south enclosure wall, with chambers mirroring those of the pyramid. This seems to be the direct ancestor of the later subsidiary pyramids.

The entrance to the tomb chambers lay within the temple. These centred on a burial chamber constructed at the bottom of a vertical shaft. This room was unusual in being entered via a hole in the roof, blocked by a piece of stone similar to a sink plug. A series of galleries surrounded the burial chamber, some decorated with blue faience plaques, others also with reliefs of the king — the first and last time a king would be shown in his own tomb until the New Kingdom. Under one side of the pyramid was a series of shaft tombs intended for members of the king's family.

The earliest modern explorers found parts of one or more mummies within the pyramid, and a number of other portions of a body were found in the burial chamber in the 1930s. Their age is uncertain; the location of the finds suggests that they are contemporary with the pyramid and thus those of the king, but recent carbon-14 tests have thrown doubt on this supposition. These remains apart, non-architectural material recovered from the pyramid proper has been limited to a wooden box

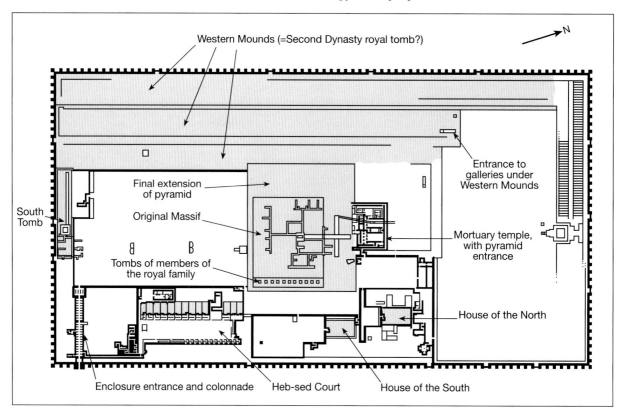

bearing the king's name. The tombs of the royal family under the east side of the pyramid revealed a number of alabaster sarcophagi, one containing human remains, seal impressions and large numbers of stone vessels, many dating back to the First and Second Dynasties.

Apart from the pyramid at its centre, Djoser's complex was, in essence, a simple combination of the formerly separate elements of the royal tomb into one unit, eternalized in stone. The union of the burial place with the complete cult complex was to continue until the beginning of the New Kingdom, although with many changes and developments.

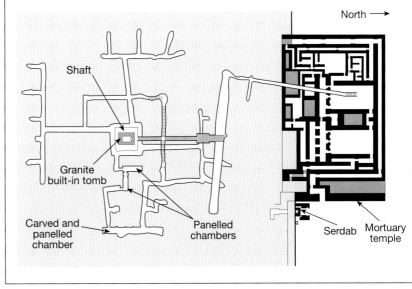

Above: Plan of the sub-structure and mortuary temple of the Step Pyramid.

The Step Pyramid is the only such monument whose architect is known. He was Imhotep, Chancellor of Egypt; his name appears on the base of a statue of Djoser from the pyramid complex – a unique honour for a commoner. During the Late Period, Imhotep was deified as a god of medicine, and as such was the subject of many small metal votive figures found in the Sacred Animal Necropolis, north of the Step Pyramid. Imhotep's tomb was probably in this area.

Left: The Step Pyramid is the only such monument to have an extensively decorated substructure, a number of rooms being lined with faience tiles and given inscribed doorways.

Principal Explorations
The first 'archaeological' investigations were made by the Egyptians of the Twenty-sixth Dynasty, who drove a new entrance passage into the long-plundered monument, apparently to some of the reliefs within. Although the pyramid had been seen by travellers, the first modern penetration of the substructure was probably by Segato and Minutoli in 1820. Perring carried out a more detailed investigation in 1839, but it was not until 1924–29 that Firth (continued by Quibell and Lauer) began comprehensive excavation work. Many of the buildings have been reconstructed, but several areas remain to be fully investigated.

EL-DEIR AT ABU ROWASH

MODERN DESIGNATION: El-Deir

LOCATION: Abu Rowash

DATE: *c.* 2643–2633 BC

OWNER: Sanakhte Nebka?

BASIS OF ATTRIBUTION: The king lacks a known tomb, and the monument's design seems appropriate to a royal tomb of this date.

DIMENSIONS: Base 20 x 20 metres; height 4.15+ metres

Djoser's successor seems to have been Sanakhte — until recently thought to have been his predecessor. It is possible that a mysterious monument at Abu Rowash may be his tomb. It was a great brick enclosure, probably 280 by 150 metres, with a solid brick structure in the centre, built upon a rocky knoll, and still over 4 metres high in 1902. Early Old Kingdom pottery was found there, and the scale and form of the monument strongly suggest that it was a royal tomb of the Second or Third Dynasty. As it was only after Djoser that royal tombs are known to have moved away from Saqqara within the Memphite region, the latter date is more likely. Sanakhte is the leading candidate as he would otherwise have no tomb.

Principal Explorations

First noticed by Vyse in 1837, and excavated by Palenque in 1902 and by Makramallah in 1931, the latter exploration being a rescue excavation following the installation of a drainage pipe. No further work on the site is recorded. Additional damage is known to have resulted from irrigation schemes.

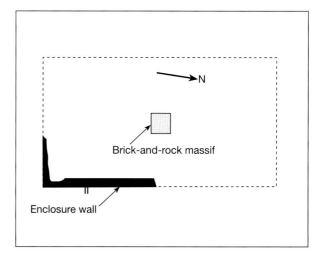

Right Plan of El-Deir, which may represent the tomb of Sanakhte.

Right: Abu Rowash overlooks the beginning of the delta; the Brick Pyramid (page 47) is represented by the darker outcrop at the top left of the photograph.

MODERN DESIGNATION: Unfinished Pyramid

LOCATION: Saqqara

DATE: *c.* 2633–2626 BC

OWNER: Sekhemkhet Djoserti

BASIS OF ATTRIBUTION: The king is named on seal-impressions within the substructure.

DIMENSIONS: Base 120 x 120 metres

SEKHEMKHET'S PYRAMID

Although unfinished, possibly due to the early death of the king, this monument seems to have been intended to be similar to Djoser's, with a large panelled enclosure. The enclosure was enlarged at least once before being abandoned, and had what was presumably intended to be a ritual mastaba tomb in its southern part. This was, however, used for the burial of a two-year-old child, probably during the Third Dynasty.

In the centre of the enclosure are the remains of a seven-stepped pyramid, whose construction had been abandoned at an early stage. Its entrance lay in the centre of the north face, the approach ramp cutting through the terrace upon which the mortuary temple would have been built. Interestingly, two attempts had been made to cut the subterranean corridors. The first was abandoned after 10 metres; the floor of the ramp was then raised and a new cutting begun. This was carried forward and extended 72 metres into the bedrock. A little beyond the entrance, a doorway was cut in the right wall, from which a right-angled passage led back northward to give access to a long U-shaped corridor,

Above: *The entrance to the pyramid of Sekhemkhet; the filling around it was intended as the foundations of the mortuary temple, but this was never built.*

off which lay 132 small storage chambers. These chambers held a large number of both finished and unfinished stone vessels, among which were the seal impressions that bore Sekhemkhet's name.

Beyond the doorway leading to the store-rooms, the roof of the main passage was interrupted by the bottom of a vertical shaft. This penetrated up through the superstructure, and may have been intended for the lowering of a portcullis slab; this arrangement is common in tombs of the period. However, no such slab was found, although a set of gold jewellery was found buried in the floor of the corridor directly below it.

The corridor also contained three intact (although rebuilt) blockings, while the roughly hewn burial chamber contained an alabaster sarcophagus of unique form – it had a sliding panel at one end sealed with plaster – and the remains of what was interpreted as a funerary wreath on top of the box. Unfortunately, the sarcophagus proved to be empty, with no trace of a body anywhere in the pyramid.

Principal Explorations

The site was identified by aerial photographs, and excavated by Goneim from 1951. After Goneim's death, further work was carried out by Lauer, beginning in 1964.

Below: *Plan of the unfinished pyramid complex of Sekhemkhet.*

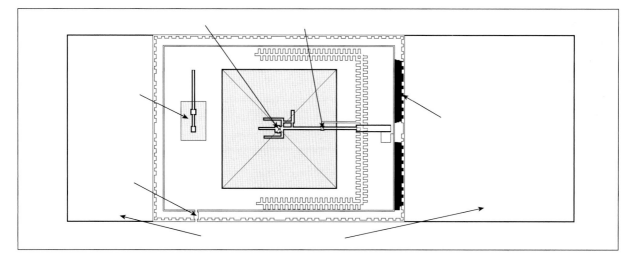

MODERN DESIGNATION:
L.XIV; Layer Pyramid
LOCATION: Zawiyet el-
Aryan
DATE: *c.* 2626–2621 BC
OWNER: Khaba
BASIS OF ATTRIBUTION:
Inscribed bowls found
in a nearby tomb; the
pyramid is dated typo-
logically directly after
Sekhemkhet's
DIMENSIONS: Base 84 x
84 metres

*Below: Plan and sections
of the Layer Pyramid.*

KHABA'S PYRA-MID (LAYER PYRAMID)

This monument lies on the edge of a steep incline from the desert down to the edge of the fields – a rather different location from earlier monuments and one unsuitable for the kind of rectangular

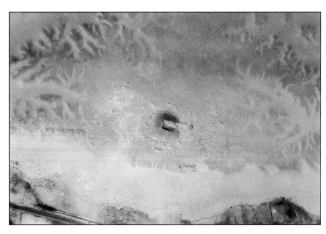

enclosure found around them. It may thus be at this point that the first major shift in the architecture of the pyramid complex occurred, with a much less elaborate cult installation (mortuary temple, causeway, etc.) centred on the eastern side, and some form of ramp leading down to the edge of the desert – blocks have been seen here that might have formed part of a valley building. Such an arrangement might explain the pyramid's novel position on the very edge of the desert.

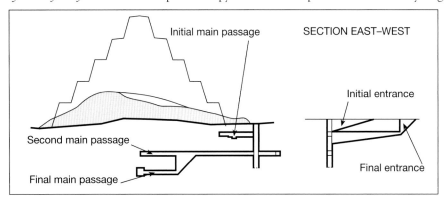

The pyramid derives its modern name, the 'Layer Pyramid', from the large breach in the north side that has revealed a neat section of its internal structure. This is of the same kind as seen in the Step Pyramid and Sekhemkhet's Pyramid: a series of facings whose successively reduced height produced steps.

The design of the substructure shows it to be almost certainly the direct successor of Sekhemkhet's monument. It has the same U-shaped set of store galleries, albeit with store-rooms on one side only, and a wholly tunnelled substructure. However, it demonstrates a number of advances over the older monument. The latter's store galleries had been approached via an awkward passage that doubled back on the entrance gallery, which would have made access difficult. In the Layer Pyramid, the entrance ramp was

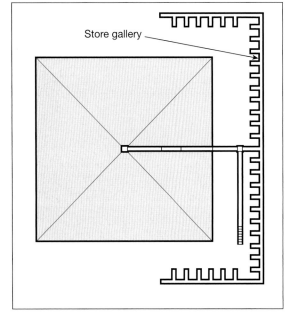

Above: The Layer Pyramid was probably the first royal tomb to break away from Archaic prototypes by abandoning the massive rectangular shape. The pyramid itself was 84 metres square. The cavity in the north face was created by early hunters seeking the entrance to the burial chamber.

turned through 90 degrees so that at the bottom of the ramp a right turn would lead direct to the store-rooms, and a left turn would lead to the burial chamber.

This basic conception was maintained through a number of modifications, all apparently intended to place the burial chamber still deeper underground, perhaps because of poor-quality rock at the highest level. Whatever the reason, galleries at two successive levels were abandoned before the final burial chamber was cut, and were apparently left unused.

Principal Explorations

First investigated in 1881 by Maspero, who located the entrance stairway but failed to enter the substructure; the first person in modern times to do that was Barsanti, in 1900. Reisner and Fisher worked on the site in 1910, but concentrated on the clearance of the tombs that lay around the pyramid, one of which (Z.500) contained stone bowls naming Khaba.

THE BRICK PYRAMID AT ABU ROWASH

This structure lies something over a kilometre south of El-Deir. Today, it appears at first sight to be no more than a rock knoll at the southern end of Abu Rowash village. However, in the 1840s, it was surmounted by various masses of mud brick. Though these have since disappeared, the emplacements for them are still clear, consistent with it having been the core of a pyramid of this material. High up on the north side, a passageway descends to an entirely rock-cut burial chamber, a method of chamber construction not found after the early Fourth Dynasty. The high entrance is also a feature of the period.

Although reverting to a much more ancient building material than the preceding monuments – brick was not used again for a pyramid until the Middle Kingdom – this was by far the biggest pyramid yet begun, and the fourth largest pyramid of all time. Construction from brick would seem at first glance to be a retrograde step, but it is conceivable that this well-tried medium was used in order to get the building completed more quickly. This could also account for the monument's proximity to the cultivation (i.e. cultivated land): to allow easy access to the bricks' raw material.

The pyramid seems never to have been finished, and by the end of the Old Kingdom enough of the rock core had been exposed by the removal of bricks to allow the construction of tombs cut into it.

The distant memory of a giant brick pyramid of the Old Kingdom may lie behind the Greek historian Herodotus' story of the

MODERN DESIGNATION: L.I; Brick Pyramid
LOCATION: Abu Rowash
DATE: *c.* 2621–2597 BC
OWNER: Huni (?)
BASIS OF ATTRIBUTION: Typological position (see text) and the historical placement of the king seem to coincide.
DIMENSIONS: Base 215 x 215 metres

Below: The Brick Pyramid at Abu Rowash still retained significant parts of its brickwork when drawn by Lepsius' team in 1842–43.

Right: By the 20th century, all that was left of the
Brick Pyramid at Abu
Rowash was the bare core
of a natural rock knoll.

Right: Reconstructed
section and plan of the
Brick Pyramid.

legendary Asychis, 'the
successor of Mykerinos
[Menkaure], who…
wishing to go one bet-
ter than his predeces-
sors, built a pyramid of
brick to commemorate
his reign, and on it cut
an inscription in stone
to the following effect:
"Do not compare me to
my disadvantage with
the stone pyramids. I
surpass them as far as
does Zeus [i.e. Amun]
the other gods. They
pushed a pole to the
bottom of a lake, and
the mud which stuck on
it they collected and
made into bricks. That
is how they built me.'"

Principal Explorations
Drawn and described
by Lepsius' team in
1842–3. Rediscovered
by Swelim, who under-
took a preliminary
survey in 1985–6.

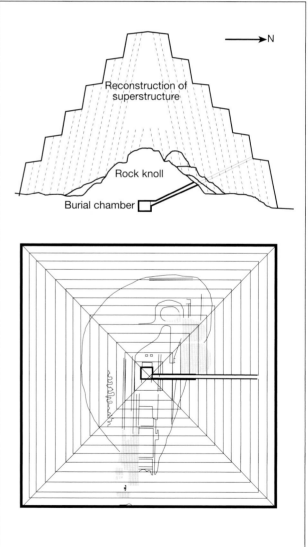

The Fourth Dynasty

The Fourth Dynasty, beginning with Seneferu around 2600 BC, marks the last part of the experimental phase of pyramid design and construction. During the dynasty's one and a quarter centuries, pyramids reached and passed the zenith of size and quality of building; there then appeared the first examples of the 'standard' pyramid complex, examples of which were still to be found as late as the Twelfth Dynasty, eight centuries later. The Fourth Dynasty saw the change from the step pyramid to the 'true' form, i.e. with smooth sides: in Egyptian,

The reason for this change has been much debated, but the consensus is that the true pyramid was a solar symbol, representing the sun's rays striking down from the sky. This fits well with the prominence of the sun cult during the remaining part of the Old Kingdom, and it is likely that, in addition to any benefits that would accrue from being buried under such a manifestation of the sun, there was some conception of the rays providing a 'ramp' to the heavens.

The Fourth Dynasty opens with the greatest pyramid builder of them all, Seneferu, who during his half-century on the throne seems to have erected no fewer than ten of these structures!

SENEFERU'S FIRST PYRAMID

 *'Seneferu endures'*

Seneferu's pyramid at Meidum is the southernmost of all the major pyramids of the Old Kingdom, presumably built near a residence of its owner. It was begun as a seven-stepped pyramid, which was then enlarged and converted to an eight-stepped one. Finally, probably after a break, it was converted into a true pyramid. Later stone robbery caused some of the outer layers of the upper part to collapse,

Below: The pyramid at Meidum represents the transition between step and true pyramids; parts of all its building phases may be seen on today's ruin. The causeway runs from a small mortuary temple towards the valley building.

MODERN DESIGNATION: L.LXV; Haram el-Kaddeb (False Pyramid)
LOCATION: Meidum
DATE: *c.* 2597–2547 BC
OWNER: Seneferu
BASIS OF ATTRIBUTION: Date of the adjacent private tombs, its design and later tourist graffiti. Earlier ideas that it might have been begun by Huni and completed by Seneferu are now generally rejected
DIMENSIONS: Base 144 x 144 metres; height 92 metres

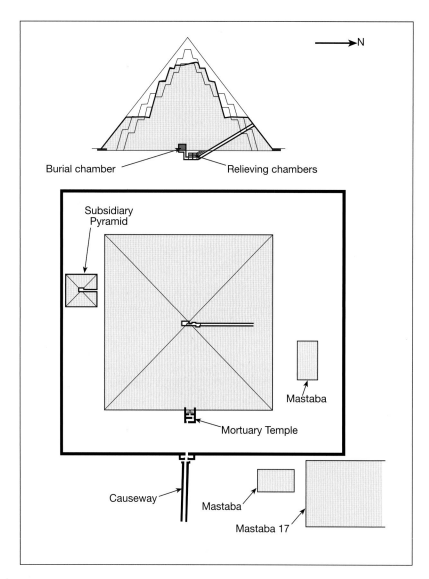

Above: Section and plan of the Meidum pyramid.

leaving the true pyramid intact at the bottom, together with a tower-like structure which preserves the fifth and sixth steps of the eight-stepped version.

A small mortuary chapel was built on the east side, with two unfinished stelae and an offering table in the sanctuary. Although the line of the causeway survives, the valley building has never been excavated. A subsidiary pyramid, now destroyed, stood in front of the south face of the main pyramid.

The substructure was constructed partly in the pyramid core and partly in a cutting in the bedrock. The burial chamber was entered from below and corbel-roofed. To relieve pressure on flat roofs, corbelled cavities were constructed above the antechambers and the lower part of the descending corridor. No sarcophagus was included and the pyramid was probably not used for a burial.

Principal Explorations

The exterior of the pyramid was described by a number of early travellers and investigators, including Perring on 29 October 1839, before being entered by Maspero in 1882. Excavations were carried out by Petrie in 1892, 1910 and 1912, and then by Rowe in 1929–30. Finally, El-Khouli worked here in 1984, as did a Supreme Council for Antiquities team at the end of the 1990s, the latter discovering the relieving chambers.

SENEFERU'S SECOND PYRAMID (BENT PYRAMID)

 *'Seneferu appears—South'*

This was the first pyramid to be begun as a true pyramid, although still employing inwardly-sloping masonry as found in step pyramids. The latter feature has contributed to its being externally the best preserved of all pyramids. It appears that structural problems manifested themselves in the substructure part way through its construction, leading to the angle — and so weight — of the upper part of the pyramid being reduced and thus creating its distinctive shape; the upper part was built from horizontal, rather than inwardly-sloping, courses.

A small mortuary temple was built on the east side, and a causeway led to the valley building at the top of a wadi leading down to the desert edge. The mortuary temple, the first surviving example of such a building, was extensively decorated with reliefs and statuary. A subsidiary pyramid lay south of the main pyramid, with a chapel to its east.

The Bent Pyramid's original substructure was similar to that of the Meidum pyramid, except that the shaft leading to the burial chamber was replaced by a steep staircase. However, a unique additional set of corridors and a chamber, approached from the west, was built within the pyramid masonry itself. This was added following the structural failures within the original complex. No sarcophagus was included in either complex and the pyramid was probably not used for a burial.

MODERN DESIGNATION: L.LVI; Bent Pyramid
LOCATION: Dahshur
DATE: c. 2597–2547 BC
OWNER: Seneferu
BASIS OF ATTRIBUTION: Name appears on inscriptions throughout pyramid complex
DIMENSIONS: Base 188 x 188 metres; height 105 metres

Left: The small mortuary temple is on the east side of the Bent Pyramid.

Below: To the north-east of the Bent Pyramid lie the remains of the valley building.

Above: *The Bent Pyramid's valley building contained a number of statues of the king; this one wears the White Crown.*

Right: *Sections and plan of the Bent Pyramid complex.*

MODERN DESIGNATION: L.XLIX; Red Pyramid; North Stone Pyramid
LOCATION: Dahshur
DATE: *c.* 2597–2547 BC
OWNER: Seneferu
BASIS OF ATTRIBUTION: Quarry marks on blocks and later inscriptions
DIMENSIONS: Base 220 x 220 metres; height 105 metres

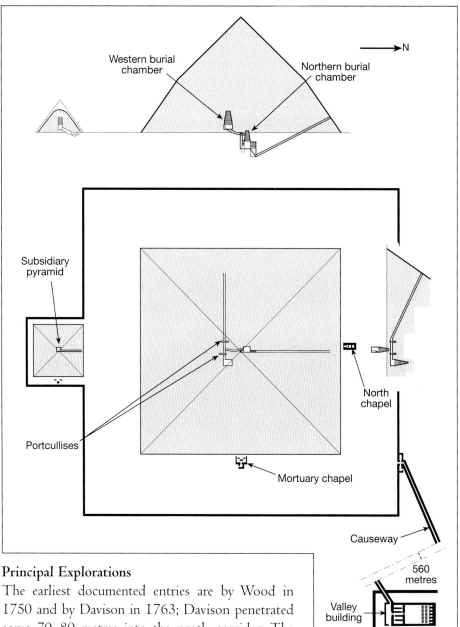

Western burial chamber

Northern burial chamber

N

Subsidiary pyramid

Portcullises

North chapel

Mortuary chapel

Causeway

560 metres

Valley building

Principal Explorations

The earliest documented entries are by Wood in 1750 and by Davison in 1763; Davison penetrated some 70–80 metres into the north corridor. The inner part and western complex were first entered by Perring in September 1839, and fully cleared and excavated by Hussein and then Fakhry between 1947 and 1955.

SENEFERU'S THIRD PYRAMID (RED PYRAMID)

'Seneferu Appears'

This, the final pyramid built for Seneferu, was constructed entirely using the lower angle that was applied to the upper part of the Bent Pyramid.

A rather more elaborate mortuary temple than those of Seneferu's previous two pyramids was provided, but a proper causeway seems never to have been constructed. The form of the valley building remains unknown, although what seemed

Above: The Red Pyramid at Dahshur, built uniformly at the lower angle used on the upper part of the Bent Pyramid.

to be parts of it were noticed during the 19th century. Likewise, no subsidiary pyramid has been found, although the pyramidion (cap-stone) of such a monument – too steeply angled for the Red Pyramid itself – has been discovered.

The substructure was built at ground level within the body of the pyramid. It comprised three spectacular corbelled rooms, the third entered from high up in the wall of the second, clearly for concealment. A sarcophagus may have been built into the floor, and fragments of a mummy, probably of Seneferu himself, were found in the pyramid.

Principal Explorations

The first recorded entries are by an anonymous Scot in 1657, and by Melton in 1661; the pyramid was subsequently surveyed by Perring in 1839 and the interior cleared by Hussein in 1947. The pyramid has been excavated by Stadelmann since 1977.

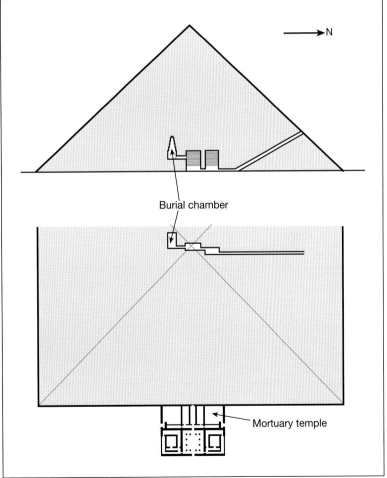

Above: Section and plan of the Red (Seneferu's third) Pyramid.

MODERN DESIGNATION:
El-Qalah
LOCATION: Seila
DATE: *c.* 2597–2547 BC
OWNER: Seneferu
BASIS OF ATTRIBUTION:
Stelae bearing the name
of the king
DIMENSIONS: Base 31 x
31 metres

PYRAMID AT SEILA

A series of small step pyramids, all apparently without any original substructure, are spread through Middle and Upper Egypt. Nothing is known of their purpose, although their positions, dotted along the Nile, might suggest the marking of some kind of royal tour. The small step pyramid at Seila is in a prominent position, at an elevation of 124 metres on top of the Gebel el-Rus, commanding a view west into the Fayoum and east over the Nile valley. A small brick chapel with an altar, statue and stelae bearing the name of its founder stands on its east side, with another chapel on the north face.

Principal Explorations

Summarily examined by Petrie, Borchardt and others; finally cleared by a team from Brigham Young University, USA, in association with Swelim, in the 1980s.

PYRAMID AT ZAWIYET SULTAN

One of the series of small step pyramids of obscure purpose, it lies close to the major ancient site of Hebenu and is, unusually, on the east bank of the Nile.

Principal Explorations

First examined by Weill in 1911 and by Lauer in 1962.

MODERN DESIGNATION:
None
LOCATION: Zawiyet
Sultan (site also known
as Zawiyet el-Maiyitin
or Zawiyet el-Amwat)
DATE: *c.* 2597–2547 BC
OWNER: Seneferu (?)
BASIS OF ATTRIBUTION:
Similarities to the pyra-
mid at Seila
DIMENSIONS: Base 22.4
x 22.4 metres

Right: Seven small pyramids were built south of the Memphite necropolis around the beginning of the Fourth Dynasty, possibly all by Seneferu. This is the example at Zawiyet Sultan in Middle Egypt.

PYRAMID AT NUBT

One of the series of small step pyramids of obscure purpose. A pit was found below the structure, but may not be associated with its original construction.

Principal Explorations

Partly cleared by Petrie in 1896.

MODERN DESIGNATION: Qurn el-Shair
LOCATION: Nubt (El-Zawayda, Naqada)
DATE: *c.* 2597–2547 BC
OWNER: Seneferu (?)
BASIS OF ATTRIBUTION: Similarities to the
pyramid at Seila
DIMENSIONS: Base 18 x 18 metres

PYRAMID AT SINKI

Another of this series of small step pyramids; this one was never completed and still retains its constructional ramps.

MODERN DESIGNATION: None
LOCATION: Sinki (Nag Ahmed Khalifa, Abydos)
DATE: *c.* 2597–2547 BC
OWNER: Seneferu (?)
BASIS OF ATTRIBUTION: Similarities to the pyramid at Seila
DIMENSIONS: Base 18.5 x 18.5 metres

Principal Explorations

Noted by Maspero and Wilbour in 1883, and then re-identified by Swelim on 27 October 1977; excavated by Swelim and Dreyer in 1980.

PYRAMID AT EL-KULA

Until recently, this pyramid was the best-known of the series of small step pyramids; this monument is odd in having its corners oriented to the points of the compass.

MODERN DESIGNATION: None
LOCATION: El-Kula (Nag el-Miamariya, Edfu-North)
DATE: *c.* 2597–2547 BC
OWNER: Seneferu (?)
BASIS OF ATTRIBUTION: Similarities to the pyramid at Seila
DIMENSIONS: Base 18.6 x 18.6 metres

Principal Explorations

The pyramid was visited by Rifaud sometime between 1816 and 1826, and by Vyse in 1836, and then examined by Maspero in 1882. This work resulted in the removal of blocks from the north side. A further investigation was made by Capart in 1946.

Left: The three-stepped pyramid at El-Kula. As with the other small pyramids, no trace of a substructure has ever been found, despite several investigations.

PYRAMID AT EL-GHENIMIA

Unlike the preceding small step pyramids, this example is of sandstone, reflecting the local geology.

MODERN DESIGNATION: Abu Sinnah
LOCATION: El-Ghenimia (Edfu-South)
DATE: *c.* 2597–2547 BC
OWNER: Seneferu (?)
BASIS OF ATTRIBUTION: Similarities to the pyramid at Seila
DIMENSIONS: Base 22 x 22 metres

Principal Explorations

Identified by Aly around 1980.

MODERN DESIGNATION:
None
LOCATION: Elephantine
DATE: *c.* 2597–2547 BC
OWNER: Seneferu (?)
BASIS OF ATTRIBUTION:
Similarities to the pyramid at Seila
DIMENSIONS: Base 25 x 25 metres

Right: The pyramid at Elephantine is now almost entirely hidden among later buildings, but is visible in the centre of this view.

PYRAMID AT ELEPHANTINE

This small step pyramid was built of local granite. The Old Kingdom element of the city lay 120 metres to the south-east, but later expansion has placed the pyramid within the ancient settlement area known as Elephantine.

A granite cone was found nearby bearing the name of Huni, which has frequently led to the pyramid being assigned to him.

Principal Explorations

Initially misidentified as the foundations of a Jewish temple early in the 20th century, its true status was recognized by Dreyer in 1979.

KHUFU'S PYRAMID (GREAT PYRAMID)

   'Horizon of Khufu'

MODERN DESIGNATION:
L.IV; G I; Great Pyramid
LOCATION: Giza
DATE: *c.* 2547–2524 BC
OWNER: Khufu
BASIS OF ATTRIBUTION:
Quarry marks inside pyramid; numerous monuments of family and officials in surrounding cemeteries
DIMENSIONS: Base 230 x 230 metres; height 146 metres

This is the so-called Great Pyramid, the largest of all the pyramids. A mortuary temple was built on the east side, directly south of which was the subsidiary pyramid. A causeway led towards the valley building, some elements of which have been detected under modern buildings below the desert escarpment. A number of boat pits lie on the south and east sides of the pyramid; when investigated in modern times, two still contained wooden boats.

The substructure seems to have been constructed in three stages. First, a rock-cut descending passage was built, leading to what was to have been the first of a series of chambers deep under the centre of the pyramid. This series of chambers seems to have been abandoned when it was decided to include a stone sarcophagus in the burial, the passages being too low and narrow to introduce such a piece. An ascending corridor was thus added, apparently cutting through extant masonry, giving access to the so-called 'Queen's Chamber'. This could have received the sarcophagus before its walls were built, but plans seem to have changed again. The chamber is interesting, in that here the roof, instead of being corbelled, is of a new pointed type, which subsequently became standard for such rooms.

Above: The Great Pyramid at Giza, built by Khufu and still the most massive free-standing monument in the world. The entrance lies close to the centre of the north face.

Right: The Grand Gallery of Khufu's Great Pyramid leads up towards the burial chamber.

Plug-blocks were to be slid down the ascending passage after the burial, and to store them a corbelled room had been begun beyond the entrance to the passage leading into the Queen's Chamber. A shaft was also built to allow workmen to exit down to the descending passage after releasing them. The corbelled room was then greatly extended to become the 'Grand Gallery', giving access to the final burial chamber – the 'King's Chamber' – approached via an antechamber protected by portcullis slabs. Above the King's Chamber a series of relieving chambers were built; both the King's and the Queen's chambers had narrow (20 centimetres square) channels angled upwards from their north and south walls, apparently aimed at the stars. The channels from the King's Chamber continue to the exterior of the pyramid, but those of the Queen's Chamber were each blocked by a slab of stone with copper attachments. In at least one case, the shaft continued beyond

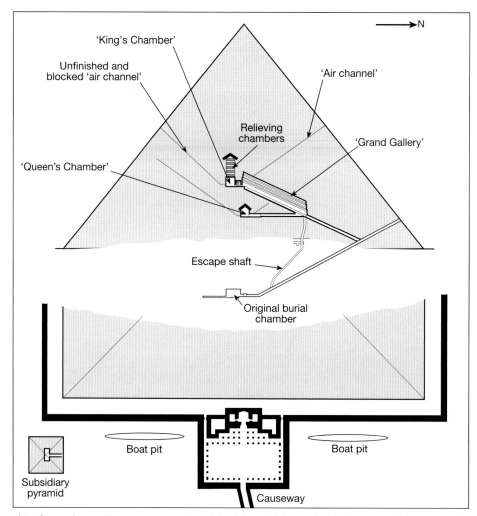

Right: Section of the Great Pyramid, and plan of the area in front of its east face.

Below: In the shadow of the Great Pyramid are the scanty remains of its subsidiary pyramid, whose entrance passage begins on the left.

this for a short distance to another blocking. This probably happened because the chamber was superseded by a new burial chamber, the position of the blocking corresponding to the level reached by the pyramid at the time the plan changed. The King's Chamber still contains the granite sarcophagus.

Principal Explorations

The pyramid was reopened by the Caliph Maamun during 813–33, when some elements of the original contents may still have been in place. The first proper survey was by Greaves in 1639. Investigations followed by Davison in 1765, Caviglia in 1817, Vyse and Perring in 1837 and a major survey by Petrie in 1880–82. The mortuary temple was excavated by Schiaparelli and Ballerini in 1903, Hassan in 1938–9 and Lauer in 1947. El-Mallakh found two pits containing dismantled boats in 1954. Hawass found the subsidiary pyramid in 1991.

DJEDEFRE'S PYRAMID

'Djedefre is a Shining Star'

Djedefre's Pyramid was built in a spectacular location, on a mountain top with views north into the delta, and south to Dahshur. The relatively modest size of the pyramid would thus have been more than offset by its visibility, lying some 20 metres higher than the Giza plateau. The structure is now very badly ruined, only the native rock core, plus a little masonry, being visible.

The remains of the mortuary temple are on the east side, and were partly constructed quickly in brick, suggesting the king's premature death. The remains of what seems to have been the subsidiary pyramid lie in the south-west corner of the enclosure, an unusual position otherwise found only at the Giza pyramid of Menkaure. The causeway leads, uniquely, from the north side of the complex to descend a 1.5-kilometre natural ridge. The valley building at the bottom has never been excavated, but must have lain close to the Third Dynasty El-Deir (Sanakhte's Tomb).

The substructure was built in a very deep T-shaped cutting, which placed the burial chamber far below the pyramid base. The corridors and chambers are, however, almost entirely destroyed. A fragment of what may have been an oval sarcophagus has been found.

Principal Explorations

The pyramid was surveyed by Perring in 1838–9 and Lepsius in 1842–3, and visited in 1881 by Petrie, who found the sarcophagus fragment. The mortuary temple was excavated by Chassinat in 1901–1903 and by Lacau around 1912. Valloggia began full clearance in 1994.

Above: The cutting for the entrance passage of Djedefre's Pyramid.

MODERN DESIGNATION: L.II.

LOCATION: Abu Rowash

DATE: *c.* 2547–2524 BC

OWNER: Djedefre

BASIS OF ATTRIBUTION: Numerous fragments of statues of the king have been found in the enclosure

DIMENSIONS: Base 106 x 106 metres

Left: Plan of the pyramid complex of Djedefre.

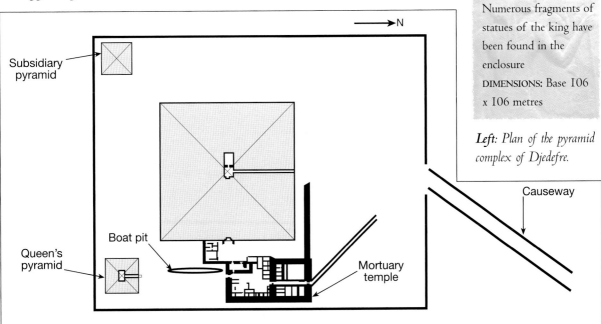

Subsidiary pyramid

N

Queen's pyramid

Boat pit

Mortuary temple

Causeway

MODERN DESIGNATION:
L.XIII; Unfinished
Pyramid; Great Pit
LOCATION: Zawiyet el-
Aryan
DATE: *c.* 2516–2515 BC
OWNER: Seth?ka
BASIS OF ATTRIBUTION:
Quarry marks on blocks
give the king's name, the
first sign of which is
difficult to read (hence
the question mark in
the name). The king is
otherwise unknown, and
the pyramid was first
dated architecturally to
the Third Dynasty. It is
now agreed to be
Fourth Dynasty, and so
similar to Djedefre's
that the king is likely to
be his successor
DIMENSIONS: Base 200
x 200 metres

*Right: The Second
Pyramid of Khaefre still
has parts of the casing
near its top.*

MODERN DESIGNATION:
L.VIII; G II; Second
Pyramid
LOCATION: Giza
DATE: *c.* 2515–2493 BC
OWNER: Khaefre
BASIS OF ATTRIBUTION:
Numerous inscribed
statues in the pyramid's
temples
DIMENSIONS: Base 215
x 215 metres; height
143 metres

SETH?KA'S PYRAMID

Nothing of the superstructure of Seth?ka's monument survives; it may never have been begun. The T-shaped cutting for the substructure had been quarried and the pavement of the burial chamber – incorporating an oval sarcophagus – laid, before all work stopped.

Principal Explorations

Located by Lepsius in December 1842; substructure identified and cleared by Barsanti in 1904–11; a clearance for the filming of the movie *Land of the Pharaohs* was made in 1954. The monument is now within a military area and wholly inaccessible.

Above: Nothing of the superstructure of the Unfinished Pyramid at Zawiyet el-Aryan survives. Only the cutting for the substructure remains.

KHAEFRE'S PYRAMID

 'Great is Khaefre'

The second largest pyramid in Egypt, the angle of elevation on Khaefre's pyramid is, at 53 degrees, slightly greater than usual. Part of the casing survives near the summit.

The mortuary temple, causeway and valley building are all fairly well preserved, and mark a major step towards the standard pyramid complex. They are all built from particularly massive limestone masonry. The valley building was faced with ashlars of granite, its T-shaped hall containing a large number of fine statues, preserved through their placement in a pit in later times.

An almost completely destroyed subsidiary pyramid stood on the south side of the main pyramid, while the complex also incorporated the Great Sphinx and its associated temple. Although usually regarded as having been sculpted in the time of Khaefre, the Sphinx may have been carved during the Archaic Period. It is also possible that its head may have been completely recarved later, possibly during the Twelfth Dynasty reign of Amenemhat II, as a similar sphinx from that king's reign

provides the best parallels for the details of the head of the Giza sphinx.

It may originally have been intended to build the pyramid somewhat north of its final location. This is suggested by its having essentially two substructures, the northernmost of the two with an entrance outside the north face and a burial chamber 30 metres north of the centre of the pyramid. Had the pyramid been further north (and of somewhat larger dimensions than finally employed), both would have been in a conventional position. The second set of galleries placed the final burial chamber roughly at ground level, marking the abandonment of deeply buried sepulchral chambers in pyramids. The new complex was linked to the old by a ramp, and protected by a portcullis slab. The sarcophagus was sunk in the floor of the burial chamber, with a cavity for the canopic containers in the floor to the

Above: Near the foot of the causeway of the Second Pyramid crouches the Great Sphinx. It is possible that this dates from a slightly earlier period than the pyramid, and that its head may have been reworked during the Twelfth Dynasty.

south-east: the first surviving example of such a canopic installation within a pyramid.

Left: The Second Pyramid has a granite pillared hall that would once have been lined by statues of the king, Khaefre.

Principal Explorations

The interior of the pyramid was opened by Belzoni in 1818, with the first major

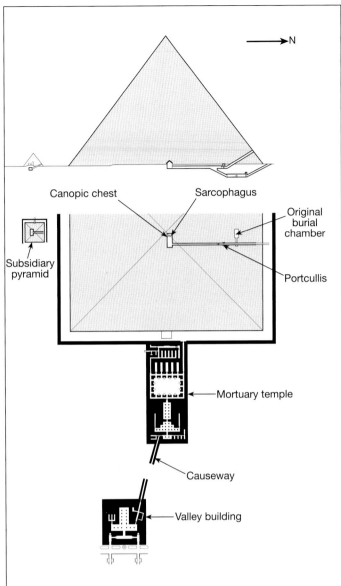

Canopic chest

Sarcophagus

Original
burial
chamber

Subsidiary
pyramid

Portcullis

Mortuary temple

Causeway

Valley building

Above: The statues of Khaefre found in a pit in the temple hall of the valley building are now in the Cairo Museum.

Above right: Section and plan of the Second Pyramid.

examination of the whole monument undertaken by Vyse and Perring in 1837. The valley building was cleared by Mariette in 1853 and 1858, and surveyed by Petrie in 1881. The complex was fully cleared by Hölscher in 1909–10.

MENKAURE'S PYRAMID

   *'Menkaure is Divine'*

The Third Pyramid is very much smaller than the other two Giza pyramids; indeed, it seems originally to have been intended to be even smaller. It has lost all its limestone casing, but a large amount of a lower casing of granite is still in place.

The pyramid's temples show a further development over the temples of Khaefre, moving towards what was later to become the standard layout. The subsidiary pyramid (L.X/GIIIc) is near the south-west corner of the main monument, a position previously used by Djedefre, and later only by Userkaf.

The substructure of the main pyramid seems to have undergone at least two changes of plan. The initial small pyramid had a simple descending passage and burial chamber but, with the enlargement of the super-structure, a new entrance corridor was provided, including a small panelled chamber and three portcullises. Still later, a new burial chamber and a niched store-room were added at a lower level. The panelled basalt sarcophagus found in the final burial chamber was lost at sea en route to England in 1838. Menkaure's burial was renewed during the Twenty-fifth or Twenty-sixth Dynasty, when a new coffin was provided for his despoiled mummy. This coffin is in the British Museum, together with human remains that might be part of Menkaure's body, although carbon-14 dates suggest a much later derivation.

MODERN DESIGNATION
L.IX; G III; Third Pyramid
LOCATION: Giza
DATE: c. 2493–2475 BC
OWNER: Menkaure
BASIS OF ATTRIBUTION
Inscription upon pyramid casing and many inscribed statues and fragments in the complex
DIMENSIONS: Base 103 x 103 metres; height 65 metres

Left: Section and plan of the Third Pyramid complex.

Below: The Third Pyramid still preserves substantial remains of the mortuary temple, from which the line of the causeway can be traced down to the valley building, now buried beneath the sand at the bottom right of the picture.

Labels in the diagram: N · Original entrance · Subsidiary pyramid (GIIIc) · GIIIb · GIIIa · Portcullises · Mortuary temple · Causeway · Valley building

Principal Explorations

Many early European and Arab travellers mention the pyramid; masonry was removed in 1196 and 1827. Caviglia attempted to tunnel into the structure in 1836, and it was finally entered by Vyse and Perring in 1837; the pyramid's temples were excavated by Reisner during 1906–24.

MODERN DESIGNATION:
L.XLIII; D 66;
Mastabat Faraun
LOCATION: Saqqara-
South
DATE: *c.* 2475–2471 BC
OWNER: Shepseskaf
BASIS OF ATTRIBUTION:
Inscribed fragment
from mortuary temple
DIMENSIONS: Base 100
x 74 metres; height 18
metres

Above: The Mastabat Faraun of Shepseskaf at South Saqqara.

Below: Plan of the Mastabat Faraun.

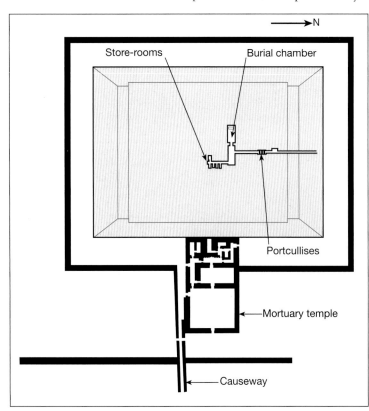

SHEPSESKAF'S TOMB

 *'Shepseskaf is Pure'*

Alone among the kings of the Old Kingdom whose monuments can be traced with certainty, Shepseskaf, last king of the Fourth Dynasty, did not begin a pyramid. Instead, he built a gigantic mastaba tomb, with raised end-pieces reminiscent of those found on the lids of many sarcophagi. This would seem to be a manifestation of the '*pr-nw*' shrine, a shape that is symbolic of Lower Egypt. The meaning of this change is unclear, although the abandonment of the solar symbol represented by the pyramid may be linked to the fact that the king's own name did not, unlike those of his immediate predecessors, contain the name of the sun-god, Re.

A conventional mortuary temple and causeway were built on the east side, but the valley building has never been explored. Likewise, nothing is known of any subsidiary tomb.

The substructure is similar to that of Menkaure's pyramid, but arranged more regularly, with the burial chamber west of an antechamber, and a room with store-niches to the south-east. The sarcophagus was smashed in antiquity.

Principal Explorations

The tomb was first entered by Mariette in the 1860s or 1870s; full clearance was carried out by Jéquier in 1924–5.

The Fifth Dynasty

Little is known of the transition between the Fourth and Fifth Dynasties, although it appears that a woman, Khentkaues I (see page 123), acted as regent at some point during the period. During the new dynasty, the principal royal necropolis was Abusir, some 11 kilometres south of Giza, although a number of kings were interred at Saqqara. The size and constructional quality of these pyramids falls well short of Fourth Dynasty norms, but in contrast, their temples are consistently larger and preserve very fine examples of relief decoration.

Above: North Saqqara: from the right are the pyramids of Userkaf, Djoser and Unas.

USERKAF'S PYRAMID

 *'Pure are the Places of Userkaf'*

Userkaf's pyramid, although relatively well built, has lost its casing, and is in fairly poor condition. Uniquely for its period, the majority of its mortuary temple is on the south side, probably as a result of the topography directly to the east not being conducive to pyramid building. The subsidiary pyramid is to the south-west, but the majority of the causeway and the valley building have not been discovered.

The substructure generally follows Shepseskaf's pattern, except that the store-room is placed halfway along the entrance corridor and lacks niches. A broken sarcophagus was found in the burial chamber.

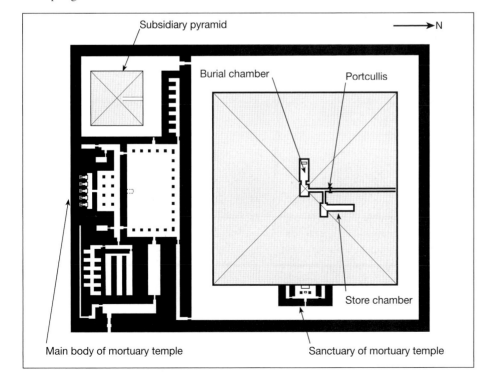

Subsidiary pyramid — N

Burial chamber — Portcullis

Store chamber

Main body of mortuary temple — Sanctuary of mortuary temple

Left: Plan of the pyramid complex of Userkaf.

MODERN DESIGNATION: L.XXXI; Haram el-Mekarbesh (Scratched Pyramid)
LOCATION: Saqqara
DATE: *c.* 2471–2464 BC
OWNER: Userkaf
BASIS OF ATTRIBUTION: Many inscribed items in the pyramid complex
DIMENSIONS: Base 73 x 73 metres; height 49 metres

Above: The pyramid of Userkaf seen from the north-east.

Principal Explorations

The pyramid was opened by Marucchi (of whom very little is known) in 1831–2, and subsequently by Perring in July 1839, via a robber's tunnel. The mortuary temple was excavated by Firth in 1928–9; work was continued between 1948 and 1955 by Lauer, who returned for further work with Labrousse in 1976–8. Finally, El-Khouli worked on the site in 1982–5.

SAHURE'S PYRAMID

 *'The Ba of Sahure Appears'*

Right: Looking up the causeway of Sahure's pyramid.

Sahure's Pyramid is in poor condition, and the area over the entrance corridor has collapsed. The mortuary temple is fairly well preserved, and follows a plan that

MODERN DESIGNATION: L.XVIII

LOCATION: Abusir

DATE: *c.* 2464–2452 BC

OWNER: Sahure

BASIS OF ATTRIBUTION: Numerous inscribed elements from the pyramid complex

DIMENSIONS: Base 79 x 79 metres; height 47 metres

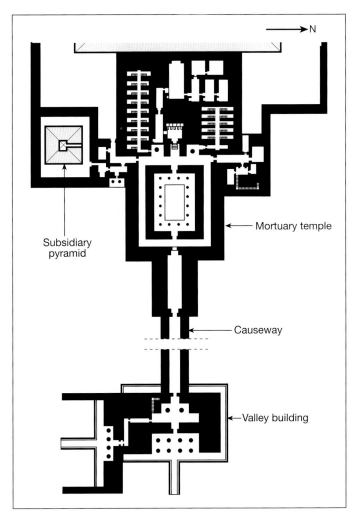

Subsidiary
pyramid

Mortuary temple ◄——

Causeway ◄——

Valley building ◄——

Above: Many fragments of the decoration of the mortuary temple of Sahure's Pyramid survive. This one of Sahure being suckled by the goddess Nekhbet is in the Cairo Museum; their eyes were once inlaid with metal and stone.

Left: Plan of the mortuary temple and valley building of Sahure.

essentially sets the standard for the remainder of the Old Kingdom. The causeway is also well preserved, although the valley building is in poor shape, and partly below the modern water table. The subsidiary pyramid was placed just south of the mortuary temple, in what was henceforth the standard location.

The interior of the pyramid was wrecked in the Middle Ages by stone robbers, leaving a partly collapsed, irregular set of cavities, with just a single fragment of basalt representing the sarcophagus. The burial chamber lay in the centre of the pyramid; on the basis of later monuments, it is likely that an antechamber lay directly east of it, from which a horizontal passage led at a modestly oblique angle towards the centre of the north face. The actual entrance was a short sloping passage, with a portcullis at its inner end.

Principal Explorations

Investigated and entered by Perring in 1839, and again by de Morgan in the 1890s; excavated by Borchardt in 1902–1908.

NEFERIRKARE'S PYRAMID

 *'The Ba of Neferirkare'*

The pyramid core was built in stepped form, and it is possible that it was never cased as a true pyramid. Only the inner part of the mortuary temple was completed in stone, the remainder having been completed in brick and wood after Neferirkare's death. An important set of papyri relating to the running of the temple were found in the mortuary temple. The causeway was later diverted to serve the pyramid of Niuserre, the valley building also being taken over by that king.

MODERN DESIGNATION: L.XXI; Great Pyramid (of Abusir)
LOCATION: Abusir
DATE: c. 2452–2442 BC
OWNER: Neferirkare Kakai
BASIS OF ATTRIBUTION: Inscribed material from complex
DIMENSIONS: Base 105 x 105 metres; height 72 metres

Above: The pyramid of Neferirkare, which may never have been cased.

Right: Plan of the mortuary temple of Neferirkare, where an important set of papyri on the running of the temple were found.

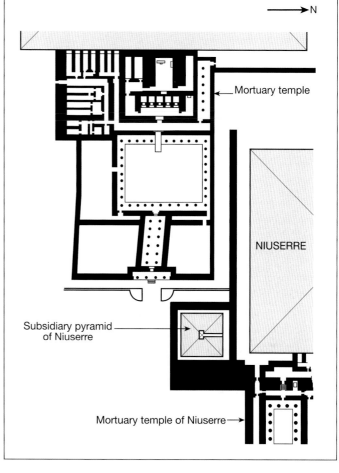

Mortuary temple

NIUSERRE

Subsidiary pyramid of Niuserre

Mortuary temple of Niuserre →

The interior of the pyramid was another victim of stone robbers, and little more than the general layout can be discerned.

Principal Explorations
Investigated and entered by Perring in 1839, and again by de Morgan in the 1890s; excavated by Borchardt in 1902–1908.

NEFEREFRE'S PYRAMID

 *'The Bas of Neferefre are Divine'*

Right: The monument of Neferefre rises only a few courses above the surrounding desert, and is dwarfed by the adjacent pyramid of Neferirkare.

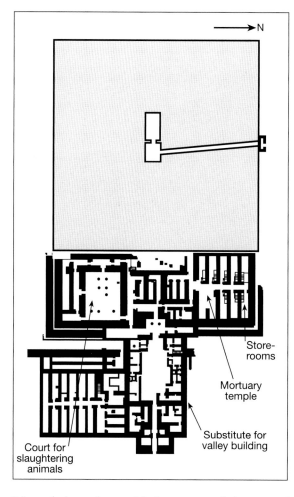

Left: Plan of the pyramid complex of Neferefre.

Although intended to follow the pattern of earlier pyramids, this monument had only risen a few courses when the king died. Accordingly, it was finished off by filling the interior with gravel, thus turning it into a mastaba of uniquely square plan. Since the causeway and valley building were barely begun, the mortuary temple, largely built in brick, was enlarged to incorporate elements usually found in the valley building. The structure is well preserved, and revealed many items, including a wooden boat, statuary and administrative papyri.

The substructure followed the usual pattern for the period, but suffered severely from stone robbery owing to its coverage by little more than rubble. Nevertheless, along with fragments of the sarcophagus, parts of the royal mummy were found, including a hand, part of the skull and other fragments. These mummified parts proved to be those of a young man.

MODERN DESIGNATION: L.XXVI; Unfinished Pyramid
LOCATION: Abusir
DATE: *c.* 2435–2432 BC
OWNER: Neferefre
BASIS OF ATTRIBUTION: Inscribed and written material from complex
DIMENSIONS: Base 65 x 65 metres

Above: Neferefre's brick mortuary temple is well preserved; the outer part has been reburied after excavations.

Principal Explorations
Summarily examined by Borchardt in 1906, who believed that there was nothing to be found. Excavated by Verner and Bartá from 1985 onwards, whose important discoveries contradicted their predecessor's conclusions.

SHEPSEKARE'S PYRAMID (?)
The outline of a barely begun pyramid lies under the sand to the north of the other Abusir pyramids. The T-shaped cut for the substructure is visible, but little else; it seems that only one or two months' work was ever carried out.

MODERN DESIGNATION: None
LOCATION: Abusir
DATE: *c.* 2442–2435 BC
OWNER: Shepseskare?
BASIS OF ATTRIBUTION: Position and lack of any other likely monument for king
DIMENSIONS: Uncertain

Principal Explorations
Located by Verner in 1980.

MODERN DESIGNATION:
L.XX

LOCATION: Abusir

DATE: c. 2432–2421 BC

OWNER: Niuserre

BASIS OF ATTRIBUTION:
Inscribed material from complex

DIMENSIONS: Base 79 x 79 metres; height 52 metres

Above: The pyramid complex of Niuserre, seen from the pyramid's causeway.

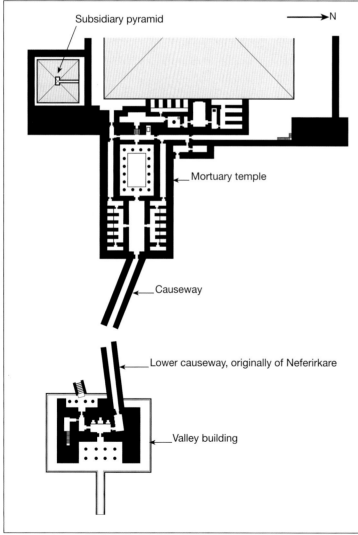

Left: Plan of the mortuary temple of Niuserre, and the valley building he usurped from Neferirkare.

NIUSERRE'S PYRAMID

'The Places of Niuserre are Established'

The pyramid is of the usual construction for its period. The lower causeway and valley building of Neferirkare's pyramid were reused, the outer parts of Niuserre's mortuary temple being placed further south than usual to facilitate the construction of the new upper (joining) section of the causeway.

Here, too, the substructure was badly damaged by stone robbers who sought large fine limestone blocks for building the monuments of Cairo.

Principal Explorations

Examined and entered by Perring in 1839, and again by De Morgan in the 1890s; excavated by Borchardt in 1902–1908.

MENKAUHOR'S PYRAMID

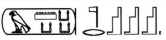

'Divine are the Places of Menkauhor'
For plan, see page 74.

Nothing of this pyramid is now visible, although its general outline has been traced by modern investigators. It is possible that the causeway or valley building – traces of which could be seen in the 1840s – may have been reused for the complex of Teti, which lies to the west-south-west and has the outer parts of its mortuary temple arranged in such a way as to suggest orientation towards the earlier structure. What little is known of its sub-structure suggests the typical early Fifth Dynasty arrangement of an oblique entrance passage, an antechamber and a burial chamber. The monument has also been ascribed to the Tenth Dynasty king Merykare (see page 79), but the size and design are more consistent with a Fifth Dynasty date.

Most of the complex area was heavily built upon during the Graeco-Roman period, partly to provide the entrance way to the avenue of the Serapeum, the cemetery of the sacred bulls, which led west from this part of Saqqara, and to the cat and dog cemeteries that lay at the edge of the escarpment.

Principal Explorations

Noted by Lepsius in 1843 and Firth in 1930, Zahi Hawass began work at the site in 2005.

ISESI'S PYRAMID

'Perfect is Isesi'
This pyramid follows the usual constructional style of the period. The mortuary temple is somewhat larger than those at Abusir, with a large 'pylon' on either side of the entrance. The causeway ascends the edge of the escarpment at a fairly steep angle; the valley building has not been found.

MODERN DESIGNATION: L.XXIX; Destroyed Pyramid
LOCATION: Saqqara
DATE: *c.* 2421–2413 BC
OWNER: Menkauhor
BASIS OF ATTRIBUTION: Design of interior, presence of monuments bearing Menkauhor's name in general area; its location near the edge of the escarpment mirrors that of the pyramid of Menkauhor's successor, Isesi
DIMENSIONS: Base *c.* 65–70 metres square

Above: King Menkauhor, as shown in an Eighteenth Dynasty relief from the tomb of Amenemonet at Saqqara.

Below: The pyramid of Isesi, seen from its mortuary temple.

MODERN DESIGNATION:
L.XXXXVII; Haram
el-Shawwaf (Pyramid
of the Sentinel)
LOCATION: Saqqara-
South
DATE: c. 2413–2385 BC
OWNER: Djedkare Isesi
BASIS OF ATTRIBUTION:
Inscribed material from
complex
DIMENSIONS: Base 79 x
79 metres; reconstruct-
ed height 53 metres

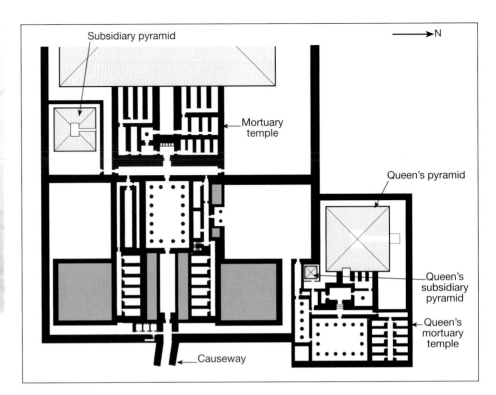

Right: Plan of the mortuary temple of Isesi and the pyramid complex of his wife.

The substructure introduces a new standard plan: the antechamber now has doors in both west and east walls, the latter giving access to a store-room, proba- bly with three niches. The burial chamber had its canopic chest sunk in the floor, south-east of the foot of the sarcophagus, which was broken by robbers; among the sarcophagus's fragments were the remains of Isesi's mummy, now in Cairo Museum.

Principal Explorations
Examined by Perring in 1839 and Lepsius in 1843, and entered by Maspero in 1880. Cleared by Varille and Abdelsalam Hussein in 1945, work being continued by Fakhry. New investigations began under Mathieu in April 2001.

UNAS' PYRAMID

 *'Perfect are the Places of Unas'*

MODERN DESIGNATION:
L.XXXV
LOCATION: Saqqara
DATE: c. 2385–2355 BC
OWNER: Unas
BASIS OF ATTRIBUTION:
Inscriptions inside and
outside the pyramid
DIMENSIONS:
Base 58 x 58 metres;
reconstructed height 43
metres

The funerary complex of Unas was built across the site of the Second Dynasty tomb of Hotepsekhemwy, the superstructure of which was demolished to make way for it. This enabled the complex to sit on the 'podium' created for the Archaic tomb.

Externally, the pyramid of Unas closely follows Fifth Dynasty patterns. Similarly, the mortuary temple is like that of Isesi, although lacking the latter's 'pylons'. Its causeway, of very considerable length owing to the complex's remote location, is perhaps the best preserved of its kind, with elements of the wall decoration in situ. The valley building is also in a fairly good state, and is interest- ing in that part of it was later used as the burial place of an early First Intermediate Period prince, Ptahshepses, in a borrowed Fourth Dynasty sarcophagus.

Internally, Unas' monument is essentially identical in design with that of Djedkare Isesi, but with some important additions: first, a chapel was built over the

Above: The pyramid complex of Unas.

Right: Plan of Unas' complex.

entrance to the substructure; second, the pyramid has the first royal substructure to be decorated since the time of Djoser. The west end of the burial chamber has a delicate panelled design, while the ceiling is adorned with five-pointed stars. Most importantly, the rest of the burial chamber, the antechamber and part of the approach corridor are covered with columns of hieroglyphs – the so-called Pyramid Texts, a compilation of religious spells (see page 14) that from this time became the standard decorative scheme for kingly pyramids until the end of the Old Kingdom. Interestingly, decoration also appears at this time in some private burial chambers, which hitherto had likewise been devoid of adornment.

Fragments of Unas' skull and left arm found in the burial chamber are now in Cairo Museum.

Principal Explorations

First entered by Maspero on 28 February 1881; the complex was cleared by Barsanti between 1899 and 1901, by Firth in 1929–30, by Hassan and Goneim in 1937–8, and by Saad and Hussein between 1939 and 1941. Hussein continued alone in 1941–3 and 1949; further work was done by Lauer and Leclant in 1974–5, Moussa in 1971 and Labrousse in 1990.

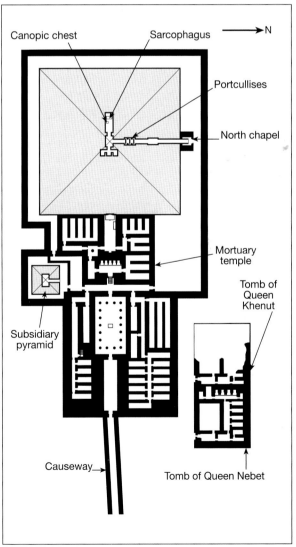

Canopic chest

Sarcophagus

N

Portcullises

North chapel

Mortuary temple

Tomb of Queen Khenut

Subsidiary pyramid

Causeway

Tomb of Queen Nebet

MODERN DESIGNATION:
L.XXX

LOCATION: Saqqara

DATE: *c.* 2355–2343 BC

OWNER: Teti

BASIS OF ATTRIBUTION:
Inscriptions throughout
the complex

DIMENSIONS: Base 79 x
79 metres; reconstruct-
ed height 52 metres

The Sixth Dynasty

TETI'S PYRAMID

'The Places of Teti Endure'

The whole pyramid complex of Teti is very similar to that of Unas. In contrast to the latter, however, it lies close to the edge of the Saqqara escarpment, and it is possible that it reused the lower part of

Above: *The west end of the gable-roofed burial chamber of Teti, showing the incised panelling, the Pyramid Texts and the star-spangled ceiling.*

the causeway of the probable pyramid of Menkauhor, just to the east. Supporting this theory is the unusual offset entrance to Teti's mortuary temple.

The substructure of Teti's pyramid is identical with that of Unas, the only substantive difference being that the sarcophagus is internally decorated with the king's name and titles. Unlike the almost pristine interior of Unas' pyramid, that of Teti's was badly damaged by stone robbers – although not as severely as the Abusir pyramids. A shoulder and arm from the king's mummy were found in the chamber when it was opened.

Below: *The area of the pyramid of Teti at Saqqara, showing the probable pyramid of Menkauhor, those of Teti's wives and some of the major private tombs of the period.*

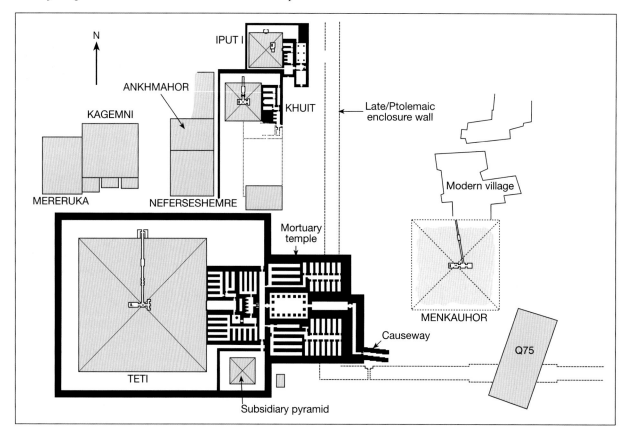

Principal Explorations

The substructure was first opened by Maspero on 29 May 1881; the mortuary temple was investigated by Quibell in 1907 and by Lauer and Leclant in 1965. The area north of the pyramid was cleared by Firth in 1921–2, the interior by Lauer and Sainte Fare Garnot in 1951–6.

PEPY I'S PYRAMID

'The Perfection of Meryre is Established'

The now very badly ruined pyramid complex of Pepy I followed usual Sixth Dynasty patterns. The interior also suffered at the hands of robbers, attempts even being made to break up the sarcophagus, which had been inscribed along the upper edge of its cof-

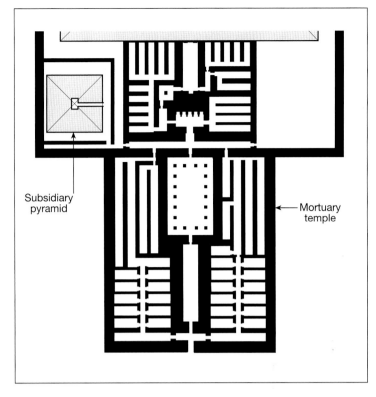

Subsidiary pyramid

Mortuary temple

fer. Besides the canopic chest, sunk as usual in the floor of the chamber, fragments of the canopic jars have come to light, together with the solidified contents of two of them. In addition, a hand and some bandages of the royal mummy survived.

Above: Plan of the mortuary temple of Pepy I.

Principal Explorations

The tomb was first entered by a local villager – via a hole in the roof of the exposed burial chamber – closely followed by Shahin in May 1880. Copies of the texts within were made soon afterwards by Emile Brugsch and also, surreptitiously, by Petrie, who found a mummified hand in the debris. This work revealed for the first time that some pyramids were decorated, as against the contemporary view that they were 'mute'. Petrie's 'pirate' copies appeared in a British periodical in April 1881, beating the official account of Heinrich Brugsch – who had copied the texts on 11 February 1881 – to the press by a month. The wrecked interior of the pyramid was cleared and restored by Lauer and Leclant in 1966–73, and the exterior parts excavated by Labrousse in 1979, 1987–8 and 1993–7.

Left: The pitiful remains of the pyramid of Pepy I, distinguishable only by the white limestone chips generated by its demolition.

MODERN DESIGNATION: L.XXXVI

LOCATION: Saqqara-South

DATE: *c.* 2343–2297 BC

OWNER: Nefersahor/ Meryre Pepy I

BASIS OF ATTRIBUTION: Inscriptions throughout complex

DIMENSIONS: Base 79 x 79 metres; reconstructed height 52 metres

NEMTYEMSAF I'S PYRAMID

 *'The Perfection of Merenre Appears'*

MODERN DESIGNATION:
L.XXXIX

LOCATION: Saqqara-
South

DATE: *c.* 2297–2290 BC

OWNER: Merenre
Nemtyemsaf I

BASIS OF ATTRIBUTION:
Inscriptions within
pyramid

DIMENSIONS: Base 79 x
79 metres; reconstruct-
ed height 52 metres

This monument is nearly as badly destroyed as that of Nemtyemsaf's predecessor, both inside and out. The sarcophagus – which, like the canopic chest, survived largely undamaged and was made of greywacke – was decorated externally with the royal names and titles, with the innovation that the edge of the lid also bore texts. A mummy was found within the sarcophagus, but it remains a matter of debate whether it belonged to the king or, as is perhaps more likely, a later intrusive burial.

Principal Explorations

Opened by Shahin in December 1880, it was examined on 4 January 1881 by the Brugsch brothers, who removed the mummy found there. This was first carried to the local railway station in a wooden box. Unfortunately, the train had to terminate short of Cairo, meaning that the Germans had to walk the last few kilometres. The box proving too heavy, the mummy was then carried without covering – until it broke in half! One brother carrying each part, they eventually caught a cab to the museum, paying customs duty on their burden as 'pickled fish' when they crossed into the city via the Qasr el-Nil bridge.

While the temples of the pyramid remain unexcavated, the interior of the pyramid was cleared and restored by Lauer in 1971–3.

Right: Nemtyemsaf I's Pyramid, seen from the west, is another pyramid in a rather poor state.

PEPY II'S PYRAMID

 *'Neferkare is Established and Alive'*

MODERN DESIGNATION
L.XLI

LOCATION: Saqqara-
South

DATE: *c.* 2290–2196
BC

OWNER: Neferkare Pepy
II

BASIS OF ATTRIBUTION:
Inscriptions throughout
complex

DIMENSIONS: Base 79 x
79 metres; reconstruct-
ed height 53 metres

Pepy II's pyramid is much better preserved than those of his immediate predecessors, and seems to have been built with rather more care. When it was at least partly built, a masonry 'girdle' 6.5 metres thick was added around the lower part of the structure; this may have been because the structure was feared to be unstable, perhaps after an earthquake. The construction of this feature meant that

Above: Pepy II's monument is in rather better condition than Nemtyemsaf's or Pepy I's.

Right: Plan of the complex of Pepy II, including the pyramids of some of his wives.

the north chapel had to be dismantled and rebuilt further out.

The complex itself represents the Old Kingdom royal tomb at its most developed, with all aspects preserved to some extent. Parts of the mortuary temple have been restored with elements of the decoration in place.

The substructure once again follows contemporary norms, and is not as badly damaged by stone robbers as most of the other pyramids of the period. In contrast to that of Nemtyemtsaf I, the (broken) box of the canopic chest was of alabaster, although the lid was still of hardstone. The sarcophagus has only one row of texts on its exterior.

Principal Explorations

The pyramid was first opened by Shahin for Maspero in February–April 1881; the complex was fully excavated by Jéquier in 1932–5.

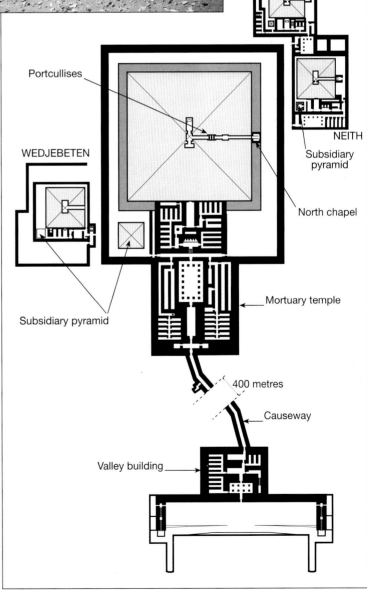

THE FIRST INTERMEDIATE PERIOD

Following the very long reign of Pepy II, there seems to have been a rapid decline in central power, manifested in a succession of brief reigns, known as the Seventh/Eighth Dynasty. This dynasty continued to reign at Memphis, but the power of the southern provincial governers grew rapidly. Ultimately, the country split with the Ninth/Tenth Dynasty ruling from Herakleopolis and the Eleventh at Thebes. A civil war presaged forcible reunification under the southern Eleventh Dynasty.

The Seventh/Eighth Dynasty

IBI'S PYRAMID

MODERN DESIGNATION:
L.XL
LOCATION: Saqqara-South
DATE: c. 2185 BC
OWNER: Qakare Ibi
BASIS OF ATTRIBUTION: Inscriptions within pyramid
DIMENSIONS: Base 32 x 32 metres

This monument reflects the collapse of royal power, the unfinished pyramid itself being no larger than a queen's example of the preceding era. Only a few parts of the superstructure survive, along with traces of a small mud-brick mortuary temple. The substructure was reduced to two rooms, albeit still decorated with the Pyramid Texts.

Principal Explorations
Excavated by Jéquier in 1929–31.

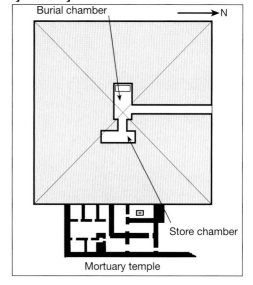

Above right: Plan of Ibi's Pyramid, which is no larger than that of an Old Kingdom queen.

Right: The scant ruins of the pyramid of Ibi.

The Ninth/Tenth Dynasty

These dynasties are little known, except that they ruled from Herakleopolis, near the mouth of the Fayoum depression. Even the names of the kings of these dynasties are uncertain, as are their burial places. One tomb is known of, thanks to written sources, and another is dated to the period on archaeological grounds.

KHUI'S PYRAMID (?)

This mysterious brick structure is of considerable size, bigger than all brick pyramids except that at Abu Rowash. Its dating is very uncertain, Khui being otherwise unknown. Of the structure's intended form, only the square plan suggests a pyramid. The substructure is unique, apparently entered via a horizontal vaulted passage in the middle of the north side.

Beyond this vaulted passage, a vestibule has a stairway running upwards to the left and a passage to the right; their destination has been destroyed, along with most of the interior of the superstructure. A passage descends from the end of the vestibule, its roof supported by a series of brick arches until it ends abruptly in a small stone-lined burial chamber. The burial chamber's floor is, very oddly, at the same angle as the passage, with its ceiling at a slightly shallower angle. This would suggest a hurried change of plan — presumably the intended burial chamber would have been further south.

MODERN DESIGNATION: Dara M

LOCATION: Dara (Arab el-Amaiem; Beni Qurra)

DATE: *c.* 22nd/21st century BC

OWNER: Khui?

BASIS OF ATTRIBUTION: Name of king found in a nearby tomb; pottery from the site is of First Intermediate Period type

DIMENSIONS: Base 130 x 130 metres

Principal Explorations

Kamal first excavated the structure in 1911; further work was done by Weill in 1946–8.

→N

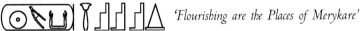

Entrance tunnel

Burial chamber

Brick arching

Above: Section of the mysterious monument of Dara.

MERYKARE'S PYRAMID

'Flourishing are the Places of Merykare'

Our knowledge of the very existence of this monument derives solely from the texts on the stelae of a number of mortuary priests of the monument. Several of the texts claim that the pyramid shared its priesthood with that of the pyramid of Teti. It is generally assumed that the two pyramids of Teti and Merykare lay near one another, although an earlier mortuary priest, Shery, was buried at Saqqara, but had cult responsibilities for Peribsen, buried over 300 kilometres away at Abydos. Merykare's pyramid has frequently been identified with L.XXIX, directly east of Teti's, but the apparent plan of that seems far more appropriate for the Fifth Dynasty's Menkauhor (see above, page 71). It is conceivable that Merykare might have usurped Menkauhor's monument, but without its proper excavation conclusions are impossible.

MODERN DESIGNATION: ?

LOCATION: Saqqara (?)

DATE: *c.*2042 BC

OWNER: Merykare

BASIS OF ATTRIBUTION: Inscriptions on stelae of mortuary priests (see main text)

DIMENSIONS: Not known

THE EVOLUTION OF THE PYRAMID: THE MIDDLE KINGDOM

Below: Apart from the pyramid itself, only a few stone fragments survive from Amenemhat III's complex at Hawara.

The Eleventh Dynasty

The first kings of the Eleventh Dynasty ruled southern Egypt only. They ruled from their capital of Thebes, and this is where they were buried. Later monarchs reunified the nation, but continued to be buried in the cemeteries that lay across the river from the Theban temples.

CHRONOLOGY OF THE MIDDLE KINGDOM

MIDDLE KINGDOM

DYNASTY XIa (2160–2066)   DYNASTY XIb (2080–1994)   DYNASTY XII (1994–1781)

Inyotef I Inyotef II Inyotef III Montjuhotpe II Montjuhotpe III Amenemhat I Senwosret I Amenemhat II Senwosret II Senwosret III Amenemhat III Amenemhat IV Sobknefe

HEAD OF
MONTJUHOTPE II

SPHINX OF
AMENEMHAT II

FACE OF
SENWOSRET III

BUST OF
AMENEMHAT III

INYOTEF I'S TOMB

The surviving portion of this tomb is a sunken courtyard, with a double colonnade across the rear, providing the façade for the royal offering place. A series of doorways at the sides gives access to the tombs of members of the court. Such tombs are known as 'saffs', from the Arabic for 'row'. Below the central royal chapel descend shafts lead to roughly hewn burial chambers.

Later documents refer to at least one of these tombs as 'pyramid', but no trace of any such element has been identified.

Principal Explorations

Surveyed in 1966 and excavated in 1970–74 by Arnold.

INYOTEF II'S TOMB

A very similar monument to the previous *saff*, but with many more chambers at the rear of the court. It is likely that the king's burial lay at the end of the sloping passage at the rear of the central chapel, but this remains unverified.

The tomb is described in Papyrus Abbott (British Museum). This papyrus is a record of an inspection of Theban royal tombs during the reign of Rameses IX, which describes the Saff el-Qisasiya as having 'the

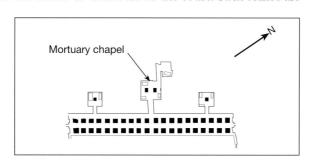

Mortuary chapel

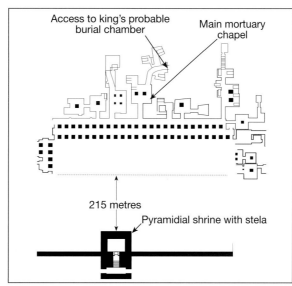

Access to king's probable burial chamber

Main mortuary chapel

215 metres

Pyramidial shrine with stela

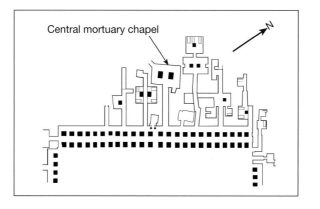

Central mortuary chapel

MODERN DESIGNATION: Saff el-Dawaba
LOCATION: El-Tarif
DATE: *c.* 2140–2123 BC
OWNER: Horus Sehertawy Inyotef I
BASIS OF ATTRIBUTION: Design and location relative to tombs of Inyotef II and III
DIMENSIONS: Courtyard 65 x 300 metres

Left: The saff tombs of the Inyotefs. From the top: Saff el-Dawaba (Inyotef I), Saff el-Qisasiya (Inyotef II) and Saff el-Baqar (Inyotef III).

STATUE OF HOR

STATUE OF KHENDJER

STATUETTE OF SOBKHOTEP V

COFFINS OF INYOTEF VII AND INYOTEF V

pyramid fallen down upon it, before which its stela stands; the figure of the king stands upon this stela, his dog between his feet'. The stela in question is now in the Cairo Museum; the brick chapel which held it, at the eastern end of the court — 250 metres from the main façade — was apparently of pyramidal form. The chapels and burial shafts of the tomb are of simple form at the rear of the courtyard. The whole tomb is today largely filled by modern houses.

Principal Explorations

The stela-chapel was located by Mariette in 1860, and the stela recovered by Maspero in 1884, further fragments being found by Daressy in 1889; Winlock obtained a number of stelae in 1913–14. The tomb was surveyed and excavated by Arnold in 1966 and 1970–74.

MODERN DESIGNATION:
Saff el-Qisasiya
LOCATION: El-Tarif
DATE: *c.* 2123–2074 BC
OWNER: Horus
Wahankh Inyotef II
BASIS OF ATTRIBUTION:
Various items of
inscribed material
DIMENSIONS: Courtyard
70 x 250+ metres

INYOTEF III'S TOMB

This tomb is essentially identical to the previous two monuments, but with a more elaborate stone-lined offering place. Sarcophagus fragments also suggest more sophisticated arrangements.

MODERN DESIGNATION: Saff el-Baqar
LOCATION: El-Tarif
DATE: *c.* 2074–2066 BC
OWNER: Horus Nakhtnebtepnefer Inyotef III
BASIS OF ATTRIBUTION: Typological comparison with the tomb of Inyotef II
DIMENSIONS: Courtyard 75 metres wide, length not known

Principal Explorations

Surveyed in 1966 by Arnold, and excavated in 1971–4.

MONTJUHOTPE II'S TEMPLE-TOMB

 *'Glorious are the places of Nebhepetre'*

This sepulchre marks a complete departure from previous royal mortuary monuments. It comprises a terraced temple, with colonnades fronting each terrace, and peristyle and hypostyle elements further back. In the centre stood a square massif

Right: Aerial view of Deir el-Bahari. Montjuhotpe II's temple is on the left, that of the Eighteenth Dynasty Hatshepsut on the right. Thutmose III's temple was still buried under the debris between Montjuhotpe's and Hatshepsut's temples when this view was taken in the 1920s or 1930s.

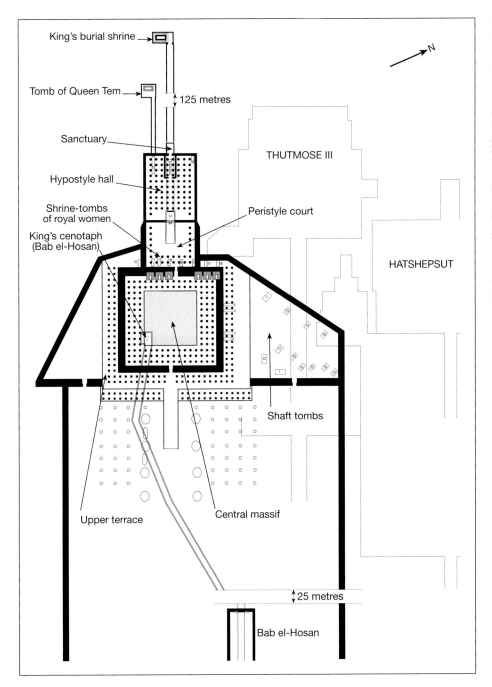

King's burial shrine

Tomb of Queen Tem

125 metres

Sanctuary

Hypostyle hall

Shrine-tombs
of royal women

King's cenotaph
(Bab el-Hosan)

THUTMOSE III

Peristyle court

HATSHEPSUT

Shaft tombs

Upper terrace

Central massif

25 metres

Bab el-Hosan

MODERN DESIGNATION:
Eleventh Dynasty
Temple; DBXI.14
LOCATION: Deir el-
Bahari
DATE: c. 2066–2014 BC
OWNER: Nebhepetre
Montjuhotpe II
BASIS OF ATTRIBUTION:
Numerous inscribed
elements from through-
out the complex
DIMENSIONS: Temple
axis 115 metres long

Left: Plan of the temple
of Montjuhotpe II, showing
the location of the later
Eighteenth Dynasty temples
of Thutmose III and
Hatshepsut.

of uncertain original form. The Abbott Papyrus (see page 106) calls the monument a pyramid, but the extant remains do not support such a reconstruction.

The temple was extensively decorated, with a sloping passageway in the rear courtyard giving access to a long, sandstone-lined passage leading to the pointed-roofed burial chamber (Tomb 14). Rather than a sarcophagus, the burial chamber held an alabaster shrine. Most of the recovered fragments of the coffin, canopic jars and mummy are in the British Museum. The monument also incorporated the burial places of members of the royal family and, in the forecourt, a dummy tomb for the king (the Bab el-Hosan). The dummy tomb held a statue, an empty coffin and some boats, and seems to have been used in Montjuhotpe II's jubilee ceremonies.

The rear part of the temple was discovered by Lord Dufferin in 1859–60 and the dummy tomb by Carter in 1901. The whole monument was then cleared by Naville in 1903–1906, and re-excavated by Winlock in 1920–24. Further work was led by Arnold in 1966–71.

Above: The entrance to the royal tomb of Montjuhotpe II in the rear courtyard of the temple.

THEBAN TOMB 281

The later of the two datings given in the information panel below is based on the advanced style of the material from the nearby tomb of Meketre (TT280), which, it has been argued, is inconsistent with the time of Montjuhotpe III. In addition, the unfinished state of the funerary complex of Amenemhat I at Lisht might suggest that this was an earlier tomb for the king at Thebes before he moved the royal capital and necropolis to the north, where subsequent royal tombs lay.

It appears that this structure was intended to be of the same kind as that of Montjuhotpe II. However, nothing was ever done other than filling and grading the platform for the temple itself and its causeway. A sloping passageway at the rear of the platform leads to a gable-roofed limestone burial chamber.

Below right: The temple platform begun by either Montjuhotpe III or Amenemhat I. The entrance to the tomb (TT281) is in the centre of the platform, towards the base of the cliff.

Principal Explorations

The burial chamber was discovered by Mond in 1903–1904, but the existence of the rest of the monument was noted only in 1914 by Winlock, who excavated the site in 1920–21.

MODERN DESIGNATION:
TT281

LOCATION: Sheikh Abd el-Qurna West

DATE: *c.* 2014–2001 or 1994–1964 BC

OWNER: Seankhkare Montjuhotpe III or Sehotepibre Amenemhat I (?)

BASIS OF ATTRIBUTION: Apparent similarity to tomb of Montjuhotpe II

The Twelfth Dynasty

AMENEMHAT I'S PYRAMID

'The Places of the Appearance of Amenemhat'

'Amenemhat is High and Beautiful'

Amenemhat I was responsible for moving the capital of Egypt back to the north, to a city known as Itjtawi. This seems to have lain near modern Lisht, where Amenemhat I built his tomb. As we have seen, it is possible that he may previously have begun a temple-tomb in the south, but at Lisht a broadly conventional pyramid complex was erected. The pyramid itself was of stone, albeit of poor quality, and incorporated numerous blocks from Old Kingdom pyramid complexes. This may simply reflect a desire for economy, but it is also possible that they were used physically to link Amenemhat with the great kings of the past. Certainly, his propaganda presented him as the founder of a new era, which would see Egypt restored to its past glories.

Little is known of the valley building and causeway, and the mortuary temple has been so thoroughly destroyed that virtually nothing is known of its plan. We can, however, assume that it remained unfinished. Surviving terracing shows that it had two levels, suggesting some affinity with Montjuhotpe II's sepulchre at Deir el-Bahari. There are indications that the design of the temple was altered in the course of construction. No trace of a subsidiary pyramid was found.

The substructure was entered from ground level on the north side, a granite-lined corridor leading to a square chamber under the

Right: Section and plan of Amenemhat I's pyramid complex.

MODERN DESIGNATION: L.LX; Northern Pyramid
LOCATION: Lisht
DATE: *c.* 1994–1964 BC
OWNER: Sehetepibre Amenemhat I
BASIS OF ATTRIBUTION: Inscribed material from complex
DIMENSIONS: Base 86 x 86 metres; reconstructed height 55 metres

N

Modern water table

372

North chapel

Upper terrace

470

Mortuary temple

954

463

956

Causeway

Possible queens' tombs

Lower terrace

Above: The pyramid of Amenemhat I at Lisht: it appears to lie on a higher level than the area of the destroyed mortuary temple, suggesting a possible arrangement akin to that found at Deir el-Bahari.

centre of the pyramid. From the centre of this room, a vertical shaft led down over 11 metres. Unfortunately, rising groundwater has inundated whatever lies below, and all attempts at pumping have failed. Likewise, no items of the king's funerary equipment have come to light.

Principal Explorations

Examined by Perring on 28 October 1839, Amenemhat I's tomb was first entered by Maspero in 1882. Excavations were then begun by Gautier and Jéquier in November 1894, followed by far more extensive ones by Lythgoe, Lansing and Mace collaboratively in 1906–1908, 1913–14 and 1920–22. The Egyptian Antiquities Organization did some clearance work at the valley building in the 1980s.

SENWOSRET I'S PYRAMID

 *'Senwosret Beholds the Two Lands'*

Amenemhat I's successor built his pyramid some 1,750 metres south of that of his father. Senwosret I's structure is innovative: it comprises a series of solidly built limestone retaining walls, with the intervening spaces filled with smaller blocks and rubble, embedded in mortar. The complex, of which the valley building remains undiscovered, closely follows late Old Kingdom norms in its design, including the last known example of a subsidiary pyramid. An unusual feature of the causeway was its partial lining with statues of the king. The outer part of the enclosure wall of the complex had finely carved bastions bearing the Horus-name of Senwosret I.

A chapel once stood over the pyramid entrance; as in Amenemhat I's pyramid, the burial chamber – some 24 metres below the pyramid base – is now under water, together with the lower end of the steeply sloped entrance corridor: the

Right: A distant view of Senwosret I's innovative pyramid.

MODERN DESIGNATION: L.LXI; Southern Pyramid

LOCATION: Lisht

DATE: *c.* 1974–1929 BC

OWNER: Kheperkare Senwosret I

BASIS OF ATTRIBUTION: Inscribed material from complex

DIMENSIONS: Base 105 x 105 metres; height 61 metres

shaft found in Amenemhat's pyramid is absent here. However, items of funerary equipment, displaced by robbers, were found above the water level, including the king's canopic jars. These are fairly unusual in having arms carved on their sides, although a private contemporary even had feet incorporated into his!

Principal Explorations

Examined by Perring on 28 October 1839, the pyramid was first entered by Maspero's workmen in 1882. Excavations were then carried out by Gautier and Jéquier in 1895–6, followed by far more extensive ones by Lythgoe and Lansing between 1908 and 1934. The latter excavations were undertaken under the auspices of the Metropolitan Museum of Art, New York, which resumed work under the direction of Arnold in 1984–7. These renewed excavations were undertaken so that Arnold could obtain the necessary information to proceed with the publication of the excavations of the pyramid complex.

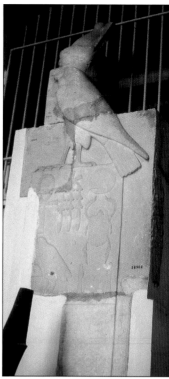

Above: One of the highly decorated panels from the enclosure wall of Senwosret I's Pyramid, bearing the king's Horus name – Ankhmesut – and praenomen, Kheperkare.

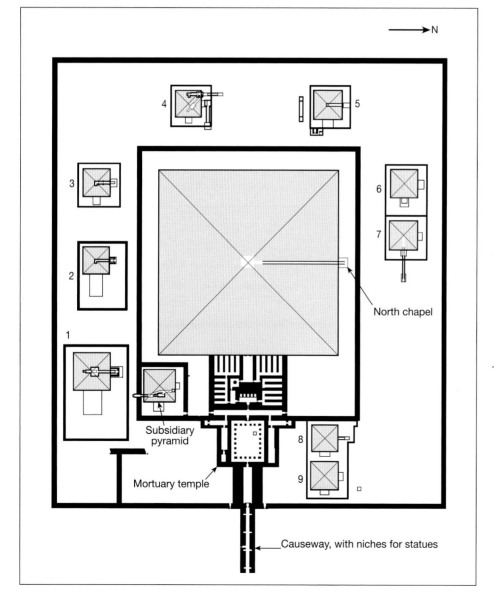

Left: Plan of the complex of Senwosret I, showing the nine pyramids belonging to members of the royal family.

Plan labels: N

4, 5, 3, 6, 7, 2, North chapel, 1, Subsidiary pyramid, Mortuary temple, 8, 9, Causeway, with niches for statues

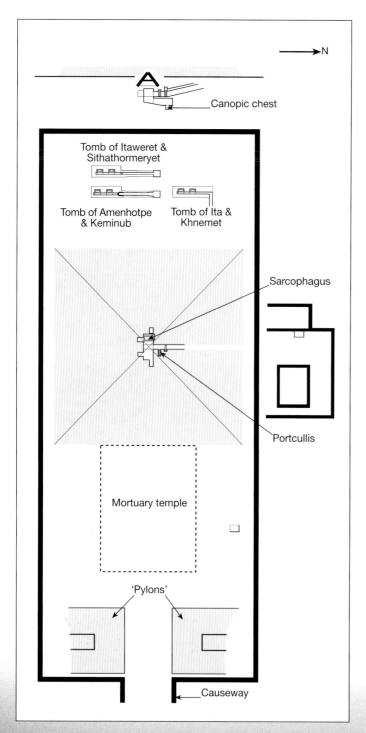

Canopic chest

Tomb of Itaweret & Sithathormeryet

Tomb of Amenhotpe & Keminub

Tomb of Ita & Khnemet

Sarcophagus

Portcullis

Mortuary temple

'Pylons'

Causeway

N

AMENEMHAT II'S PYRAMID

'The Ba of Amenemhat'

The next king abandoned Lisht, and moved north to Dahshur. In contrast with Seneferu, who had built his pyramids some 2,000 metres out into the desert, Amenemhat II built his close to the edge of the desert, on the high ridge that lies only a short distance from the edge of cultivated land. It is situated directly south of an Old Kingdom cemetery, at least four of whose tombs were annexed into the north-west corner of the king's new enclosure. The pyramid itself has been so thoroughly destroyed – the remaining limestone chippings giving it its modern name of White Pyramid – that even the dimensions of its base cannot be determined. However, it seems to have used the same structural scheme as that of Senwosret I.

The rest of the complex is also in poor condition, but it can be seen to represent further divergence from the Old Kingdom prototype. First, the enclosure is extended both to the east and west. The area to the west holds a number of innovatively designed tombs, almost certainly belonging to members of the king's family, although later dates have been suggested. The area to the east accommodated the vanished

Left: Plan of the White Pyramid complex, and a section of the pyramid's substructure.

Below: *The utterly devastated White Pyramid of Amenemhat II is barely visible on the peak of the escarpment at Dahshur.*

mortuary temple, as well as two masonry masses, which may, like similar elements at the pyramid of Djedkare Isesi, represent some kind of pylon gateway.

The substructure is, at first sight, simple, but nevertheless has a number of interesting features. A corridor from the north leads, via two portcullises, to a flat-ceilinged burial chamber. Above this, however, is a set of gabled relieving beams. Inside the chamber the sarcophagus, made up from a series of quartzite slabs, was concealed under the floor. In some previous tombs, for example that of Khaefre, sarcophagus lids had been arranged to lie flush with the floor, but in the White Pyramid, filling and paving slabs had been laid over the sarcophagus cover. Hitherto, canopic chests had always lain south or south-east of the body. This one, however, lay in the floor of a short passage that led back under the pyramid entrance passage, ending up north-east of the body. These departures were clearly intended to enhance the protection given to the corpse, the next reign seeing yet further divergence from time-hallowed tradition.

Principal Explorations

De Morgan, between December 1894 and April 1895, carried out the only substantive work on this pyramid; he found the intact burials of four princesses in the western part of the enclosure; their jewellery is now in the Cairo Museum.

SENWOSRET II'S PYRAMID

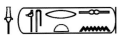 *'The Power of Senwosret'*

Senwosret II constructed his tomb in the Fayoum region, an area remote from the usual royal necropolis in the Memphis area. This would seem to have been a

MODERN DESIGNATION: L.LI; White Pyramid
LOCATION: Dahshur
DATE: *c.* 1932–1896 BC
OWNER: Nubkaure Amenemhat II
BASIS OF ATTRIBUTION: Inscribed material from complex
DIMENSIONS: Base approx. 50 x 50 metres

MODERN DESIGNATION: L.LXVI
LOCATION: Lahun
DATE: *c.* 1900–1880 BC
OWNER: Kheperkhare Senwosret II
BASIS OF ATTRIBUTION: Inscribed material from complex
DIMENSIONS: Base 106 x 106 metres; reconstructed height 49 metres

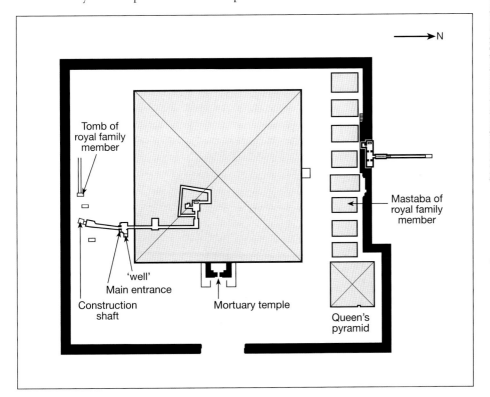

Tomb of royal family member

Construction shaft

'well'

Main entrance

Mortuary temple

Mastaba of royal family member

Queen's pyramid

Left: The plan of the pyramid complex of Senwosret II at Lahun shows the radical change that the monument represented, with the burial places decisively shifted relative to their above-ground elements.

Above: Below Senwosret II's Pyramid at Lahun is a granite burial chamber containing a sarcophagus of unusual form.

Below: The core of Senwosret II's Lahun pyramid was also something different – a rock knoll surmounted by a framework of stone, filled with mud brick.

reflection of the interest shown in the Fayoum area by kings of his dynasty, a number of whom appear to have undertaken irrigation and land reclamation work there. It centres on a large lake, Birket Qarun, fed by the Bahr Yusef, an offshoot of the Nile which splits from it at Asyut.

The king's pyramid complex marks the most momentous set of changes in Egyptian funerary practice since the early Old Kingdom. While the basic concept of the pyramid, mortuary temple, causeway and valley building remained intact, the execution of the first element (the pyramid) incorporated fundamental rethinking. First, the pyramid itself was built of mud brick for the first time since the end of the Third Dynasty. As in the Brick Pyramid at Abu Rowash, a considerable portion of the core was composed of a native rock knoll. The brick was keyed into the rock by a set of radial stone walls built on top, very similar to the system employed at the pyramid of Senwosret I, except that the filling was now of brick. The usual Tura limestone was employed for the outermost casing.

Second, the entrance to the substructure was switched to the south side, with the burial chamber shifted away from the centre of the monument. At the same time, the entrance became a shaft and the corridors and chambers a tunnelled system – apparently necessitated by the use of the rock knoll for the pyramid core which prevented the usual 'cut and cover' approach. The inability to lower in heavy blocks from above resulted in the main entrance shaft being supplemented with a larger 'construction' shaft further south. This was concealed after use under the floor of a dummy tomb, reflecting the underlying motivation of security. The same imperative is also seen elsewhere in the complex. On the north side are eight mastabas, with their cores cut from the living rock like the main pyramid, and the queen's pyramid (page 132). However, none has its substructure below the pyramid, and the burial passages of the mastabas lie in front of the south face of the king's pyramid.

Senwosret II's substructure is

fairly simple, but has some curious features, including a deep shaft near the entrance leading down to the water table and a corridor that runs round three sides of the burial chamber. The chamber itself, gable-roofed and of granite, holds a sarcophagus with an irregular undersurface and a thick lip round the rim. Perhaps an early plan had called for the sarcophagus to be partly sunk in the burial chamber floor. When excavated, the room was found to contain an alabaster offering table, the gold cobra from the king's crown and a pair of leg bones, the last traces of the pharaoh himself.

Above: Among the contents of Senwosret II's Pyramid at Lahun was an alabaster offering table.

The rest of the complex has been badly depleted, although the settlement of Lahun that adjoined the valley building has preserved much information on the daily life of the Middle Kingdom. This includes documents as well as domestic items.

Principal Explorations

The site was examined by the French and Prussian expeditions of the 1820s and 1840s, as well as by Perring on 31 October 1839, but it was not until 1889–90 that excavations properly began, carried out by Petrie. He resumed work in 1913–14, completing his excavations in 1920–21. Further excavations have been carried out by Millet from 1989 onwards.

SENWOSRET III'S PYRAMID

 *'Pure is Senwosret'*

The next monarch forsook the Fayoum in favour of the ancient cemetery of Dahshur, building his tomb 1,500 metres north of that of Amenemhat II. Senwosret III's monument is, however, another innovative achievement, although not quite in the same way as that of Senwosret II. It continues the use of brick for the actual pyramid, but without the use of a rock knoll; today, the pyramid is in a poor state, having been badly mutilated by 19th-century excavators.

The pyramid complex underwent at least two phases of building. The first followed a design not dissimilar to that found at Lahun, with royal family tombs placed within the enclosure, north and south of the king's pyramid (see page 133). However, the final version produced a rectangular enclosure strikingly similar in appearance to that of Djoser of the Third Dynasty. Not only was the enclosure wall panelled, but the king's sarcophagus had a panelled motif applied to its lower part that seems to have been intended to replicate the actual pattern of bastions seen on Djoser's monument. In addition, the entrance to the enclosure was in the south-east corner, an arrangement not seen since the Third Dynasty. Finally, in two shafts at the northern end of the complex, in an area enclosed by the final enlargement, were two Third Dynasty alabaster sarcophagi, apparently not used for burials. They are identical with examples found under the Step Pyramid, and it

MODERN DESIGNATION: L.XLVII; North Brick Pyramid

LOCATION: Dahshur

DATE: *c.* 1900–1880 BC

OWNER: Khakaure Senwosret III

BASIS OF ATTRIBUTION: Inscribed material from complex

DIMENSIONS: Base 105 x 105 metres; reconstructed height 78 metres

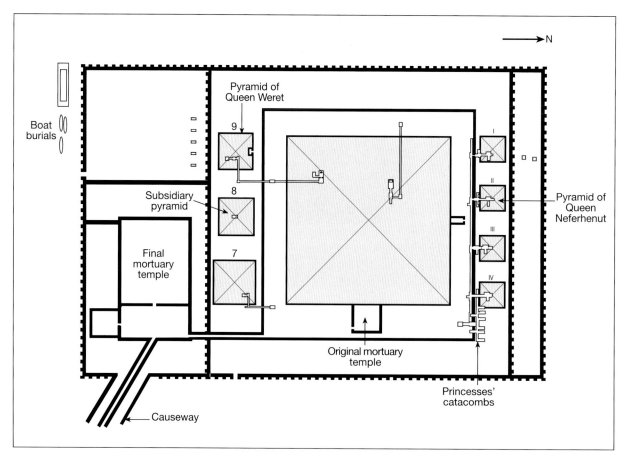

Pyramid of
Queen Weret

9

Boat
burials

Subsidiary
pyramid

8

Final
mortuary
temple

7

Original mortuary
temple

Causeway

N

I

II

Pyramid of
Queen
Neferhenut

III

IV

Princesses'
catacombs

Above: The plan of the complex of Senwosret III is heavily reminiscent of Third Dynasty practice, and represents a major shift from the practice of most of the previous millennium.

seems likely that they were actually removed from there. If so, they may have been installed as a concrete link with the earlier monument, which Senwosret III so clearly wished to recall in the design of his tomb. The Old Kingdom blocks used in Amenemhat I's pyramid may be analogues.

On the other hand, Djoser's pattern was not followed slavishly, there being no major temple on the north side of the pyramid, nor the 'Heb-sed' complex seen there. Instead, in addition to the original eastern mortuary temple, there was a large temple in the (later) southern portion of the enclosure.

Senwosret III may also have revived the subsidiary pyramid. Pyramid 8 in the centre of the south face has just a single shaft with a small chamber that contains only an uninscribed canopic chest; clearly it was some kind of ritual structure.

The substructure of the pyramid was approached via a shaft

Left: The pyramid of Senwosret III; in the foreground is the corner of the outer enclosure wall.

on the west side. It is of a fairly simple form, similar to Fifth/Sixth Dynasty royal sepulchres. Interestingly, the granite walls of the burial chamber were whitewashed, contradicting the usual Egyptian practice of flaunting the use of hard stones.

It remains uncertain whether Senwosret III was ever buried in his pyramid: no traces of an interment were found, while the king, most unusually, had a second tomb at Abydos. This tomb at Abydos was of a highly unusual design, with no superstructure other than a temple, and is known to have been an important focus of the royal cult in later years.

Principal Explorations

The pyramid was examined by Perring in September/October 1839, and in the early 1880s Maspero made an unsuccessful attempt to enter it. Excavations were carried out by de Morgan in 1894, the pyramid being entered and important caches of jewellery found in the tombs of some of the king's daughters. Jéquier did some work on the causeway in 1924 before fresh excavations were begun by Arnold in 1990.

Arnold's work has greatly increased knowledge of the layout of the whole complex, and revealed another group of jewellery (see page 133).

Above: Senwosret III also had a funerary complex at Abydos, comprising a temple and town on the edge of cultivation, and then a complex under the edge of the cliffs. In the foreground can be seen the lines of walls that enclose an area dominated by a huge crater that marks the entrance to a rock-cut tomb. To the left, the two mounds are tombs S9 and S10 (see pages 103–4).

Right: Plan of the Abydos complex. Debate continues as to whether Senwosret III was buried there, rather than at Dahshur. The rock-cut tomb descends to a considerable depth, and has a number of features designed to deter thieves, including the concealment of the sarcophagus and canopic chest behind walling.

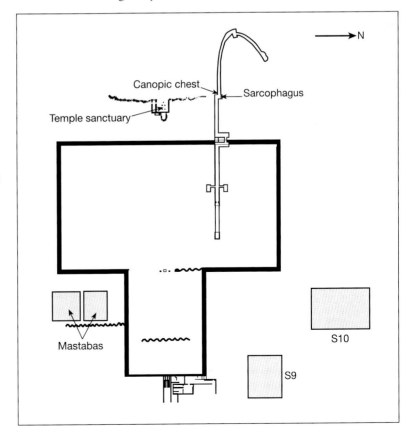

MODERN DESIGNATION:
L.LVIII; Black Pyramid
LOCATION: Dahshur
DATE: *c.* 1842–1794 BC
OWNER: Nimaatre
Amenemhat III
BASIS OF ATTRIBUTION:
Inscribed material from
complex
DIMENSIONS: Base 105
x 105 metres; recon-
structed height 75
metres

*Right: Amenemhat III's
Black Pyramid at Dahshur.*

*Below: Amenemhat III's
pyramid plan shows a
range of interesting features
in the south-west quadrant.*

AMENEMHAT III'S FIRST PYRAMID (BLACK PYRAMID)

A site due east of the Bent Pyramid was chosen for Amenemhat III's burial place. The brick pyramid itself, although badly ruined, remains a distinctive and impressive monument. The surviving part of the core is surrounded by heaps of pulverized, decomposed brickwork, some of it resulting from a major collapse during the 20th century. The elaborately decorated pyramidion survives in the Cairo Museum.

Here the pyramid complex reverts to a more standard form, although lacking any potential subsidiary pyramid. On the other hand, the substructure is more elaborate than before, with the tombs of two of the king's wives wholly within the pyramid's structure: Aat and an anonymous lady had chambers with their own entrances, but no separate superstructure. This complex was connected to the king's tomb chambers, with its own entrance on the opposite (west) side. For the first time pyramid entrance passages have stairs, greatly easing descent; in addition, the corridors have an average height of some 2 metres, contrasting with the low ceilings of Old Kingdom pyramids.

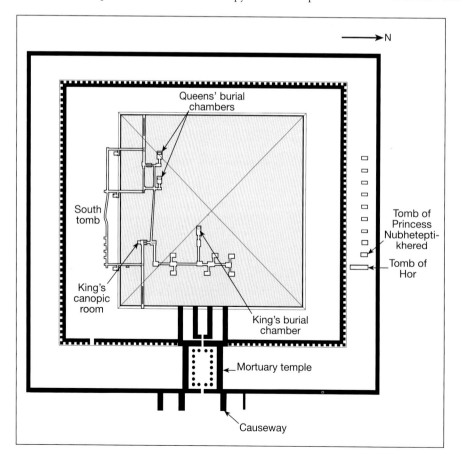

Queens' burial chambers

South tomb

King's canopic room

King's burial chamber

Tomb of Princess Nubhetepti-khered

Tomb of Hor

Mortuary temple

Causeway

N

The king's main complex comprises a burial chamber near the centre of the pyramid, approached by a corridor flanked with store-rooms. Curiously, the canopic chest was intended to lie some 40 metres from the burial chamber. Apparently as a substitute for subsidiary pyramids for the king and his queens, a series of corridors were placed under the south face of the pyramid and equipped with chapels and three dummy canopic chests. These unique features were not revived in any pyramid.

The Black Pyramid's substructure displays numerous indications of structural failure, and the monument was not used for the king's burial, a new pyramid being built at Hawara (see below). However, the queens' interments do seem to have gone ahead, with further burial places improvised in the corridors and vestibules of the king's chambers. These improvised sepulchres may date to the Thirteenth Dynasty, when two shaft tombs on the north side were converted into royal tombs.

Principal Explorations

Examined by Perring in 1839, the complex was first excavated by de Morgan from December 1894 onwards; he first entered on 15 March 1895, having found the interior by means of tunnelling under the pyramid from the north. However, he neglected much of the enclosure, and the whole complex was re-excavated by Arnold from 1976 to 1983.

AMENEMHAT III'S SECOND PYRAMID

 *'Amenemhat Lives'*

Having abandoned his original pyramid, Amenemhat III turned to the Fayoum for his new sepulchre. At Hawara, he erected a pyramid complex with several

Below: Amenemhat III's Second Pyramid at Hawara is also of radical design, incorporating a huge temple (the 'Labyrinth') on its south side. This partly restored plan is based on the extremely scanty traces that have survived into modern times.

MODERN DESIGNATION: L.LXVII
LOCATION: Hawara
DATE: c. 1842–1794 BC
OWNER: Nimaatre Amenemhat III
BASIS OF ATTRIBUTION: Inscribed material from complex
DIMENSIONS: Base 105 x 105 metres; reconstructed height 58 metres

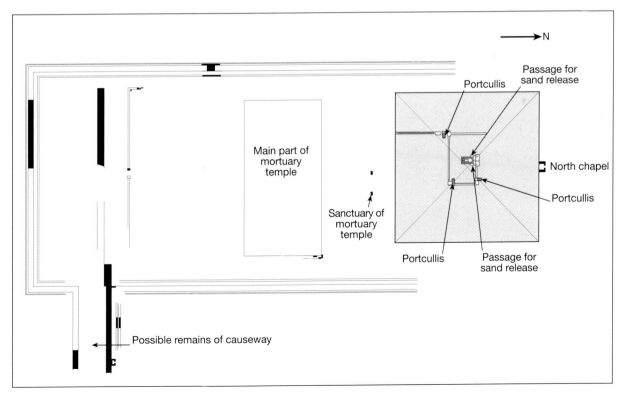

Above: The focus of the huge temple, the Labyrinth, of Amenemhat III's Second Pyramid at Hawara seems to have been a series of granite shrines near the south face of the pyramid; each shrine held two royal figures.

innovative features, and it is the best-preserved of the brick pyramids.

The temple complex lay predominantly on the south side of the pyramid itself, and covered an area of over 60,000 square metres. Subsequent destruction has made its plan difficult to work out, although its north part included a number of quartzite shrines, each with two royal figures inside. The entrance seems to have been in the south-east corner, and thus the whole structure may – like that of Senwosret III – be paying tribute to the pyramid complex of Djoser.

The entrance to the pyramid substructure is on the south side, and has even more elaborate protective devices than the Black Pyramid. Each change of direction is via a sliding quartzite portcullis slab in the ceiling, while the burial chamber is a single block of the same stone. Access was via a trench in the antechamber floor leading to a gap between the burial chamber's end wall and one of the roofing slabs, kept raised until the funeral. The slab was supported on props, bedded in a series of sand-filled 'chimneys'. The latter had plugs at the bottom: when these were removed, the sand would flow out, the props would sink down, and the slab would seal the chamber. Security was further enhanced by filling an apparently blind corridor near the pyramid entrance with stone blocks.

However, robbers mined the obstacles in the corridor and robbed the burial chamber; the king's body was burned. His granite sarcophagus, with the panelled lower part introduced in the previous reign, lay in the centre of the room, a canopic chest beyond its foot. An additional sarcophagus had been created by placing granite slabs between the east side of the king's sarcophagus and the wall, and adding a lid. An offering table in the room showed this extra sarcophagus to have been made for Princess Neferuptah. Her body was, however, removed prior to her father's death, and placed in a new pyramid, built two kilometres to the south (see page 134).

Principal Explorations

The mortuary temple was damaged early in the 19th century during the digging of the Wahbi Canal, which cut off a whole corner. It was examined by Perring on 1 November 1839 and first mapped by Lepsius in May–July 1843; it was excavated in 1888–9 and 1910 by Petrie, who is the only person to have entered the pyramid. Unable to find the entrance, he extended a robber's tunnel that ultimately led to the burial chamber; he then found the entrance by working his way outwards. Petrie was hindered by the rise of the water table since antiquity, which had filled many galleries with mud and water almost up to the ceiling. Subsequent increases in water levels meant that by the time the entrance was reopened by the Supreme Council for Antiquities in the 1990s, it was not possible to reach even the bottom of the entrance staircase.

The Thirteenth Dynasty

The tombs of the last two monarchs of the Twelfth Dynasty, Amenemhat IV and Queen Sobkneferu, are unknown. Our knowledge of the kings of the next dynasty is also very patchy and inconclusive. The Thirteenth Dynasty comprises a long series of monarchs who reigned for only short periods, and only a handful of them left known sepulchres. In addition, there are a number of pyramids of this date without identified owners. Accordingly, the ordering of these monuments is heavily reliant on the interpretation of the evolution of their architecture.

Two structures at Abydos may possibly be royal tombs of the Thirteenth Dynasty; they might reflect the shift in the dynasty's political mass southwards as Palestinian power built up in the delta. Ultimately, the Thirteenth Dynasty was to end with the takeover of northern Egypt by the 'Hyksos' Fifteenth Dynasty of Palestinian origin, an area ruled first by the Palestinian Fourteenth Dynasty. The Hyksos Fifteenth Dynasty seem to have violently displaced the earlier line *c*. 1650.

AMENEMHAT IV, V OR VI'S PYRAMID (?)

Near the ruined pyramid of Amenemhat II is an area of limestone rubble, some 40 metres square, with the line of a causeway leading from it. The rubble is probably the remains of a casing; together with the survival of the causeway, it suggests a considerable degree of completion at some stage.

Principal Explorations

No clearance has ever taken place, although the named fragment was recovered by Moussa in the 1970s; the site was damaged by pipe-laying in 1975.

MODERN DESIGNATION: L.LIV

LOCATION: Dahshur

DATE: *c*. 18th century BC

OWNER: Amenemhat IV, V or VI?

BASIS OF ATTRIBUTION: A fragment bearing the name Amenemhat was found in the area, although it might be a 'stray' piece from the nearby pyramid of Amenemhat II

DIMENSIONS: Base *c*. 40 metres square

Left: *The wastes of South Dahshur were used as a royal necropolis, including the burial of Qemau, during the Thirteenth Dynasty. Qemau's Pyramid lay on a low hill at the right-hand end of this view.* (see page 98).

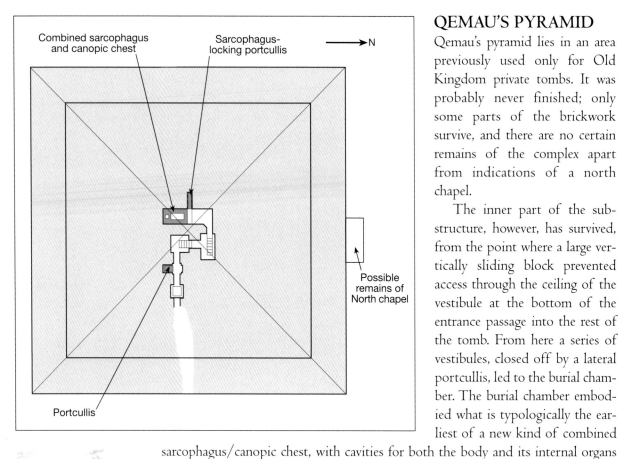

Combined sarcophagus and canopic chest

Sarcophagus-locking portcullis

→ N

Possible remains of North chapel

Portcullis

MODERN DESIGNATION:
Pyramid of Ameny-Qemau

LOCATION: Dahshur-South

DATE: 18th century BC

OWNER: (Ameny-)Qemau

BASIS OF ATTRIBUTION:
The king's canopic jars found in the pyramid

DIMENSIONS: Base 53 x 53 metres

Above: The substructure of Qemau's pyramid had a number of security features, including a combined sarcophagus and canopic chest whose lid was locked in place by a lateral portcullis.

QEMAU'S PYRAMID

Qemau's pyramid lies in an area previously used only for Old Kingdom private tombs. It was probably never finished; only some parts of the brickwork survive, and there are no certain remains of the complex apart from indications of a north chapel.

The inner part of the substructure, however, has survived, from the point where a large vertically sliding block prevented access through the ceiling of the vestibule at the bottom of the entrance passage into the rest of the tomb. From here a series of vestibules, closed off by a lateral portcullis, led to the burial chamber. The burial chamber embodied what is typologically the earliest of a new kind of combined sarcophagus/canopic chest, with cavities for both the body and its internal organs within the same block. This formed the floor of the room, and was sealed by a lid that was slid on top from the antechamber area directly north of the sarcophagus. The lid was locked into place by a sideways-sliding portcullis slab; as the lid was in contact with the chamber walls on three sides and the portcullis on the other, tomb-robbers had to resort to smashing the north end of the lid to gain access to the coffin, and then push the remains northwards to rifle the canopic cavity.

Principal Explorations

The site was cleared by Muses and Gabra in 1957, but the excavations were brought to a premature end that summer with Muses arrest for contravening antiquities law. Maragioglio and Rinaldi made an examination of the remains in the late 1960s.

TWO ANONYMOUS PYRAMIDS

Two possible ruined pyramids have been noted under the sand north-east and north-west of Qemau's monument. Nothing more is known.

Principal Explorations

First noticed by Arnold and Stadelmann in the mid-1970s.

MODERN DESIGNATION: A & B

LOCATION: Dahshur-South

DATE: 18th century BC

OWNER: Not known

BASIS OF ATTRIBUTION: Location in an area otherwise known to have been used during the Thirteenth Dynasty

DIMENSIONS: Not known

THE NORTH PYRAMID OF MAZGHUNA

The early Thirteenth Dynasty royal necropolis spread further southward from Dahshur to Mazghuna, where two pyramids have been found. Although a very thick layer of limestone chips covered its site, the northern pyramid was entirely destroyed before 1910. Nothing of the core was then traceable, although Lepsius included it on his map. In view of the lack of any brick debris, it is possible that the structure may have been of stone, unlike preceding pyramids. The only part of the complex that has been traced in detail is a 116-metre section of the foundations of the exceptionally wide causeway.

The actual entrance to the pyramid has been destroyed, the first preserved part being steps descending from the north. However, since the size of the pyramid is very uncertain, it is not clear where the actual entrance was. In contrast to the state of the superstructure, the roofing of the rest of the substructure is intact, the plan being reminiscent of that of Qemau, albeit with additions; the arrangement of the combined sarcophagus/canopic chest, portcullis and antechamber is exactly the same. It seems likely that the pyramid had never been used for a burial, as the sarcophagus lid was found still stored in the antechamber.

Principal Explorations

Examined by Lepsius in spring 1843 and entered by de Morgan in the 1890s, the pyramid was cleared by Mackay in 1910–11.

THE TOMB OF HOR

The Tomb of Hor has been dated to the middle of the Thirteenth Dynasty. It is an enlarged version of a simple shaft tomb on the north side of Amenemhat III's Black Pyramid, with the addition of a new stone burial chamber. Except for the omission of a portcullis and the use of a

Right: Plan of the North Pyramid of Mazghuna. This pyramid has the widest known causeway, but a totally destroyed superstructure. Its dimensions could vary anywhere between the two potential baselines shown. A mound just north of the causeway may represent a queen's pyramid.

MODERN DESIGNATION: L.LIX; North Pyramid
LOCATION: Mazghuna
DATE: 18th century BC
OWNER: A later king than Qemau
BASIS OF ATTRIBUTION: Slightly more developed than Qemau's pyramid
DIMENSIONS: Base *c.* 58 metres square?

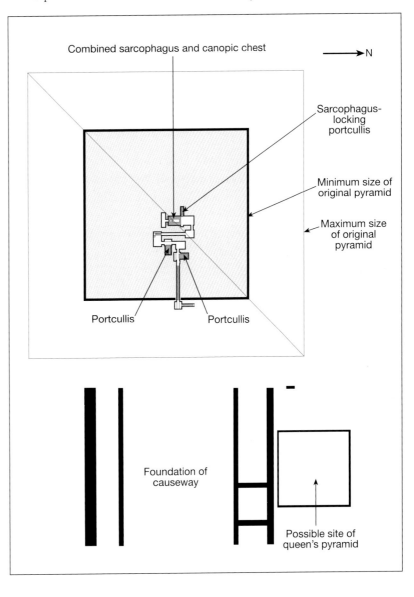

Combined sarcophagus and canopic chest

N

Sarcophagus-locking portcullis

Minimum size of original pyramid

Maximum size of original pyramid

Portcullis

Portcullis

Foundation of causeway

Possible site of queen's pyramid

separate sarcophagus and canopic chest, the arrangement mirrors that found in contemporary pyramids (e.g. Qemau's). The existence of this tomb suggests that other kings of the period may have had similar sepulchres, explaining why there are so few known pyramids in relation to the number of kings.

The great interest of this tomb derives from the fact that it suffered relatively lightly at the hands of the tomb-robbers, thus providing us with our only sizeable body of information on what accompanied a Middle Kingdom monarch to the grave. The antechamber contained principally a celebrated ka-statue in its shrine, two alabaster stelae, one with an offering formula, a case for staves, and a number of pottery and (dummy) wooden vessels. Inside his sarcophagus, the king's rifled body lay within a badly decayed rectangular coffin, decorated with an eye-panel and inscribed gold strips.

Although stripped of much of his finery, Hor retained some of his equipment: his once-gilded mask, and the remains of two falcon collars and a dagger. The mummy itself had been reduced to a damaged skeleton. Alongside him lay a stave, two long sceptres, an inlaid flail, two small alabaster vases and a wooden mallet. The wooden inner canopic chest, which closely matched the coffin and still contained four human-headed canopic jars, was found still sealed.

Principal Explorations
The tomb was discovered by de Morgan on 16 April 1894.

THE SOUTH PYRAMID OF MAZGHUNA
This brick monument lies some 400 metres from the North Pyramid. The pyramid itself has been entirely destroyed, along with much of the roofing of the substructure; only a thin coating of limestone chips marked the site. The brick enclosure wall was of a wavy form, with a simple mortuary temple of the same material on the east side; another structure in the south-east corner of the enclosure seems to have been some form of gatehouse, through which the pyramid itself could be approached. Quarry marks indicate that work was being carried on in the third year of an unnamed king.

The outer part of the descending corridor is lost, but the corridor gives access to the interior via two granite portcullises of a design and workmanship identical with that seen in the North Pyramid. The arrangement of the innermost part is reminiscent of that found in Amenemhat III's Second Pyramid at Hawara, but with the difference that the chamber, sarcophagus and canopic chest are now made from a single block. Compared with earlier sarcopha-gus/canopic chests, the block was considerably deeper, leaving a considerable void above the cavities for the coffin and canopic vessels, while a straightforward lid was abandoned in favour of two more massive blocks. One block was intended as a fix-ture, cut away below to give additional head-room for the burial party, but the other was supported by a pair of quartzite props, equipped with 'sandraulics' like the Hawara pyramid. The whole arrangement is thus a cross between that found in the North Pyramid and Qemau's Pyramid on one hand, and that of the Hawara pyra-mid on the other. The burial chamber had been broken open by pushing the entrance block northwards, having demolished the southern wall of the antechamber: only a fragment of a make-up pot and an inlay survived when the pyramid was excavated.

Principal Explorations
Identified and cleared by Mackay in 1910–11.

KHENDJER'S PYRAMID
The enclosure seems originally to have had the same 'wavy' wall as the South Pyramid at Mazghuna, but this was then replaced with a niched one of stone. Remains of an eastern mortuary temple and a north chapel have both been located. It is known that the pyramid was completed, as fragments of the pyramidion were found nearby.

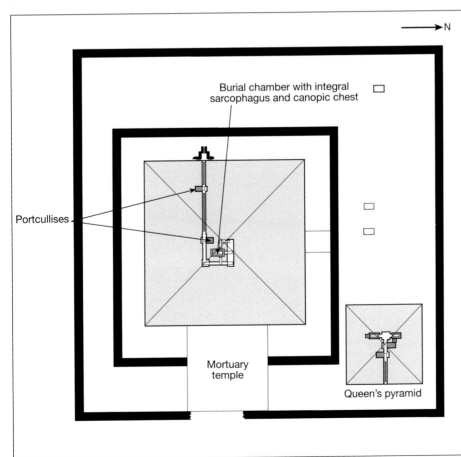

N

Burial chamber with integral sarcophagus and canopic chest

Portcullises

Mortuary temple

Queen's pyramid

Left: The pyramid complex of Khendjer in southern Saqqara-South, with its Queen's pyramid in the north-east corner.

MODERN DESIGNATION: L.XLIV

LOCATION: Southern Saqqara-South

DATE: 18th century BC

OWNER: Userkare Khendjer

BASIS OF ATTRIBUTION: Inscribed pyramidion

DIMENSIONS: Base 53 x 53 metres; height 37 metres

Right: The cap-stone of Khendjer's Pyramid is now on display in the Cairo Museum.

Internally, the structure represents a further development of the arrangements found in the South Pyramid of Mazghuna.

Principal Explorations

The site was visited by Lepsius in 1843. The pyramid was entered by de Morgan during the 1890s and excavated by Jéquier in 1929–31.

PYRAMID OF AN UNKNOWN KING

MODERN DESIGNATION: L.XLVI; Unfinished Pyramid

LOCATION: Southern Saqqara-South

DATE: 18th century BC

OWNER: Unknown king

BASIS OF ATTRIBUTION: The elaboration and scale of the monument would suggest that it is the latest of the known Middle Kingdom pyramids

DIMENSIONS: Base 91 x 91 metres

The fifth excavated pyramid of the Thirteenth Dynasty lies just south of Khendjer's Pyramid, and was apparently never finished. As well as being by far the largest pyramid of the dynasty, its substructure is one of the most elaborate of any Egyptian sepulchral monument, with a series of vestibules, changes of level and portcullises. One of its most remarkable features is its two burial chambers. The principal one was carved out of a block of quartzite, with a conventional-looking sarcophagus and canopic chest within, but carved as one with the chamber. Closure of the chamber was to be by the now customary 'sandraulic' means, but the tomb was never used.

The other burial chamber lay to the west and had an arrangement of sarcophagus/lid/portcullis similar to Qemau's, but reversed, with a separate canopic chest. The chamber has been described as a queen's, but no equivalent installation is known elsewhere. Given the elaboration of the substructure, which was clearly inspired by the desire for security, the most attractive solution is that it was actually a decoy, intended to draw plunderers away from the real burial.

Right: The antechamber of the Unfinished Pyramid: the upper doorway leads to the dummy burial chamber, while the opening contains a shaft used by those triggering the 'sandraulic' sealing system for the burial chamber. The burial chamber is beyond the left-hand wall.

Principal Explorations

The site was visited by Lepsius in 1843. The pyramid was entered by de Morgan during the 1890s and excavated by Jéquier in 1929–31.

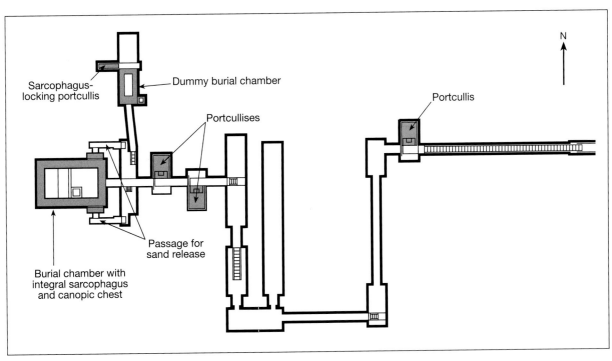

ABYDOS TOMB S9

Back in the Twelfth Dynasty, a large temple-tomb complex had been built in the southern part of the Abydos cemetery for Senwosret III (see page 91). Two tombs, with their superstructures largely destroyed, lie just north-east of this structure, and it has been suggested that the forms of their substructures may mark them out as royal tombs of the Thirteenth Dynasty – whether or not their superstructures were mastabas or pyramids.

This sepulchre employs the twisting, quartzite portcullis-blocked plan seen in all the pyramids of the dynasty, together with the combined burial chamber/sarcophagus/canopic chest typified by the pyramid of Khendjer. However, in the case of S9 no 'sandraulics' were employed: lowering of portcullises and the access block

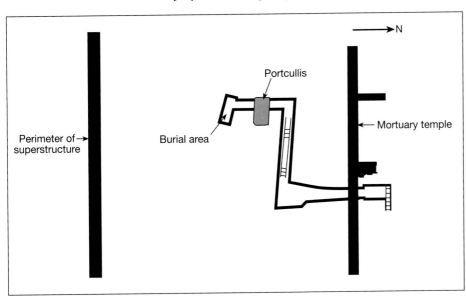

Above: Plan of the sub-structure of the Unfinished Pyramid at Saqqara-South, the most elaborate example to be found in any pyramid.

MODERN DESIGNATION:
S9
LOCATION: Abydos
DATE: 18th century BC
OWNER: King of the later Thirteenth Dynasty (?)
BASIS OF ATTRIBUTION: Similarity in design of substructure to other royal tombs of the dynasty
DIMENSIONS: Not known

Left: Tomb S9 at Abydos; its location is shown on page 93. Its substructure design is similar to those of the Thirteenth Dynasty.

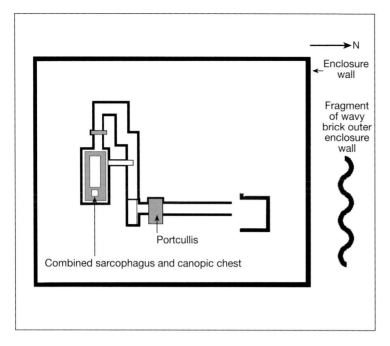

N

Enclosure wall

Fragment of wavy brick outer enclosure wall

Portcullis

Combined sarcophagus and canopic chest

Above: Tomb S10 at Abydos. As with Tomb S9 on page 103, this could be a royal tomb from the Thirteenth Dynasty.

Below: The pyramidion of the lost pyramid of Iy was found in the Nile delta, but is now in the Cairo Museum.

of the burial chamber was apparently done by the manual removal of the supports. In the case of the burial chamber block, this was done by means of a narrow service passage (only 50 centimetres wide by 55 centimetres high) from the approach corridor; perhaps owing to the constriction, the job was botched, leaving the burial chamber partly open.

Only some elements of the mud-brick complex survive, including what may be sections of the chapel and inner enclosure. Part of a 'wavy' outer enclosure wall has also been traced.

Principal Explorations
The tomb was partly cleared by Amélineau in 1896, and then excavated by Weigall in 1901–1902. Further work was begun by Dawn McCormack in 2004.

ABYDOS TOMB SIO
This tomb is less regular than S9, more badly damaged, and seems to have lacked an integrated burial chamber. Indeed, although a huge quartzite sarcophagus lid remains, no coffer survives; the coffer may have been of limestone. On the other hand, a typical late Middle Kingdom stairway flanked with benches is to be found in the main corridor of the tomb. A fragment of canopic jar was found.

MODERN DESIGNATION: SIO
LOCATION: Abydos
DATE: 18th century BC
OWNER: King of the later Thirteenth Dynasty?
BASIS OF ATTRIBUTION: Similarity in design of substructure to other royal tombs of the dynasty
DIMENSIONS: Not known

Principal Explorations
The tomb was excavated by Weigall in 1901–1902. Further work is planned.

IY'S PYRAMID
Only the pyramidion of this tomb has been found (Cairo Museum TR 5/1/15/12). It came from Kataana in the delta, but it is likely that it was taken there as booty by the Hyksos kings. In contrast to the elaborate pyramidia of Amenemhat III and Khendjer, it merely bears an image of the king offering to Ptah.

MODERN DESIGNATION: None
LOCATION: Uncertain
DATE: c. 1700 BC
OWNER: Merneferre Iy
BASIS OF ATTRIBUTION: Pyramidion bears king's name
DIMENSIONS: Not known

THE SECOND INTERMEDIATE PERIOD

The Thirteenth Dynasty's grasp on power seems gradually to have slipped until, around 1650 BC, the whole of Lower (northern) Egypt came under the rule of the Palestinian Hyksos Fifteenth Dynasty. The full extent of their power is still the subject of debate, but there is evidence that their nominal power stretched a long way into the south, possibly embracing even Thebes for a relatively short period.

While the Palestinians ruled in the north, the rump of the old royal line moved south to Thebes, where it is now referred to as the Sixteenth/Seventeenth Dynasty. At Thebes the native Egyptian line initiated the royal cemetery at Dira Abu'l-Naga. There, they erected what – with one exception – were to be the last kings' pyramids to be built in Egypt.

Below: Western Thebes, with Deir el-Bahari on the left and the southern end of Dira Abu'l-Naga on the right.

Below: Dira Abu'l-Naga, the royal necropolis of the Seventeenth Dynasty. After the abandonment of pyramids by royalty, some private individuals began to place pyramids above their rock-cut chapels. The remains of some of these lie high up the slope to the right. In the distance is El-Qurn, the natural pyramid that towers above the New Kingdom Valley of the Kings (see pages 112–13).

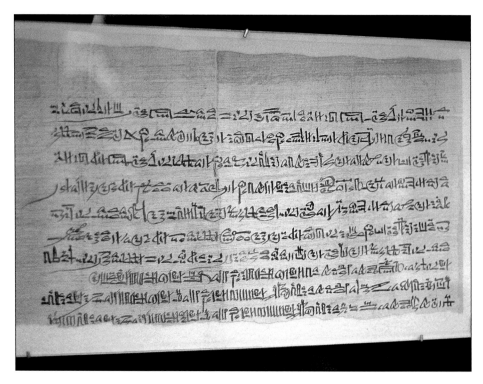

MODERN DESIGNATION:
None
LOCATION: Dira Abu'l-
Naga
DATE: Early 16th centu-
ry BC
OWNER: Sekhemre-
shedtawi Sobkemsaf I
BASIS OF ATTRIBUTION:
Known only from
Abbott Papyrus
DIMENSIONS: Not
known

SOBKEMSAF I'S PYRAMID

In Year 16 of the Twentieth Dynasty, Pharaoh Rameses IX (*c.* 1100 BC) appoint-ed a commission to investigate claims that a number of royal tombs had been robbed. Ten royal sepulchres were accordingly examined, six of them being Seventeenth Dynasty kings' pyramids at Dira Abu'l-Naga.

The report of the commission, the Abbott Papyrus, now in the British Museum, is our sole source of information on three of the pyramids, including the pyramid of Sobkemsaf I. Sobkemsaf I's burial chamber was stated to have been found 'without its lord' and his queen, 'thieves having laid hands on them'. The robbers were later apprehended. The transcript of the trial of the robbers, including their confession, is in the Leopold II-Amherst Papyrus, which is now split between Brussels and New York:

We found the pyramid of King Sobkemsaf I, this being unlike the pyramids and tombs of the nobles that we were used to rob. We took our copper tools and forced a way into the pyramid of this king through its innermost part. We found the substructure, and we took our lighted candles in our hands and went down. Then we broke through the blocking that we found at the entrance to his crypt, and found this god lying at the back of his burial place. And we found the burial-place of Queen Nubkhaes, his wife, situated beside him, it being protected and guarded by plaster and enclosed by a stone blocking. This we also broke through, and found her resting there in the same way.

We opened their sarcophagi and their coffins in which they were, and found the noble mummy of this king equipped with a khepesh-sword; many amulets and jewels were upon his neck, and his headpiece of gold was upon him. The noble mummy of the king was completely bedecked with gold, and his coffins were adorned with gold and silver inside and out and inlaid with all kinds of precious stones ...

INYOTEF V'S PYRAMID

The ancient commission found an incomplete tunnel being made into Inyotef V's pyramid. The pyramid's steep angle of elevation is shown by the surviving cap-stone, now in the British Museum. This cap-stone bore the king's names, and also those of his parents. Unfortunately, the parents' names were largely destroyed when the upper and lower parts of the cap-stone were broken away.

Nothing else is known of the pyramid's superstructure, but the entrance to the substructure seems to have been a brick-lined pit, about 20 feet deep, halfway up the Dira Abu'l-Naga hill. From the entrance pit a corridor led to a chamber in which two coffins lay, 'covered with cloth and dirt thrown over them', according to the local plunderers who found them in modern times. Both coffins are now in the Louvre Museum: one was that of Inyotef V himself, the other a private coffin, hurriedly adapted to hold the body of King Sekhemreheruhirmaet Inyotef (VII). The latter seems to have been the next-but-one king, buried in a recent predecessor's tomb after the briefest of reigns. Inyotef V's canopic chest, presumably found with the coffin, is also in the Louvre, Paris.

Principal Explorations

The tomb has never been scientifically located and investigated, but local plunderers penetrated the substructure in the late 1840s. Their testimony was recorded by Wilkinson between 1849 and 1855.

MODERN DESIGNATION: None

LOCATION: Dira Abu'l-Naga

DATE: Early 16th century BC

OWNER: Sekhemre-wepmaat Inyotef V

BASIS OF ATTRIBUTION: Abbott Papyrus; items of funerary equipment

DIMENSIONS: Not known

Above: The pyramidion from the tomb of Inyotef V in Dira Abu'l-Naga can be seen in the British Museum. Further fragments have now been found near the pyramid of Inyotef VI, indicating that Inyotef V's must have been close by.

Left: The coffins of Inyotef VII (left) and Inyotef V, from the latter's burial chamber, are on display in the Louvre, Paris.

INYOTEF VI'S PYRAMID

MODERN DESIGNATION:
None
LOCATION: Dira Abu'l-
Naga
DATE: Early 16th centu-
ry BC
OWNER: Nubkheperre
Inyotef VI
BASIS OF ATTRIBUTION:
Abbott Papyrus;
inscribed material
DIMENSIONS: Base 11 x
11 metres; restored
height 13 metres

Inyotef VI's pyramid is the only one of these Second Intermediate Period pyramids to have been properly investigated in modern times. The white-plastered brick pyramid was built on the slope of the hill, its sides rising at an angle of between 65 and 68 degrees; a pair of obelisks bearing the king's name stood outside the chapel. The burial chamber was not in the immediate area of the pyramid and its location is currently unknown. It seems to have lain some distance from the pyramid, and presumably resembled the substructure of Inyotef V's tomb (page 107).

Principal Explorations

Although an attempt had been made under Rameses IX to tunnel into the tomb from the tomb-chapel of Shuroy (see picture below), the burial chamber seems to have remained intact until 1827. It was then entered by local plunderers, who removed the coffin and mummy, apparently destroying the latter through carelessness. The coffin was then sold to the British Consul, Henry Salt, and later purchased as part of Salt's collection by the British Museum.

Mariette rediscovered the pyramid in 1860, but failed to publish any details. The obelisks were removed by Maspero in 1881; sadly, both pieces were lost in the Nile en route to Cairo.

The site was then lost until 1919–20 when Winlock identified the tomb, which the Abbott Papyrus indicates as being the start of a robber's tunnel heading for the pyramid. Finally, in 2001, Polz used the same data to locate the pyramid directly next to the tomb of Shuroy (TT13).

Below: The site of the pyramid of Inyotef VI lies on the slope directly behind the modern shelter; this shelter protects the entrance to the tomb-chapel of Shuroy (TT13).

TAA I'S PYRAMID

The king's tomb was found untouched by Rameses IX's commissioners; their report suggests that his tomb was near the southern end of Dira Abu'l-Naga. Taa I's mummy and coffin have never come to light.

MODERN DESIGNATION: None
LOCATION: Dira Abu'l-Naga
DATE: Mid-16th century BC
OWNER: Senakhtenre Taa I
BASIS OF ATTRIBUTION: Known only from Abbott Papyrus
DIMENSIONS: Not known

TAA II'S PYRAMID

Although found untouched by Rameses IX's commissioners, the king's mummy and coffin were later removed for reburial. The king's mummy showed severe head wounds, suggesting death in battle. The mummy and coffin were ultimately placed in the tomb of the High Priest Pinudjem II near Deir el-Bahari (TT320), some time after Year 11 of Shoshenq I (c. 932 BC); found there in 1881, they are now in the Cairo Museum.

MODERN DESIGNATION: None
LOCATION: Dira Abu'l-Naga
DATE: c. 1558–1553 BC
OWNER: Seqenenre Taa II
BASIS OF ATTRIBUTION: Known only from Abbott Papyrus
DIMENSIONS: Not known

Above: The horrific head wounds that caused the death of Taa II, and which were probably inflicted during a battle against the Hyksos, are still visible on Taa II's mummified head, now in the Cairo Museum.

KAMOSE'S PYRAMID

Similarly found untouched by Rameses IX's commissioners, the king's mummy and coffin were also later removed and found buried in debris near the mouth of the Valley of the Kings. Discovered in 1857, the coffin is now in the Cairo Museum, although the mummy crumbled to dust. The Abbott Papyrus implies that Kamose's pyramid was the southernmost in the cemetery, and, near the likely spot, Winlock discovered a small pyramid that he believed could be that of the king. The identification is not, however, in any way certain.

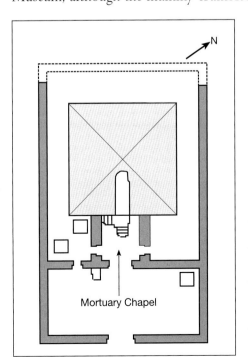

Mortuary Chapel

N

MODERN DESIGNATION: None
LOCATION: Dira Abu'l-Naga
DATE: c. 1553–1549 BC
OWNER: Wadjkheperre Kamose
BASIS OF ATTRIBUTION: Known from Abbott Papyrus, which implies its location at the southern end of Dira Abu'l-Naga
DIMENSIONS: Not known

Left: Plan of a small pyramid at the southern end of Dira Abu'l-Naga which has occasionally been attributed to Kamose.

THE EVOLUTION OF THE PYRAMID: THE NEW KINGDOM ONWARDS

Below: The tombs were generally elaborately decorated, with the 'Books of the Underworld' and depictions of the king before the gods. This is the tomb of Horemheb (KV57).

The reunification of Egypt around 1550 BC marked a major change in royal funerary practices, which would soon end 1,000 years of pyramid-building for the tombs of the Egyptian kings, although there would be a short-lived revival some eight centuries later.

THE NEW KINGDOM

One final pyramid was erected, however, by the first king of the Eighteenth Dynasty, Ahmose I. Ahmose had been responsible for the final expulsion of the Palestinian Hyksos Fifteenth Dynasty and the re-establishment of royal power. The succeeding kings established Egyptian hegemony over much of Syria–Palestine, with the height of Egyptian power coming under Amenhotep III. A gradual decline followed Amenhotep III's reign, exacerbated by conflicts within the royal family during the late Nineteenth Dynasty and economic difficulties in the Twentieth Dynasty.

AHMOSE I'S PYRAMID

Ahmose I built a funerary monument a few hundred metres south of Senwosret III's Abydene complex; as with that monument, it is uncertain whether Ahmose I's was actually used for a burial or – more likely – was a cenotaph. Ahmose I's complex comprises a number of elements. First, a rubble-cored, but limestone-sheathed, pyramid stands near the boundary between desert and cultivated land; its angle one can assume to have been 63 degrees. A temple adjoining its east side was once decorated with extensive, but now fragmentary, battle scenes, perhaps recording the king's defeat of the Hyksos; a smaller chapel lies just to the north. At the opposite end of the complex's 1.4-kilometre axis, further into the desert, was another temple, rising in terraces against the cliff face. In the expanse of desert between the pyramid and the temple, Ahmose constructed two monuments. The first was a brick chapel dedicated to the king's grandmother, Tetisherit, containing a fine stela, now in the Cairo Museum. The second was a subterranean tomb of unusual form. It is cut for the most part only a few metres below the surface; a pit entrance gives access to a twisting passageway that eventually opens into a great hall, its roof formerly supported by 18 columns. Below the hall, a further passage, probably unfinished, leads deeper into the matrix.

MODERN DESIGNATION: Kom el-Sheikh Mohammed

LOCATION: Abydos

DATE: *c.* 1549–1524 BC

OWNER: Nebpehtyre Ahmose I

BASIS OF ATTRIBUTION: Inscribed material from the complex

DIMENSIONS: Base 80 x 80 metres

Left: *The pyramid of Ahmose I at Abydos is the last such monument built by a native king of Egypt. No passages are known within the pyramid, and the substructure lies far out in the desert beyond the monument.*

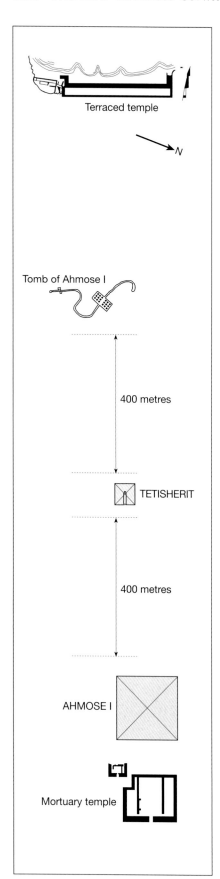

Terraced temple

N

Tomb of Ahmose I

400 metres

TETISHERIT

400 metres

AHMOSE I

Mortuary temple

Little was found by the excavators: only a few bricks, stamped with Ahmose's praenomen, and a number of fragments of gold leaf came to light in the debris of the pillared hall. An interesting point is that the pyramid's core contained rubble from the construction of the tomb.

Principal Explorations

Although Amélineau seems to have examined the area in 1896, the pyramid was first excavated by Mace in 1899–1900, and the rest of the complex by Currelly in 1902, the substructure being discovered through the clue supplied by the hollow in the ground created by the pillared hall's collapse. New investigations were begun by Harvey in 1993.

The Eclipse of the Pyramid

Ahmose I's pyramid was the last pyramid to be built by a native Egyptian king – the last of a line stretching back over 1,000 years to Djoser and Imhotep. His successors, beginning with Thutmose I, revived the Archaic Period practice of separating the burial chamber from the offering place. The latter was set near the desert edge at Thebes, in the form of a large mortuary – or rather 'memorial' –

Left: *Plan of the Ahmose I complex at Abydos, with his mortuary temple, his pyramid, the pyramidal chapel of the royal grandmother, Tetisherit, the subterranean tomb and the terraced temple against the cliffs.*

Below: *Once kings had ceased to use pyramids, they began to be adopted by rapidly descending echelons of the social ladder. This example, at Deir el-Medina, belonged to one of the workmen employed on building the royal tombs in the Valley of the Kings during the Nineteenth Dynasty.*

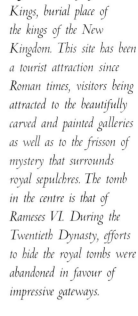

Left: The Valley of the Kings, burial place of the kings of the New Kingdom. This site has been a tourist attraction since Roman times, visitors being attracted to the beautifully carved and painted galleries as well as to the frisson of mystery that surrounds royal sepulchres. The tomb in the centre is that of Rameses VI. During the Twentieth Dynasty, efforts to hide the royal tombs were abandoned in favour of impressive gateways.

temple, while the substructure lay over a kilometre away behind a curtain of cliffs in what has come to be known as the Valley of the Kings. There, galleries penetrated deep into the bedrock, resurrecting ancient practice by bearing the decoration that is the ultimate descendant of the Pyramid Texts. But there was no pyramid erected over the offering place or burial place. Indeed, the pyramid now became the marker for the tombs of private individuals: small brick structures built above the rock-chapels along the front of the Theban necropolis. Yet, in one sense, kings continued to rest under a pyramid: for over the Valley of the Kings rears El-Qurn, the sacred mountain home of the goddess Mertseger, 'the Lover of Silence', and the most magnificent of all natural pyramids.

THE THIRD INTERMEDIATE AND LATE PERIODS

Below: With the Third Intermediate Period, the royal cemeteries moved to the north, where they comprised stone chambers sunk in the soil of temple courtyards. Here, at Tanis, we have the tombs of Pasebkhanu I and Osorkon II (NRT-III and I).

The Valley of the Kings accommodated royal tombs until the end of the Twentieth Dynasty. After this, around 1070 BC, with the foundation of the Twenty-first Dynasty, the capital of Egypt moved north to Tanis (San el-Hagar) in the delta. Tanis lies many miles from any place suitable for rock-cut monuments, and accordingly the new royal cemetery comprised stone-built structures sunk just below the ground surface, and probably topped by chapels. These tombs are of modest dimensions, containing at most a handful of chambers and generally decorated with books of the underworld.

The Tanite tombs lay in the forecourt of the city's principal temple, and after Thebes effectively became an independent polity in the middle of the Twenty-second Dynasty, at least one king had a tomb within the temple complex of Medinet Habu there. Similar tomb locations were used for nearly all later known royal cemeteries, although the physical remains of only one such sepulchre, of Nefarud I at Mendes (Twenty-ninth Dynasty), has been examined.

Resurrection in Sudan: the Twenty-fifth Dynasty

The exception to the rule of temple burial comes from the Twenty-fifth Dynasty. The latter part of the Third Intermediate Period saw increasing fragmentation of Egypt, reversed only with the annexation of the country by the Egyptianized rulers of Sudan (Kush). Although buried in their home country, these kings resumed the use of pyramids, albeit of the steeply angled type used by the Seventeenth Dynasty kings, and later nobles, at Thebes.

PI(ANKH)YE'S PYRAMID

The pyramid of Piye is wholly vanished, together with the chapel. However, the substructure still survives, consisting of a corbel-roofed room approached by a stairway. Although sets of canopic jars and *shabtis* (see glossary, pages 265–6) were provided, instead of a sarcophagus a rock-cut bench lay in the middle of the burial chamber with a cut-out in each corner to receive the legs of a bed. Interment on a bier has been characterized as a typical feature of Nubian burials since Kerman (Second Intermediate Period) times.

Principal Explorations
Excavated by Reisner in 1918–19.

MODERN DESIGNATION: Ku17

LOCATION: El-Kurru

DATE: *c.* 752–717 BC

OWNER: Seneferre Pi(ankh)ye

BASIS OF ATTRIBUTION: Funerary figure with name of king

DIMENSIONS: Base 8 x 8 metres

Right: The remains of the corbelled roof of the burial chamber of Pi(ankh)ye at El-Kurru (Ku17).

SHABAKA'S PYRAMID

Also entirely destroyed above ground, Shabaka's tomb displays rather better workmanship than Piye's, both in its architecture – which is fully rock-cut – and its funerary equipment, which includes a fine set of canopic jars. The burial chamber also preserves traces of paintings.

Principal Explorations
Excavated by Reisner in 1918–19.

SHABATAKA'S PYRAMID

The sepulchre of Shabataka marks something of a regression. The workmanship of his canopics is poor, while the burial chamber reverts to corbelled roofing; the tomb also has an unusual right-angled turn in its descending stairway. The tomb lies apart from the other Twenty-fifth Dynasty sepulchres, and is among the burial places of the ancestors of the royal line which date perhaps as far back as the early Third Intermediate Period.

Principal Explorations
Excavated by Reisner in 1918–19.

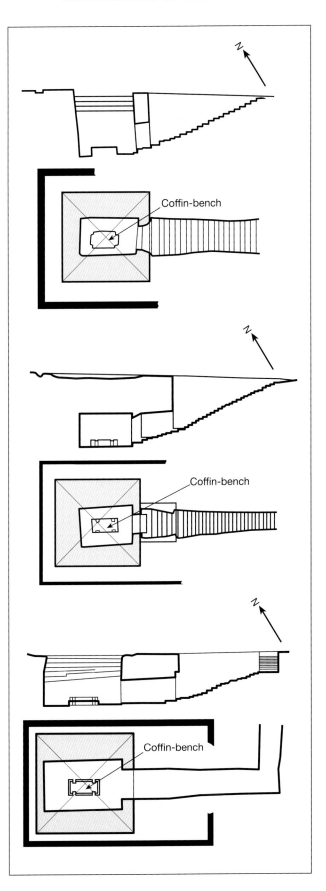

Left: Sections and plans of the pyramids of P(iankh)ye, Shabaka and Shabataka; they were far smaller than any king's pyramid of earlier periods.

MODERN DESIGNATION: Ku15
LOCATION: El-Kurru
DATE: *c.* 717–703 BC
OWNER: Neferkare Shabaka
BASIS OF ATTRIBUTION: Various inscribed items
DIMENSIONS: Base 11 x 11 metres

MODERN DESIGNATION: Ku18
LOCATION: El-Kurru
DATE: *c.* 703–690 BC
OWNER: Djedkare Shabataka
BASIS OF ATTRIBUTION: Funerary figure with name of king
DIMENSIONS: Base 11 x 11 metres

MODERN DESIGNATION:
Nu1
LOCATION: Nuri
DATE: *c.* 690–664 BC
OWNER: Khunefertumre
Taharqa
BASIS OF ATTRIBUTION
Substructure contained
large amounts of
funerary equipment
bearing his name.
DIMENSIONS: Base 52 x
52 metres

*Right: Although now badly
ruined, Taharqa's Pyramid
at Nuri is the largest of all
the Sudanese monuments.*

*Below: Plans of the
pyramids of Taharqa
and Tanutamun.*

Coffin-bench

TAHARQA'S PYRAMID

Rather than make use of the now somewhat crowded family cemetery of El-Kurru, Taharqa made a fresh start at Nuri, a little way downstream. His pyramid was built in two phases, the first having a 29.5-metre base, with which the substructure was aligned; the final version had a different axis. Apart from its size, with a base nearly seven times that of the monument of Piye, Taharqa's pyramid has the most elaborate substructure of any Kushite royal tomb. A conventional stairway, over which a mortuary chapel may have been built, led into a small antechamber, which in turn gave access to a six-pillared burial chamber with vaulted aisles. A curious corridor completely surrounded the subterranean rooms at a slightly higher level, accessible via a flight of steps at the far end of the sepulchral chamber, or via a pair of stairways just outside the doorway of the antechamber. The usual bench lay in the centre of the burial chamber; the nest of coffins that had lain on this had been largely destroyed, but quantities of their gold foil and stone inlay remained, plus a fragment of skull.

The canopic jars are of a very fine quality, and introduce new textual formulations, which became standard in subsequent Egyptian burials. A vast number of *shabtis* (see glossary, pages 265–6) were recovered in a variety of hard and soft stones, and many in remarkably large sizes – up to 60 centimetres in height.

Principal Explorations
Excavated by Reisner in 1918–19.

TANUTAMUN'S PYRAMID
The last Kushite to rule Egypt was Tanutamun. For his pyramid site he moved back to El-Kurru, adopting a much simpler substructure, curiously without the previously obligatory coffin-bench. Like Shabaka's tomb, Tanutamun's had a burial chamber adorned with paintings, in his case sufficiently well preserved to identify the topics covered. The vignettes and texts essentially follow the age-old association of royal burials with solar matters, the entrance doorway being surmounted by painted apes adoring the sun-god in his bark; a similar motif appears on the rear wall.

Principal Explorations
Excavated by Reisner in 1918–19.

Later Kushite Pyramids
Tanutamun's rule in Egypt ended with an Assyrian invasion in 656 BC. However, his successors continued to rule in what is modern Sudan for centuries more. Pyramids also continued to be built, although their contents and ornamentation show a steady shift towards a distinctly Kushite interpretation of the ancient motifs. Canopic jars initially remained in use, supplemented for a short period by (for the first time in Kush) stone sarcophagi, but both types of container had disappeared soon after the reign of Melanaqeñ, sixth successor of Tanutamun. At first the royal tombs were primarily built at Nuri, but they later shifted further south to Gebel Barkal and Meroë. It was at Meroë that the last Nilotic pyramid was built, around AD 350, 3,000 years and 1,600 kilometres from the first such monument at Saqqara.

MODERN DESIGNATION: Ku16

LOCATION: El-Kurru

DATE: 664–*c.* 656 BC

OWNER: Bakare Tanutamun

BASIS OF ATTRIBUTION: Decoration of burial chamber and inscribed material

DIMENSIONS: Base 8.25 x 8.25 metres

Below: Sudanese pyramids, including these examples at Nuri, have a particularly high angle of elevation, apparently copied from the royal and private pyramids at Thebes.

THE PYRAMIDS OF THE QUEENS

Below: The monument of Khentkaues I, ancestress of the Fifth Dynasty, is of a very odd form, with a rock-cut lower section and masonry upper part — not quite a mastaba, and not quite a pyramid!

Very little is known of the tombs of royal wives prior to the beginning of the Fourth Dynasty. One, the First Dynasty Meryetneith, had a large tomb and funerary enclosure at Abydos, but this was by virtue of her having been Regent for her young son, Den. Another, Neithhotep, probably the mother of Aha, had a panelled mastaba at Naqada, while Herneith, perhaps a wife of Den, was in all likelihood the owner of a tomb at Saqqara (S3507).

On this basis, it may well be that during the early years of Egypt's history, queens were generally buried apart from their royal spouse, following other members of the court. However, it is likely that some who predeceased their husbands shared the king's tomb, given the discovery of probably-female bejewelled human remains in the tomb of Djer.

Two Second Dynasty princesses are known to have been buried at Saqqara, with three other royal offspring of the dynasty interred across the river at Helwan, a huge necropolis of the Archaic Period. It is possible that the vast mastaba tomb KI at Beit Khallaf might be that of Queen Nymaathap, given the presence of her name on a number of seal-impressions there. The building is some 85 metres long, 45 wide and 8 high, and incorporates one of the earliest brick arches known.

However, no further queen's tomb is evident until the reign of Khufu. Tombs of other family members are present during the time of Seneferu, all being mastabas erected some distance from the Dahshur and Meidum pyramids. This general geographical separation of the king's tomb from that of others breaks down under Khufu, who created a whole series of cemeteries close to his Great Pyramid at Giza for his family and associates. The cemetery in front of the pyramid, the East Cemetery, incorporated three small pyramids, the first of a series of such monuments that stretches on into the Thirteenth Dynasty. There are many gaps in the record, however, where other types of tomb were used or no sepulchre(s) have yet been identified.

REIGN OF KHUFU: *c. 2547–2524* BC
GIa

This is the northernmost of the small pyramids adjacent to the Great Pyramid. Its superstructure is largely ruined, and on the east side is a small chapel. The interior consists of a descending passage giving access to a vestibule, from which a right turn leads into the burial chamber, its door some distance above the floor.

The pyramid's possible attribution is based on the proximity of G7000X, a shaft tomb just north-east of the pyramid, which held the canopic chest, empty

SITE/DESIGNATION: Giza L.V; GIa+G7000X
OWNER: Hetepheres, mother of the king (?)
DIMENSIONS: Base 47.4 x 47.4 metres

Right: This plan of the southernmost of the three pyramids built by Khufu for his wives at Giza, GIc, is typical of the original layout of these monuments. However, in the Third Intermediate and Late periods, the Old Kingdom chapel (seen here in black) was greatly enlarged to form the temple of 'Isis, mistress of the Pyramids' (seen here in grey). At the same time, the pyramid itself became associated (rightly or wrongly) with Princess Henutsen.

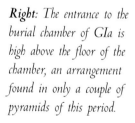

SITE/DESIGNATION:
Giza L.VI; GIb
OWNER: Not known
DIMENSIONS: Base 49.5
x 49.5 metres

sarcophagus and funerary furniture of Hetepheres, wife of Seneferu and mother of Khufu. A recent suggestion is that these may have been 'leftovers' following the creation by Khufu of a new set of equipment for the queen in her new role as King's Mother, at the same time as he provided for her the first pyramid created for someone other than a king – GIa.

Principal Explorations

The pyramid was opened by Vyse and Perring in 1837, and further examined by Reisner in the 1920s; the shaft was discovered by Reisner in 1925.

GIb

GIb is very similar to GIa; part of the decoration of the chapel is now in Boston, USA.

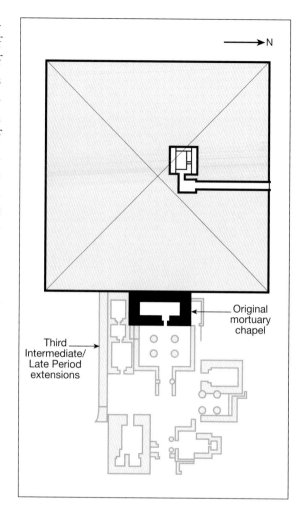

Original mortuary chapel

Third Intermediate/ Late Period extensions

Principal Explorations

Opened by Vyse and Perring in 1837, and further examined by Reisner in the 1920s.

Right: The entrance to the burial chamber of GIa is high above the floor of the chamber, an arrangement found in only a couple of pyramids of this period.

GIc

Although very similar to the monuments GIa and GIb, the pyramid of GIc is, however, much better preserved. However, during the Twenty-first Dynasty, its chapel was greatly enlarged as the temple of Isis-Mistress-of-the-Pyramids. A Twenty-sixth Dynasty stela from here attributes the pyramid to Henutsen, who is not known from any contemporary monument.

SITE/DESIGNATION: Giza L.LVII; GIc
OWNER: Henutsen, daughter of king (?)
DIMENSIONS: Base 47 x 47 metres

Principal Explorations

Opened by Vyse and Perring in 1837, and further examined by Reisner in the 1920s; the later temple on the east was excavated by Hassan in the 1930s.

Above: GIc is the best preserved of the three queens' pyramids in Giza. Here, GIb reveals part of the stepped core.

REIGN OF DJEDEFRE: *c.* 2547–2524 BC

The pyramid lies south of the boat pit in Djedefre's complex and retains five courses of masonry just under 2 metres high. A shaft 1.5 metres deep in the middle of the north face gives access to a corridor that leads to one chamber to the east and two chambers to the west.

Objects found included some faience tiles, a calcite vessel, a dish bearing the name of Khufu, pottery fragments and two lids that might have come from canopic jars. The burial chamber contained fragments of a limestone sarcophagus.

SITE/DESIGNATION: Abu Rowash
OWNER: Not Known
DIMENSIONS: Base 12 x 12 metres

Principal Explorations

Discovered by Valloggia in April 2002.

REIGN OF KHAEFRE: *c.* 2515–2493 BC

No pyramids were built for Khaefre's wives; some of these ladies, as daughters of Khufu, retained tombs in the cemetery east of the Great Pyramid, but at least two began rock-cut tombs south of Khephren's pyramid causeway at Giza. This was a considerable innovation, marking a step away from the brick- or stone-built tomb superstructures that had been standard for many years. One, lying in a former quarry south of the king's mortuary temple, belonged to Queen Persenet (LG88). The other, the 'Galarza Tomb', lay close to the bottom of the causeway of the king's pyramid, and was apparently begun for Khamerernebty I, but substantially modified by her daughter, Khamerernebty II, wife of Menkaure; the changes are believed to have had a major influence in the subsequent evolution of the rock-cut tomb at Giza.

REIGN OF MENKAURE: *c.* 2493–2475 BC

At least one of the king's spouses, Khamerernebty II, was an owner of the 'Galarza' rock-cut tomb at Giza. However, the royal complex incorporated two 'family' pyramids, in addition to the king's own subsidiary pyramid (GIIIc).

GIIIa *For plan, see page 63.*
This pyramid is well preserved; a large mud-brick chapel was constructed on the east side, on foundations intended for a stone structure. The passage into the sub-

Below: The eastern two pyramids of the three that lie south of Menkaure's monument in Giza were, after the pyramids of the queens of Khufu, the next monuments to be associated with a king's queens.

SITE/DESIGNATION:
Giza GIIIa; L.XII
OWNER: Not known
DIMENSIONS: Base 44.4
x 44.4 metres

structure was blocked by a granite portcullis, beyond which a short corridor led into the burial chamber; a sarcophagus was sunk into the floor.

G I I Ib *For plan, see page 63.*

This pyramid, which has the appearance of a stepped structure, likewise has a brick chapel, its walls plastered and whitewashed. The substructure is unusual in that its entrance lies well beyond the perimeter of the pyramid, while the chambers are far to the north of its centre. This may imply that the pyramid was originally planned to lie to the north of its final location, perhaps before the king's pyramid was enlarged (see page 63). The chambers revive the practice of Khufu's time by having a right-angled turn into the burial chamber. The latter contained a granite sarcophagus, with the skeleton of a young woman.

Principal Explorations
Opened by Vyse and Perring in 1837, and re-examined by Reisner in 1906–10.

REIGN OF SHEPSESKAF (?): *c.* 2475–2471 BC

Built just north of the valley building of Menkaure, this monument comprised a square structure atop a rock-cut podium in which were excavated a chapel with inscribed door-jambs and, below the chapel, a burial chamber. It seems likely that the 'podium' was intended as a simple mastaba, albeit mainly cut from the living rock, and given inscribed panelling reminiscent of that found on tombs of the Archaic Period. The chapel and burial chamber arrangements were elaborations of the corresponding rock-cut features of late Fourth Dynasty royal family members' tombs.

Principal Explorations
The tomb was excavated by Hassan in 1932.

Right: The plan of the tomb of Khentkaues I, believed to be the mother of two kings, shows the chapel cut in the base of the super-structure, and the elaborate burial chamber below.

SITE/DESIGNATION:
Giza GIIIb; L.XI
OWNER: A young woman
DIMENSIONS: Base 31.5 x 31.5 metres

SITE/DESIGNATION:
Giza GIV; LG100; Fourth Pyramid
OWNER: Khentkaues I, mother of two kings (?)
DIMENSIONS: Base 45.8 x 43.7 metres

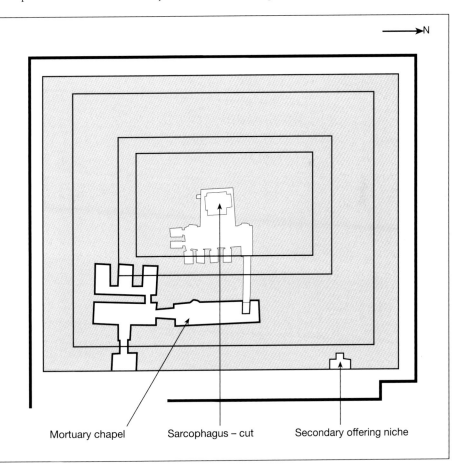

Mortuary chapel — Sarcophagus – cut — Secondary offering niche

SITE/DESIGNATION:
Saqqara
OWNER: Neferhetepes,
Userkaf's mother (?)
DIMENSIONS:
Base 26 x 26 metres

Right: *The queen's pyramid associated with the sepulchre of Userkaf, seen here across the ruins of his mortuary temple, has lost much of its upper part, leaving the substructure open to the elements (see page 21).*

REIGN OF USERKAF: *c.* 2471–2464 BC

The pyramid lies south-east of the king's, and is badly ruined, with the gable-roofed burial chamber exposed and partly destroyed. The chapel was considerably more elaborate than those of earlier queens' pyramids, with a triple set of the niches that had appeared in Khentkaues I's chapel, and these would appear in most subsequent queens' offering places.

Principal Explorations

Excavated by Firth in 1928–9; work was continued between 1948 and 1955 by Lauer, who returned for further work with Labrousse in 1976–8.

SITE/DESIGNATION:
Abusir
OWNER: Khentkaues II,
Neferirkare's wife
DIMENSIONS: Base 26 x
26 metres

REIGN OF NEFERIRKARE: *c.* 2452–2442 BC

The area south of the mortuary temple of Neferirkare included the pyramids of three queens. One belonged to his own reign, and was that of his wife, Khentkaues II. Its chapel was later enlarged, apparently to serve, in addition, the cult of Khentkaues I, the dynasty's ancestress. The pyramid itself is of standard form and badly ruined, containing a few fragments of the queen's sarcophagus.

Principal Explorations

Excavated by Verner in 1976–86.

Left: *At Abusir, the chapel of the pyramid of Khentkaues II, wife of Neferirkare, was greatly enlarged, apparently to accommodate the cult of Khentkaues I. The queen's pyramid is in a poor state.*

REIGN OF NIUSERRE: *c.* 2432–2421 BC

L.XXIV

A ruined monument of the standard plan of its time, the pyramid displays interesting examples of builders' marks, shown where the facing masonry has been destroyed. The remains of a sarcophagus and parts of the mummy of a young woman were found within.

Principal Explorations

Excavated by Verner in 1994–6.

L.XXV

Of similar size and form to L.XXI, little is yet known of this ruined monument.

Principal Explorations

To be excavated by Czech Archaeological Mission.

Above: Fragments of the sarcophagus of a young woman from Niuserre's reign lie in the burial chamber of L.XXIV; the lugs on this end of the lid were intended to make it more manoeuvrable.

SITE/DESIGNATION: Abusir L.XXIV; J
OWNER: Not known
DIMENSIONS: Base 26 x 26 metres

REIGN OF MENKAUHOR: *c.* 2421–2413 BC

Since the king's probable pyramid complex has never been cleared, nothing is known of any adjacent queenly pyramid(s). However, a likely wife of the king, Meresankh IV, was buried in a mastaba (Tomb 82) some 600 metres to the south-west, close to the north wall of Djoser's enclosure.

SITE/DESIGNATION: Abusir L.XXV
OWNER: Not known
DIMENSIONS: Not known

REIGN OF ISESI: *c.* 2413–2385 BC

L.XXXVIII *For plan, see page 72.*

Lying north of the king's pyramid temple, this structure has one of the most elaborate mortuary chapels known for a queenly monument; however, it is badly ruined.

Principal Explorations

Noted by Perring and Lepsius in the 19th century; partly excavated by Fakhry in 1952, and surveyed by Maragioglio and Rinaldi in the 1960s.

SITE/DESIGNATION: Saqqara-South L.XXXVIII
OWNER: Not known
DIMENSIONS: Base 26 x 26 metres

REIGN OF UNAS: *c.* 2385–2355 BC

For plan, see page 73.

Neither of the king's wives had a pyramid. Instead, Nebet and Khenut occupied a large double mastaba north-east of the royal mortuary temple. This area also held the tombs of a number of royal offspring.

REIGN OF TETI: *c.* 2355–2343 BC

For plans, see page 74.

The tombs of the wives of Teti seem initially to have been designed as mastabas, although they ultimately took the form of pyramids. The shaft-based substructure of Iput I's original mastaba was retained after the conversion, the mouth of the shaft being covered by the pyramid, which was thus built after Iput's death. The pyramid's core was later dug out to be the chapel of a New Kingdom sepulchre.

The chapel has a plan that, while reminiscent of earlier examples, has certain unique features. The burial chamber contained the sarcophagus of the queen, together with her canopic jars. Although the tomb had been robbed, Iput's skeleton was found in the burial chamber.

Principal Explorations
Discovered by Loret in 1897–9 and further excavated by Firth in 1920–22 and Hawass in 1992–3.

The neighbouring tomb of Khuit was designed as a pyramid, and although the chapel has areas of similarity with that of Iput I, the substructure of the pyramid is in complete contrast, being of conventional form, and a miniature version of the pyramid of Teti himself. The burial chamber contained a sarcophagus, a cavity for the canopic chest and the remains of a later mummy.

Some traces to the south of the pyramids of Iput and Khuit may represent a mastaba of a third wife of Teti, but this remains uncertain.

Principal Explorations
The chapel of the complex was excavated by Loret in 1897–9, and by Firth in 1922; the pyramid itself was found by Hawass in 1996–8.

SITE/DESIGNATION:
Saqqara
OWNER: Iput I
DIMENSIONS: Base 21 x 21 metres

SITE/DESIGNATION:
Saqqara
OWNER: Khuit
DIMENSIONS: Base 21 x 21 metres

Right: The wives of Teti were buried in this area, north-east of the king's pyramid.

Below: The double mastaba that accommodated the wives of Unas: Khenut and Nebet.

REIGN OF PEPY I: *c.* 2343–2297 BC

A group of six queenly pyramids lies close to the south-west corner of Pepy I's complex; at least four, probably five, of them belong to spouses of that king. Their plans all vary somewhat, although most seem to have chapels reminiscent of the previous reign, while the entrance to that of Inti was flanked by obelisks. The pyramids' interiors also vary in the orientation of their store-room and the portcullis arrangements. All were plain apart from the pyramid of Ankhenespepy II, which was adorned with Pyramid Texts, their first appearance in a queenly tomb.

Principal Explorations

Discovered and excavated by the French Mission to Saqqara from 1988 onwards. It is very possible that other queens' pyramids may yet be found in the area.

Below: The queens' cemetery south-west of Pepy I's Pyramid.

SITE/DESIGNATION: Saqqara-South
OWNER: Ankhenespepy II, wife of the king and also of Nemtyemsaf I
DIMENSIONS: Not available

SITE/DESIGNATION: Saqqara-South
OWNER: Nebwenet, wife of the king
DIMENSIONS: Base 22 x 22 metres

SITE/DESIGNATION: Saqqara-South
OWNER: Inenek-Inti, wife of the king
DIMENSIONS: Base 24 x 24 metres

SITE/DESIGNATION: Saqqara-South
OWNER: Meryetyotes IV, wife of the king
DIMENSIONS: Not available

SITE/DESIGNATION: Saqqara-South, 'Western Pyramid'
OWNER: Probably a wife of the king
DIMENSIONS: Not available

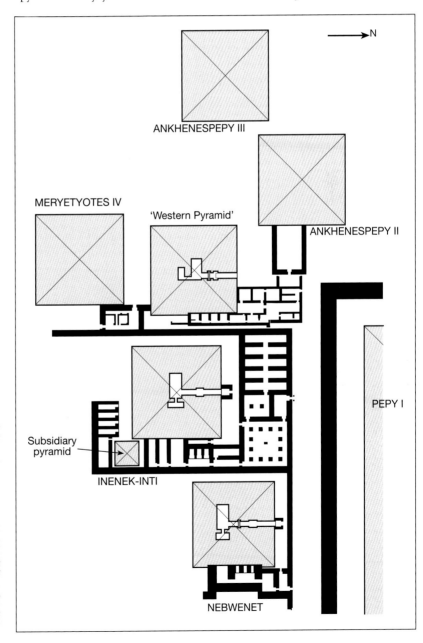

REIGN OF NEMTYEMSAF I: *c.* 2297–2290 BC

The only tomb known to belong to a spouse of Nemtyemsaf I is that of Ankhenespepy II, who had previously been married to Nemtyemsaf's father, Pepy I, and was buried in Pepy I's complex. No other wives are recorded, but a map drawn by the Prussian expedition to Egypt in the 1840s shows three approximately square mounds around the king's pyramid. Two of these are the right size for queens' pyramids, and moreover lie in almost the same position relative to the king's monument as do the tombs of Teti's queens to his.

REIGN OF PEPY II: *c.* 2290–2196 BC

One of the wives of Pepy II, Ankhenespepy III, was buried in the complex of Pepy II's father, Pepy I. Such a burial away from a husband (who had his pyramid 1.5 kilometres to the south-west) is very unusual; it is possible that this may represent the reuse of an earlier monument following Ankhenespepy's premature death.

Principal Explorations
Excavated by the French Mission in the late 1990s.

Three queens' pyramids lie adjacent to the complex of Pepy II itself. Each monument had steeply angled sides, substructures decorated with Pyramid Texts and large decorated chapels, including subsidiary pyramids. Between the subsidiary pyramid of Neith and her main pyramid, 16 wooden model ships were found. Iput's chapel had its entrance flanked by obelisks, and has the additional interest of, in later times, being used as the tomb of a queen. One of the store-rooms of one of the pyramids had a funerary stela carved into one of its walls, and a sarcophagus placed in the chamber for the burial of another wife of Pepy II, Ankhenespepy IV.

Principal Explorations
Excavated by Jéquier in the late 1920s.

Right: *Plan of Iput II's complex, representing the final development of a queen's pyramid. The westernmost of the store-rooms on the south side of the monument housed the sarcophagus of Queen Ankhenespepy IV.*

SITE/DESIGNATION: Saqqara-South
OWNER: Ankhenespepy III, wife of Pepy II
DIMENSIONS: Not available

SITE/DESIGNATION: Saqqara-South L.XLII
OWNER: Wedjebten, wife of the king
DIMENSIONS: Base 23.9 x 23.9 metres
For plan, see page 77.

SITE/DESIGNATION: Saqqara-South
OWNER: Iput II, wife of the king
DIMENSIONS: Base 22 x 22 metres

SITE/DESIGNATION: Saqqara-South
OWNER: Neith, wife of the king
DIMENSIONS: Base 24 x 24 metres
For plan, see page 77

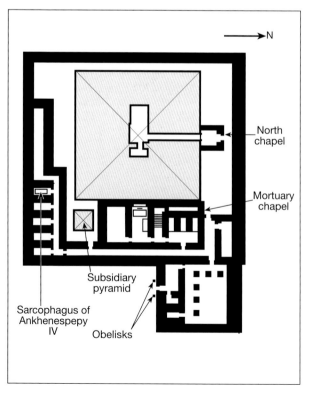

North chapel

Mortuary chapel

Subsidiary pyramid

Sarcophagus of Ankhenespepy IV

Obelisks

REIGN OF MONTJUHOTPE II: *c. 2066–2014* BC

After Pepy II's reign, tombs of royal family members are almost unknown from the Sixth to the Tenth dynasty. The next royal wives' sepulchres are to be found during the Eleventh Dynasty but, like those of the kings, they do not take the form of pyramids. In the saff tombs, they take the same chapel/shaft form as those of their husbands. At Deir el-Bahari, within the royal mortuary temple, a number of Montjuhotpe II's spouses had small, cupboard-like, free-standing decorated stone chapels with a shaft and burial chamber behind. One wife had a burial chamber at the end of a sloping passage close to that of the king himself.

REIGN OF AMENMEHAT I: *c. 1994–1964* BC

The resurrection of the kingly pyramid under the Twelfth Dynasty was not initially accompanied by pyramids for queens. Amenemhat I's complex (see page 85) incorporated only mastabas for his court, including, north of the mortuary temple, two mastabas (945 and 946). These were located in a similar place to the position of royal family tombs in many of the complexes of the late Old Kingdom and also in the slightly later pyramid complex of Senwosret I. South of the mortuary temple lie two large tombs, the southern of which (493) has its own enclosure, approached by a ramp from a lower level, with a massif (possibly a small pyramid) fronted by a chapel. Its position and form seem appropriate to a wife (or conceivably the mother) of the king.

Left: Iput II's Pyramid and chapel, with the false door still in position.

Above: The granite gateway of Iput II's complex.

Below: A number of the tombs of Montjuhotpe II's wives at Deir el-Bahari contained exquisite sarcophagi; this one, now in the Cairo Museum, belonged to Kawit.

SITE/DESIGNATION:
Lisht 1
OWNER: Neferu III, mother of the king
DIMENSIONS: Base 21 x 21 metres

SITE/DESIGNATION:
Lisht 2
OWNER: Itakayet, a daughter of the king
DIMENSIONS: Base 16.8 x 16.8 metres

SITE/DESIGNATION:
Lisht 3
OWNER: A daughter of the king (?)
DIMENSIONS: Base 16.8 x 16.8 metres

SITE/DESIGNATION:
Lisht 4
OWNER: A daughter or wife of the king (?)
DIMENSIONS: Base 16.8 x 16.8 metres

REIGN OF SENWOSRET I: *c.* 1974–1929 BC

Lisht 1 *For plans, see page 87.*

Under Senwosret I, the king's family were once more granted pyramidal monuments, which then continued to be used for many queens into the Thirteenth Dynasty. Nine small pyramids lie outside Senwosret's inner enclosure wall, the first of which has been assigned to Neferu on the basis of inscribed fragments found near the south-east corner of its enclosure. Neferu's pyramid was entered from a deep shaft in the middle of the north face, directly in front of an extension of the pyramid casing, against which a chapel formerly abutted. From the bottom of the shaft a passage leads to an antechamber, in the floor of which is sunk the entrance to the burial chamber, with a niche at its end.

Lisht 2 and 3

Itakayet's structure had a chapel that contained a number of 32-sided columns and decoration including offering-lists and -bearers, mortuary rituals, birds in the marshes and the tomb-owner seated before an offering-table. The substructure is of an elaborate form that is also found in the adjacent Pyramid 3. This form involved employing both an entrance shaft and a 'construction' one, covered over by the erection of the chapel against the north face of the pyramid. In Pyramid 2, the burial chamber was little more than an extension of the corridor, with a canopic niche in the left-hand wall, but in Pyramid 3, two sets of sliding stone doors were incorporated to block access, and a quartzite sarcophagus and canopic chest were placed in the chamber. Fragments of bone were found in the chamber and a piece of a female statue was found in the chapel, but nothing is known of the owner of the pyramid.

Lisht 4

Four more small pyramids stood on the west and north sides of the king's pyramid. Pyramid 4 had two discrete sets of corridors and chambers, approached by separate shafts. The shaft in the north-east corner gave access to two levels of chambers, the upper of which had had an additional burial place and sarcophagus inserted just outside the main burial chamber. The burial chamber was so small that it could not have contained anything more than a wooden coffin and canopic chest.

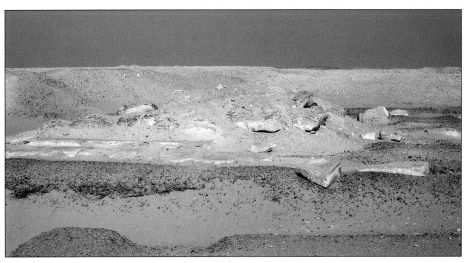

Left: Pyramid 5 in Senwosret I's complex.

SITE/DESIGNATION:
Lisht 5
OWNER: A daughter or wife of the king (?)
DIMENSIONS: Base 16.3 x 16.3 metres

SITE/DESIGNATION:
Lisht 6
OWNER: A daughter or wife of the king (?)
DIMENSIONS: Base 17.5 x 17.5 metres

SITE/DESIGNATION:
Lisht 7
OWNER: A daughter or wife of the king (?)
DIMENSIONS: Base 15.75 x 15.75 metres

SITE/DESIGNATION:
Lisht 8
OWNER: A wife of the king (?)
DIMENSIONS: Base 15.75 x 15.75 metres

SITE/DESIGNATION:
Lisht 9
OWNER: A wife or daughter of the king (?)
DIMENSIONS: Base 15.75 x 15.75 metres

Lisht 5

Although a number of tomb shafts lie around this pyramid, none leads to a conventional pyramid substructure. A shaft on the north side was unfinished, and another, on the west side, has corridors (on two levels) leading under the pyramid. These corridors, however, are collapsed and the burial chamber has never been reached.

Lisht 6 and 7

These two pyramids seem to have been built as a co-ordinated pair, and were begun around Year 13 of Senwosret I. The chapel of Pyramid 6 contained the remains of larger-than-life statues of the anonymous owner. The substructure of Pyramid 6 has not been identified, while the sloping corridor at the bottom of Pyramid 7's entrance shaft was choked with mud and never fully excavated as the water table lay just below.

Lisht 8 and 9

These two pyramids directly north of Senwosret's mortuary temple would appear to be candidates for containing queenly burials. Their dual nature, with a common enclosure wall, is reminiscent of the tombs of Nebet and Khenut in Unas' complex, not to mention Tombs 945 and 946 in that of Amenemhat I.

Pyramid 8's chapels have disappeared, but the substructure was entered via a shaft on the centre of the north side, from the bottom of which a passageway led to a chamber under the centre of the pyramid, with a coffin-cut in the middle of the floor, and another room beyond. The adjacent Pyramid 9 had a core of brick, an unusual feature which, together with the evidence of the pottery found in its foundation deposits, suggests that it may have been built during the reigns of Amenemhat II or Senwosret II, presumably for a wife or daughter of Senwosret I who had lived into one of these reigns. The location of the substructure is uncertain, since none of the shafts in the vicinity lead to rooms that obviously relate to the pyramid.

Principal Explorations

All these sites were excavated by the Metropolitan Museum of Art between 1923 and 1933; Pyramids 1, 2, 4 and 8 had previously been investigated by Jéquier and Gautier in 1895–6.

REIGN OF AMENEMHAT II: *c.* 1932–1896 BC

Amenemhat II's complex does not seem to have incorporated pyramids for his wives, although the present state of the site may skew our perception of the situation. The two large stone and brick massifs on either side of the entry from the causeway are of uncertain purpose, but if they are tombs, their prominent position might argue for their being those of queens. Also of uncertain nature is a structure just outside the main enclosure wall, directly north of the king's pyramid, whence were recovered the remains of columns, various reused fragments and what may be an offering table of highly unusual form. If this structure does represent a tomb, a prominent owner seems likely, perhaps a queen, since the northern part of the enclosure was chosen in the next reign for the wife's probable tomb.

The one wife's burial which was recorded is in a novel form of tomb only found in this complex. Three of these exist, comprising a built structure of masonry sunk in a pit, covered by a brick relieving arch. A passage runs the entire length of the tomb, off which two niches open, each containing a sunken sarcophagus, its lid just below the level of the floor of the passage. From the west side of each sarcophagus-cut, three low openings give access to an offering/canopic chamber, returning under the paving of the passage above. At the time of the burial, the niche was filled with stone slabs, locked in place by a vertical keystone.

With their passages filled with plug blocks, the tombs effectively became solid masses of stone; doubtless this explains the fact that two of them remained intact. The third tomb was plundered by robbers breaking through the brick vault directly above the burial chambers; in its southern sarcophagus had been interred the mummy of Queen Keminub. Curiously, the northern sarcophagus was not that of a royal lady, but apparently belonged to a high official named Amenhotep. Such tombs seem unlikely to have had a monumental superstructure, and certainly not pyramids.

Below: The burial chamber of Tomb 621 was almost certainly the substructure of the Lahun queen's pyramid.

SITE/DESIGNATION:
Lahun 621
OWNER: A wife of the king, probably Neferet II or Khnemetneferhedjet I
DIMENSIONS: Base 26.6 x 26.6 metres

REIGN OF SENWOSRET II: *c.*1900–1880 BC

For plan, see page 89.

A queen's pyramid once more appears in the complex of Senwosret II. It lies just north-east of the king's, at the head of a line of mastabas of other family members. The pyramid itself is largely destroyed. No galleries lay below: what appears to have been its substructure lay some 60 metres to the north-west, presumably reflecting the security concerns of the time. Its plan is reminiscent of a king's substructure of the late Old Kingdom, but with stairways in some passages. Its sarcophagus is interesting in being among the earliest of the Middle Kingdom to adopt the palace-façade motif.

Principal Explorations
Excavated by Petrie in 1920–21.

REIGN OF SENWOSRET III: *c.* 1900–1880 BC

For plans, see page 92.

The pyramid complex of Senwosret III has, like that at Lahun, a row of royal family tombs lying along the north side of the enclosure. In this case, however, their substructures lie below the four pyramidal superstructures, comprising four individual sepulchres joined by a single east–west gallery. The only one that revealed the name of an owner was Tomb II, which contained the bones and palace-façade ornamented sarcophagus of Queen Neferhenut. While each tomb on the gallery differs from the others in detail, all resemble the queen's in basic form: a chamber leading off the main east–west corridor, a stairway and passage sunk in the floor leading to a burial chamber with two subsidiaries. A canopic niche lies at the end of a short passage west of the stairway.

Two further likely queens' pyramids lay to the south of the king's pyramid, the westernmost belonging to Weret, mother of Senwosret III. The entrance to Weret's pyramid lay some distance to the north-east of the superstructure, the shaft joining a north–south passage halfway along its 60-metre length. To the north, the passage gave access to an antechamber, a canopic room and a burial chamber, the latter with a fine granite sarcophagus displaying a panelled lower part. This all lay under the body of the king's pyramid, some 50 metres away from the queen's own monument. Under the latter, the southern part of the passage led to a small subterranean shrine.

While relief fragments were recovered from Pyramid 7, it was not possible to 'name' it. However, it had a substructure entered once again from far outside, but with a burial chamber under the monument itself.

Principal Explorations

These monuments were first investigated by de Morgan in February–March 1894; they were re-excavated by Arnold in 1994, who discovered the burial chamber of Weret, with jewellery, in November 1994.

Below: *The rock-cut mastabas on the north side of the pyramid of Senwosret II at Lahun; the queen's pyramid lies at the far end of the row.*

SITE/DESIGNATION: Dahshur L.XLVII/I
OWNER: Not known

SITE/DESIGNATION: Dahshur L.XLVII/II
OWNER: Neferhenut, wife of the king

SITE/DESIGNATION: Dahshur L.XLVII/III
OWNER: Not known

SITE/DESIGNATION: Dahshur L.XLVII/IV
OWNER: Not known

SITE/DESIGNATION: Dahshur L.XLVII/9
OWNER: Weret, mother of the king

SITE/DESIGNATION: Dahshur L.XLVII/7
OWNER: Not known

Above: The pectoral collar and restored chest area of Neferuptah's (daughter of Amenemhat III) inner coffin, now on display in the Cairo Museum.

REIGN OF AMENEMHAT III:
c. 1842–1794 BC

Amenemhat III's Black Pyramid at Dahshur further develops the arrangements of the substructure of Weret's Pyramid. Two of his wives were laid to rest wholly under his pyramid, without any separate superstructures. The queens' chambers are primarily approached via a stairway and passage from the west side of the Black Pyramid.

As we have seen above (page 96), Amenemhat III's daughter, Neferuptah, seems to have been temporarily buried in the king's burial chamber under his pyramid. She was later reburied in a pyramid two kilometres to the south, which had been designed with a burial chamber that would be roofed over and embedded in the mass of brickwork and the pyramid built over it, without any entrance passageway. This preserved the tomb intact until 1955, although the body had been destroyed by a rise in the water table. The burial chamber was divided in two by a partition wall, a huge sarcophagus lying in the southern section. The northern part held an offering table, a silver vase and a series of pots. The first two items were inscribed, as were further silver vessels from the compartment that held the sarcophagus. Another offering table and the canopics had been left behind in the main Hawara pyramid.

Principal Explorations
Noted by Habachi in 1936 and excavated by Farag and Iskander in April–May 1956.

SITE/DESIGNATION:
Hawara-South
OWNER: Neferuptah, daughter of the king
DIMENSIONS: Base 35 x 35 metres

Right: Section of the pyramid of Neferuptah, showing its lack of any entrance passage.

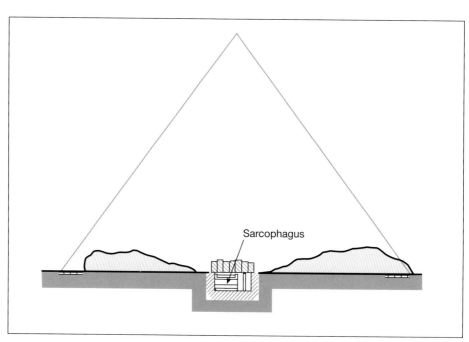

Sarcophagus

REIGN OF UNKNOWN KING: 18th century BC

For plan, see page 99.
A small pyramid was noted by Lepsius in 1843 north-east of the North Pyramid; nothing is known other than its location.

REIGN OF KHENDJER: 18th century BC

A small pyramid lay north of the site of the mortuary temple. It contains two burial chambers, reached via two portcullises; each chamber had a close-fitting sarcophagus and canopic chest. Neither chamber was ever used.

Principal Explorations
Excavated by Jéquier in 1929–31.

Later Queens' Burials

No queen's pyramid is known in Egypt subsequent to the reign of Khendjer. Indeed, very little is known of queenly interments until the Eighteenth Dynasty. Early in the Eighteenth Dynasty, a number of queens had fairly substantial rock-cut tombs of their own at Thebes, but later others seem to have been buried simply in side-rooms of kings' tombs. It was not until the Nineteenth Dynasty that a fairly consistent pattern emerges of consorts owning substantial decorated burial places in what is now known as the Valley of the Queens, where some of the royal family had been buried since the New Kingdom.

The Third Intermediate Period saw a major change in burial patterns at all levels of society, with a move towards communal burial and the large-scale abandonment of monumental chapels and burial apartments in favour of simple shaft tombs, only occasionally accompanied by modest offering places. Thus, a number of kings were accompanied by their wives in their tombs in temple courtyards. Similar, independent tombs are also found belonging to certain Third Intermediate and Late Period queens, but there are insufficient surviving examples to be able to confirm what pattern, if any, there was.

The only exception was during the Twenty-fifth Dynasty, when pyramids were re-adopted for queens' burials at El-Kurru and Nuri in the Sudan – and the queens continued, like the kings, to be interred in them following the Kushite withdrawal from Egypt. At El-Kurru, Piye's wife, Kheñsa, was buried in Ku4 and Tabiry in Ku53; adjacent were four other similar tombs, one belonging to Neferukakashta (Ku52).

Three other definite royal ladies' tombs have been identified at El-Kurru. Qalhata's Ku5 and Abar's Ku6 are some way south-east of the pyramid of Shabataka (Ku18), while the third, Ku3, of Ñaparaye, is interesting in that her husband, Taharqa, was not buried in the same cemetery, but at Nuri. On the other hand, another wife, Atakhebasken, was buried in Nuri (Nu36), where many of the subsequent queens' pyramids were erected.

SITE/DESIGNATION: Mazghuna
OWNER: Not known
DIMENSIONS: Not known

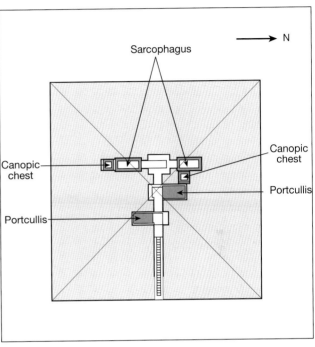

SITE/DESIGNATION: Saqqara-South L.XLV
OWNER: Probably two wives of the king
DIMENSIONS: Base 25.5 x 25.5 metres

Above: Plan of the pyramid of two wives of Khendjer of the Thirteenth Dynasty.

HIEROGLYPHS

IN THE HIEROGLYPHS, the ancient Egyptians produced what are perhaps the most attractive of all scripts. These images of human beings, animals, birds, insects and a vast range of inanimate objects could be carved and painted in exquisite detail, ornamenting a building or object as well as serving as a medium for imparting a particular piece of information. They also had the quality of being capable of being written in any chosen direction, even further enhancing their decorative utility.

To the outside world, they have also imparted a sense of mystery, that these images must conceal great secrets, unknowable to the uninitiated. During the long centuries that followed the death of their last ancient reader, probably early in the fifth century AD, speculations multiplied, with 'solutions' that had the sole common denominator of being more or less wrong.

The reality was that the hieroglyphs were simply a writing system, just as capable of expressing a laundry list or love poem as an impenetrably deep religious text. Alongside the superbly drawn signs on the wall of a temple or a tomb were hand-written versions that bore only a passing resemblance to their picture-prototype. From these developed further forms whose final shape was wholly divorced from the original glyph.

Hieroglyphs and their derivatives were in use for three and a half millennia, and saw many adjustments and changes during that immense period of time. However, the basic forms of the hieroglyphs were little changed, and although one can tell at a glance between texts of 3000 BC and AD 300, the signs are

the same, albeit writing an appreciably different version of the Egyptian language. From their contents, it has proved possible to reconstruct the history, society and economy of Egypt in remarkable detail. Nevertheless, the surviving written documents represent an infinitesimally small tithe of those which once existed. Thus, every new discovery may be of fundamental importance in fleshing out the picture, a small fragment perhaps revealing wholly-unknown events and persons. Such 'new' material is not just the result of archaeological excavations in Egypt. Much material, found long ago, remains unstudied in museum basements and archives, and expeditions into such dusty recesses are just as important as those to the ruins of the Nile valley.

Other 'explorations' concern the very meaning of the carved or written words. Although the basics of the Egyptian language had been re-established by the latter part of the nineteenth century, the subtleties on which the true meaning of a language depends are still the subject of active research.

The sections that follow are intended to explore some of the wide range of topics that surround Egyptian hieroglyphs. It is not about how to read them – there are many fine (and not so fine) books available designed to teach this skill. It is intended to reveal what hieroglyphs meant to the ancient inhabitants of the Nile valley, to the early scholars who struggled to understand them in the years after they went out of daily use, and to those who have over the past two centuries managed to read them once more and bring back to life the civilization to which they belonged.

THE ORIGINS OF EGYPTIAN LANGUAGE

Beginnings

Above: *The Nile at Nag Hammadi, where lush fields give way to barren high desert. The Nile has always been Egypt's great highway, linking the Mediterranean with the heart of Africa.*

Opposite: *Ancient and Modern. The mud brick settlements along the banks of the Nile have hardly changed since remote antiquity.*

The beginning of writing in ancient Egypt can perhaps be traced back to Tomb 100 at Hierakonpolis (see page 34), the earliest known decorated tomb. This was adorned with a series of painted boats, buildings, and men hunting and fighting. The existence of the unique decoration is clearly indicative of ownership at the highest elite level, which is why it is probable that Tomb 100 belonged to one of the early 'kings' of southern Egypt.

The decoration of Tomb 100 has close affinities with the images painted on pottery of the period, in particular in its focus on boat imagery. It is with further marks on pots that progress towards writing can be seen. The vessels from the latter part of the Predynastic Period do not have the standardized painted decoration characteristic of Naqada II, but ink marks on the plain wares from the Naqada III royal tombs at Umm el-Qaab seem to be amongst the earliest manifestations of the hieroglyphic script. These ink marks form graphic depictions of various types of creature; scholars have interpreted these images as expressing the name of the tomb owner.

The most important of these large royal tombs is known as U-j (see pages 34 and 36). It also contained a large number of inscribed labels bearing further early forms of hieroglyphs, and numerical notations. These labels seem to give the names of various administrative entities, presumably the points of origin of the produce to which they were once attached. The precise dating of these earliest hieroglyphs is unclear, but they certainly lie somewhere within the 150 years that directly preceded the unification of Egypt, around 3050 BC.

THE FOUNDATION OF EGYPT

PREDYNASTIC PERIOD

Badarian Period
5000–4000 BC
First evidence for pottery in Egypt

BLACK TOPPED RED POT
FROM ABYDOS TOMB 1730

Naqada I Period
4000–3500 BC
Development of culture

RED-LINED POT

Naqada II Period
3500–3150 BC
First major towns

SLATE
PALETTE

Naqada III Period
3150–3000 BC
First hieroglyphs

ARCHAIC PERIOD

Dynasty I
3050–2815 BC
*Unification of Egypt;
royal tombs at Abydos*

Dynasty II
2815–2660 BC
*Royal tombs at
Saqqara*

OLD KINGDOM

Dynasty III
2660–2600 BC
First pyramids

Dynasty IV
2600–2470 BC
*Great pyramids
at Giza*

STEP PYRAMID

PYRAMIDS AT GIZA

Left: The border of Egypt proper lay at Aswan, where granite outcrops produced a series of rapids, known as the First Cataract, which interrupted navigation southward. Here, on the island of Elephantine, was erected a city, the governors of which led the trading expeditions that were mounted into the African hinterland.

No one can be certain what stimulated the development of this early script. A frequent assumption is the influence of the script developing in Mesopotamia at the time. Like the Egyptian hieroglyphs, the first forms of writing found in Sumer (southern Iraq) are based around the use of images of actual objects and creatures to express concepts. However, rather than being painted on or incised into objects, Mesopotamian writing is found pressed into clay tablets, which were then fired to make them into a permanent record (see page 149). Mesopotamian writing rapidly moved on from the use of pictures to the essentially abstract cuneiform script, while hieroglyphs maintained their original conception for over 3,000 years, although cursive (simplified) versions also evolved.

While there is evidence for contact between this area and Egypt in Predynastic times, there are no precise dates. There are major differences in the structure, form and usage of the scripts (the earliest Sumerian tablets are administrative, rather than funerary), making direct borrowing unlikely. More probable is that merchants and other travellers disseminated the idea that sounds and ideas could be expressed through drawing pictures. From this came the local development of a wholly independent writing system that shared its roots with the other, but then went off in its own direction during the coming millenia.

Below: The Roman Period temple from Kalabsha, rebuilt in the 1960s overlooking the High Dam, or Sadd el-Ali, at Aswan. Early in the twentieth century, a series of dams was built across the Nile to control its flow.

In 1960, the greatest was begun south of Aswan. Its construction led to the flooding of a 500-km (320-mile) stretch of the Nile upstream, creating Lake Nasser. Many archaeological sites were inundated, leading to a major international campaign to survey and excavate them. A number of temples, including this one, were dismantled and moved to safe locations.

Left: The rock-cut temples at Abu Simbel, the most famous of all monuments rescued when the High Dam at Aswan was built. Colossal statues adorn the facade; in the foreground hieroglyphs that spell out some of the king's names.

Above: Early Egyptian desert grave. The earliest Egyptian burial places were oval graves scooped out of the gravel of the desert edge. In some cases, the bodies buried in them became naturally dried. They were the prototypes for the artificially desiccated mummies that came later.

Previous page: The Valley of the Kings at Western Thebes, the site of most of the tombs of the kings of the New Kingdom. This view shows the tombs of Amenmesse and Rameses III on the left, Rameses VI and Tutankhamun in the centre, and Merenptah on the right.

Right: Tomb 100, at Hierakonpolis in southern Egypt, the first known decorated tomb. One wall is adorned with paintings of boats and hunters, the former reminiscent of contemporary pottery-painting; it dates to the Naqada II period.

The key event of early Egyptian history came around 3050 BC, when the whole country was finally united. While there seems now ample evidence for a southern kingdom, the existence of the northern kingdom implied by much later tradition remains questionable. The most important monument for the Unification is the Narmer Palette (*see page 145*), discovered at Hierakonpolis in 1898, and now in the Cairo Museum. Stone palettes were used for the grinding of cosmetics; decorated versions were particularly popular in late Predynastic times. In material and workmanship, the Narmer Palette follows the pattern of a series of late Predynastic slate palettes. However, it has a much more formal decorative structure, providing a prototype for many subsequent pharaonic monuments; it also incorporates early hieroglyphs. The reverse of the palette shows the Horus Narmer smiting an enemy, above whom one of the earliest known hieroglyphic groups provides a caption.

The kind of combination of images and hieroglyphics found on the Narmer Palette is close to pure picture-writing, but is also moving towards expressing narrative through abstract images. Such a combination of a pictorial scene, with signs and groups of signs making up words, is a basic feature of the whole body of documents from the earliest years of Egyptian dynastic history. The words included are not formed into sentences, yet act with the associated depictions to convey information about an event. At this point the writing system was possibly a consciously artificial one, not intended to reproduce

the contemporary spoken language directly. However, as it effectively included nouns and verbs, and was made up of signs that would become familiar in later times, the potential was there for the later full flowering of the Egyptian script and written language.

The earliest surviving texts written in an unequivocal series of sentences date from Dynasty III (2660 BC–2597 BC), the first royal house of the Old Kingdom, when temple reliefs included proper divine speeches, and private titularies within noble tombs, showing the main features of the mature script.

The evolution of the written language during the immediately preceding period is not easy to trace, particularly since the key period, the second half of Dynasty II, was disfigured by civil war, which means that the number of available sources is severely limited. Tantalizingly, the earliest connected sentence in Egyptian appears on a sealing of the reign of Seth Peribsen, directly before the outbreak of the conflict.

EGYPTIAN NAMES AND TITLES

The study of Egyptian names is a major subject in itself, and their transcription into/from other languages and scripts was the key element in the first modern decipherment of hieroglyphic texts. Names are also the ideal vehicle for new enthusiasts to begin to recognize hieroglyphs, through royal cartouches, and also private names, whose endings (⚲ or ⚲ for a male, and ⚲ for a female) provide an excellent means of impressing one's companions!

Above: *Early slate palette. Images on the palettes from the last years of prehistory seem to have depicted the triumphs of chieftains, and included motifs that lie in the ancestry of hieroglyphs.*

THE NARMER PALETTE DECODED

The central tableau on the reverse of the palette shows King Narmer, wearing the conical White Crown, holding an enemy by the hair, and preparing to kill him with a mace, held aloft in his other hand. Directly behind the captive is the image of a harpoon, above what is known to be the hieroglyph for a body of water. This combination clearly gives the name of the captive, or more likely the group of enemies which he represents.

However, alongside this 'simple' depiction is the complex figure above the captive. The lower part is the hieroglyph for marsh-country, to which has been added a human head; the implication is thus 'people of the marsh-country'. The hawk that has this head tethered by the nose is a synonym for the king, so that the whole group reads 'the king has captured the marsh-country', apparently commemmorating the unification of Egypt.

Poised at the top of both sides of the palette are the repeated heads of a bovine goddess. These flank a rectangular frame, with a panelled lower section, containing the images of a chisel and a catfish. Together they comprise one of the earliest known 'serekhs', a rectangular frame within which is the name of King Narmer.

REVERSE OF THE NARMER PALETTE

NAMING THE KING

THE NOMEN, OR BIRTH NAME, provides the basis for the names which modern writers use for the kings of Egypt, distinguishing rulers of the same personal name by the use of ordinals (so, 'Amenemhat II', 'Thutmose IV', etc). However, there are two basic conventions used to transcribe the names so used. One is simply to vocalize the basic transcription of the Egyptian sounds into the Latin alphabet, as described in the next chapter (*see pages 162–3*). The other is to use the form in which a given royal name has been transmitted in Greek via writers of Classical times, provided that it is recognizably based on the original Egyptian. This method has the advantage of providing a regular spelling, as the vowelling of direct transcriptions is by no means universally agreed. On the other hand, many modern Egyptologists (particularly in the USA) recoil on principal from such artificial forms as the Greek transcriptions, which in any case may be so garbled as to bear no resemblance to the Egyptian, or where no Greek equivalent is known. Thus, depending on the author being read, the same king may be referred to by a number of apparently different names. A few examples are given below; this book will use the 'Egyptian transcription' throughout for clarity.

ACADEMIC TRANSLITERATION	VOCALIZED 'EGYPTIAN TRANSCRIPTION'	VERSION USED BY GREEK WRITERS
ḏsr	Djoser; Djeser; Zoser	Tosothros
ḫw-fw	Khufu	Kheops
imn-m-ḫ3t	Amenemhat	Ammenemes
s-n-wsrt	Senwosret; Senusert	Sesostris
iʿḥ-ms	Ahmose	Amosis; Amasis
imn-ḥtp	Amenhetep; Amunhotpe; Amunhotep	Amenophis
ḏḥwty-ms	Djehutymose; Djhutmose; Dhutmose; Thutmose	Tuthmosis
nsi-b3-nb-ḏdt	Nesibanebdjed	Smendes
p3-sb3-ḫʿ-n-niwt	Pasebakhanut	Psusennes
psmṯk	Psamtik	Psammetikhos
nḫt-nb-f	Nakhtnebef	Nektanebo

The Kingship

At the top of the Narmer Palette is a rectangular frame, known as a serekh. It is an element found until the very end of ancient Egyptian history. Its role was to contain the first of the series of formal names by which a king was known. By the middle of Dynasty V, these names totalled five.

The name contained within the serekh was known as the *Horus name*, assumed at the time of the king's accession and representing him as the incarnation of Horus, the patron of the Egyptian monarchy. It was the primary means of designating the king during most of Dynasties I – III, but was then gradually displaced from premier position by other names within the titulary. By the New Kingdom, it was generally only found where the full list of a king's titles was being given. By that time it had become a long series of phrases, closer to a title than a simple name. For example while a typical early Horus name, Hotep-sekhemwy (that of the founder of Dynasty II) meant 'The Two Powers [the gods Horus and Seth] are content', that of Osorkon II (Dynasty XXII) was Kanakht-merymaat-sekha-su-Re-er-nesu-tawy, 'Strong Bull, beloved of Maat, whom Re has caused to appear as king of the two lands'.

The second name in the titular canon, the *Nebty name*, represented the king as protegé of Edjo and Nekhbet, respectively the great goddesses of northern and southern Egypt. Like the Horus name, it goes back to the earliest days, and was for some time the sole additional name used. At first, it may have been used to prefix the king's 'real' name, that given to him at birth. Later, however, the birth name gained its own distinct prefix, and the Nebty became a separate name. It was one of the less-used ones, and during the New Kingdom experienced the same kind of lengthening as the Horus name.

Above Carved mace-heads depicted the activities of some of the earliest kings. Here, King 'Scorpion', who ruled just before the unification of the country, is shown cutting the first breach in the wall of an irrigation embankment.

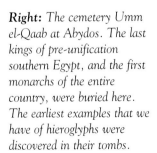

Right: The cemetery Umm el-Qaab at Abydos. The last kings of pre-unification southern Egypt, and the first monarchs of the entire country, were buried here. The earliest examples that we have of hieroglyphs were discovered in their tombs.

The third name in the canon, known as the *Golden Falcon name*, is the most obscure. Prefixed by the hieroglyphs for 'falcon' and 'gold', it first appears in Dynasty IV, but it is not until the Middle Kingdom that each king seems to have taken an individual example. Its significance has been much debated, and although the falcon is usually identified with Horus, this is by no means universally agreed. Likewise, although the 'gold' sign is probably to be taken at face value, an old suggestion made it a reference to the Predynastic city of Nubt (the word for 'gold' is '*nub*'), whose god was Seth. In Egyptian mythology, Seth was the enemy of Horus, and thus the whole title could be read as 'Horus [victorious] over Seth'. Although this may have been felt to be the implication in Ptolemaic times, it is now seen as being unlikely at the outset, on ideological grounds. The meaning of the title remains obscure; it may be pointed out, however, that gold was the material of the flesh of the gods, and thus the implication of the title may be 'the golden king'.

The Royal Rings

The remaining two names are the best known, and from the late Old Kingdom onwards were the principal means of identifying a king, easily recognizable by their enclosure in the oval frame, known as the cartouche. This modern name is based upon the shape's resemblance to a military gun cartridge ('cartouche' in French). It actually represents a tied rope, and is derived from the circular shen-sign (Ω), which seems to have represented the circuit of the sun, and is frequently found clasped in the talons of divine birds of prey.

The names are known by the Latin terms, *nomen* and *prenomen*. The nomen, which stands last in the canon of royal names, was the king's birth-name, sometimes embellished by an epithet such as beloved of a god. It is first found (without the cartouche) in the second half of Dynasty I, preceded by the title *nesu-bity*, 'He of the Sedge and the Bee'. It has traditionally been translated as 'King of Upper and Lower Egypt', but it now seems certain that this is wrong, the Sedge and Bee not being heraldic emblems of the north and south of Egypt, but signifying some other element of duality within the concept of kingship.

The first examples of the contemporary use of the cartouche are found during Dynasty III, although it is used retrospectively to enclose earlier kings' personal names in king lists, or other texts that need to refer to ancient rulers. By the end of Dynasty V, its prefix is changed to *si-Re* (son of the [sun god] Re). From the New Kingdom onwards, an alternative was *neb-khau* (Lord of Diadems/Appearances). At some periods, *si-Re* is written within the cartouche, in front of the actual name, but this was never usual.

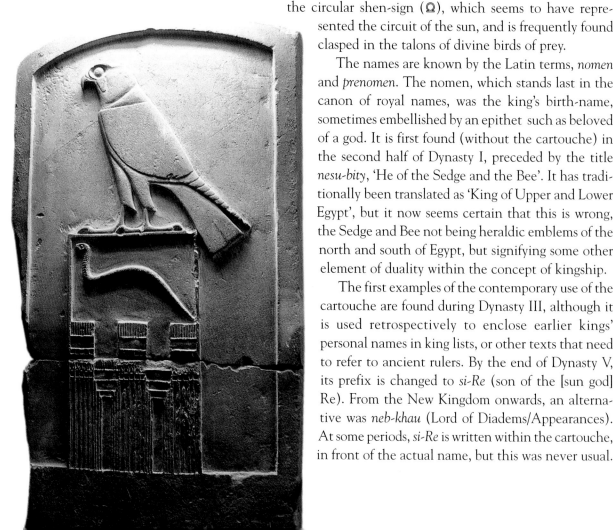

Below: Monumentally sized hieroglyphs are found on the stelae that marked out the offering places adjacent to the royal tombs at Abydos. The finest gives the Horus-name of the Horus Djet, set in an enclosure with a panelled lower part. This is known as the serekh, topped with the hawk of the god Horus, patron of the king.

Left: *Label from the tomb of Den at Umm el-Qaab. It refers to his jubilee. Tomb labels are another source of early hieroglyphs.*

Prenomen and Prenomina

Unlike modern monarchs, ancient Egyptian kings of the same personal name did not use numerals to mark out individuals – William IV or Louis XIV, for example. Instead, distinction was on the basis of the whole suite of names, in particular the other cartouche name, the *prenomen*. It was preceded by one of two titles signifying dominion over the two aspects of the Egyptian realm, one of which, nesu-bity, we have already met alongside the nomen.

The prenomen is first found during Dynasty V, but was not consistently adopted by kings until the early part of Dynasty VI. It then became the standard shorthand way of designating a king until Dynasty XXVI, when the nomen took over once again. Thus, in texts where there was only space for one part of the royal titulary, a king such as Tutankhamun would be referred to by his prenomen, Nebkheperure, rather than his nomen – Tutankhamun-heqaiunshemay (Tutankhamun, ruler of the southern Heliopolis). With but a tiny handful of exceptions, the prenomen always incorporated the name of the sun-god Re. In addition, related kings might take prenomina of a basically similar form. For example, many rulers of Dynasty XVIII had names of the X-kheper(u)-Re structure; others of the Second Intermediate Period popularized a Sekhemre-X shape, X representing the variable element of the name.

In general, Egyptian kings tried to choose prenomina that had not been used before, although a number were clearly meant to recall that of an illus-

Below: *A clay tablet from Ancient Sumer (now southern Iraq) dating from around the end of the third millennium BC. The cuneifrom marks on it indicate that Egypt was not the only country developing writing at that time.*

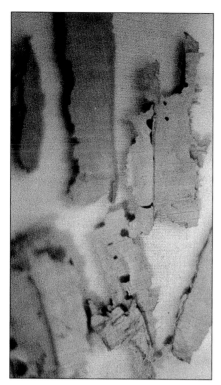

Above: *Paper made from the papyrus plant was the most characteristic Egyptian writing material. The very earliest example of this comes from the middle of Dynasty I, discovered in the tomb of a nobleman at Saqqara. Unfortunately, it is blank. Although various other materials were in use, Egypt never adopted the clay tablet as a writing medium.*

trious predecessor. One instance is Thutmose IV, whose 'Menkheperure' was just one letter different from Thutmose III's 'Menkheperre'. There was occasionally a repeat of an earlier usage, but normally accompanying a different nomen, and used many years after the death of the previous user. However, during the Third Intermediate Period, the system broke down, and prenomina were re-used within a few years of their last employment, but also with effectively the same nomen as before! In most cases, a minor variation in the epithets used allows historians to distinguish between two all-but-identically-named kings (e.g. Usermaetre-setpenamun Osorkon-meryamun-sibast [Osorkon II] vs. Usermaetre-setpenamun Osorkon-meryamun-sieset [Osorkon III]), but it can be extremely difficult. Indeed, in one such case it took some 50 years to recognize that there were two kings sharing the prenomen Hedjkheperre and the nomen Shoshenq.

Epithets

The distinction was made possible in part as a result of the study of the usage of epithets within royal names. The earliest cartouches held simple names – the penultimate king of Dynasty V had the nomen Isesi, and the prenomen Djedkare. This pattern was largely maintained until Dynasty XVIII, when kings began to add epithets to both their nomina and prenomina. In the latter case, they tended to be used only on specific occasions, not becoming an integral part of the name. For example, in a temple of the god Ptah, a king might be 'setep-en-Ptah', 'chosen of Ptah'. The same pattern is seen initially in nomina, but they become permanent parts of the cartouche by the middle of Dynasty XVIII. Amenhotep II, for example was 'netjer-heqa-On' ('divine ruler of Heliopolis'), Amenhotep III 'heqa-Waset' ('ruler of Thebes') and Amenhotep IV 'netjer-heqa-Waset' ('divine ruler of Thebes'). Almost without exception, all subsequent kings embedded one or more epithet into their nomina, the most frequent being 'mery-Amun' ('beloved of Amun'), but various other options were possible.

The prenomen first permanently incorporated an epithet under Amenhotep IV. Some of the immediately subsequent kings followed suit until a few years into the reign of Rameses II. He then added 'setep-en-Re' ('chosen of Re') to the simple Usermaetre. Epithets were then used in every ruler's prenomen until the latter few years of the Third Intermediate Period, when names reverted to their Old and Middle Kingdom simplicity.

Both nomina and prenomina remained thus (followed also by the other names within the titulary) until the last years of Egyptian independence. However, the Macedonian kings of the Ptolemaic dynasty, and their imperial Roman successors, adopted extremely elaborate cartouches that became effectively strings of epithets. In particular, the prenomen lost any trace of an easily-recognizable 'core' name. Alexander the Great had begun this by naming himself simply Setpenre-meryamun ('Chosen of Re, Beloved of Amun', both previously used purely as epithets), as did Ptolemy I. Philip

Arrhidaios and Ptolemy II used more traditional prenomina, but Ptolemy III then made the leap of using the vast prenomen Iwaennetjerwysenwy-setpenre-sekhenankhenamun ('Heir of the two sibling gods, chosen of Re, living power of Amun'); his successors emulated this length. Ptolemaic and Roman cartouches are thus easily recognized, as they usually contain double or more the number of signs of native Egyptian royal names. They also abandon the long-standing incorporation of the name of the sun god Re into the prenomen. Ptolemaic-Roman nomina are also long, with multiple epithets, commonly including 'ankhdjet-meryptah' ('living for ever, beloved of Ptah').

Roman cartouches reflect the emperor's purely nominal status as pharaoh, with major divergences from conventional formulations. Only a few of the earliest emperors, down to Domitian (AD 51–96), employed Horus, Nebty and Golden Falcon names, and not all used two cartouche names. The convention that the nomen contained the personal name was also not always obeyed, and there is often much variation between a single emperor's attestations. One set of names used by Claudius (10 BC–AD 54) had the prenomen Heqaheqau-autokrator-meryesetptah 'Ruler of Rulers, Autocrat, beloved of Isis and Ptah' and the nomen Tiberios Klaudios. In contrast, Titus (AD 39–81), eldest son of Vespasian, once used the prenomen Autokrator Titos Kaisaros, with the nomen Wespasianos-entykhu.

Below: The king Menkaure (Dynasty IV) with the goddess Hathor and the god of the province of Thebes. Kings were considered to be gods with their own place in the Egyptian pantheon, but were often shown smaller than other deities, indicating their lesser importance.

Father and Son

One variant on the usual patterns is found during Dynasty XIII, when a number of kings adopted what have been termed 'filiative' nomina, names that included the names of their fathers. Perhaps influenced by disputes as to legitimacy amongst certain claimants of the throne, these cartouches incorporated the names of a king's father, and sometimes even grandfather. An excellent example of the latter is Ameny-Inyotef-Amenemhat, better known as Amenemhat VI. Interestingly, his father Inyotef is not known to have been a king, but the 'Ameny' (a well known short-form of 'Amenemhat') refers back to his ruling grandfather, Amenemhat V.

These names can often place kings whose precise place in history is otherwise unknown. For example, 'Qemau-Sihornedjhiryotef' was long known, but 'Ameny-Qemau' was only identified when his ruined pyramid was discovered in 1957. The filiative nomina allowed Sihornedjhiryotef to be identified as Qemau's son, and Qemau as the probable son of Amenemhat V. This also showed that the three generations did not rule in succession, being separated by other kings, raising interesting questions about the political events of the time.

THAT WHICH THE SUN ENCIRCLES

THE CARTOUCHE IS DERIVED from a circular tied rope, known as the shen (Ω), symbolizing all that is encircled by the sun, and usually found grasped in the talons of bird-gods. In its oval form, it signified the pharaoh's universal dominion, and is the most common enclosure for royal names found on the monuments. The earliest examples date from the beginning of the Old Kingdom, and continue in use until the latter part of the Roman Period.

For much of Egyptian history, they were only used by kings, but from the later Middle Kingdom began to be used for other members of the royal family, in particular the queen. Finally, in the Graeco-Roman Period, they were occasionally used for gods' names as well.

Above: *The prenomen cartouche of Senwosret I (Kheperkare); at this period, cartouches tend to be fairly simple.*

Above: *By the late New Kingdom, prenomina had been expanded by a series of epithets, two in this case (Sethnakhte: Userkhaure-setepenre-meryamun).*

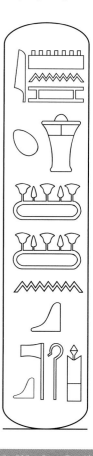

Left: *The titulary of Senwosret I: the right-hand column contains his Horus-name (in a serekh) and the prenomen; the left has the Nebty-name and nomen.*

Below: *Shoshenq IV is called Shoshenq-sibast-meryamun-netjerheqaon. Nomina had also gained numbers of epithets by the middle of Dynasty XXII.*

These filiative nomina are useful, because the dynasty in which they are found is particularly murky historically, and they help confirm the situation of certain monarchs. However, we know sufficiently little about the motivation behind the names that the attempt which has been made to argue that kings of the period without filiative nomina were thus usurpers, or had been nominated crown prince by a childless predecessor, cannot be proven.

Queens and their titles

The title that we usually read as 'Queen', *hemet-nesu*, means literally 'King's Wife'; queens reigning in their own right were called 'King', but usually with a feminine grammatical suffix. It is also sometimes used for 'King's Mother', who would of course frequently be the wife of a king in any case. The words for 'prince' and 'princess' were likewise simple filiatives. Two rather special titles were 'God's Father' and 'God's Mother', which could on occasion designate the parents of a king of non-royal birth. The former title, however, could hold other meanings, and has to be interpreted with care.

Above: Scene from the tomb of Prince Amenhirkopshef in the Valley of the Queens, showing the god Shu (left) and the prince's father, Rameses III.

The columns of text on the left and centre bottom read together: 'Speech by Shu, son of Re: "I give to you Upper Egypt"'. The cartouches in front of the king read: 'Lord of the Two Lands, Usermaatre-meryamun, the Lord of Appearances, Rameses-heqaon.'

*Below: The priest
Bakenkhonsu, who enjoyed
a long career that culminated
in the High Priesthood of
Amun-Re, regarded as King
of the Gods during the New
Kingdom. The priesthood's
importance was not limited to
the religious sphere. The
temple estates owned vast
tracts of the country, and
thus those who ran them had
considerable temporal power.*

The Officials of the State

Private individuals in Egypt were particularly keen on the use of titles. Those of high social status bore long strings of them. Since literacy was greatly prized, and limited to a small minority of society, the title of 'scribe' features highly. Literacy was the key to authority, taught by private tutors and in temple schools to, in essence, the offspring of the existing literate elite. This elite included elements of the artisan class, but most of those who could read and write in ancient Egypt can generally be classified as 'officials'.

While many titles are functional, others seem to have been intended for locating a person in the overall pecking order – 'ranking' titles. The latter were most common in the Old Kingdom, when a number of formerly functional titles seems to have become simply signifiers of status. Study of titles allows us to reconstruct much of the way in which the Egyptian state was organized, and how this changed over time. In the earliest times, the senior official under the king was the Chancellor. The translations used for many titles are purely conventional; 'Chancellor' is used for the Egyptian *sedjawty-bity*, which literally translates as 'Seal-bearer of the King' (*cf. below*). However, 'Chancellor' better expresses the implications of the title-holder's place in the state hierarchy, particularly in the early years of Egyptian history. Likewise, the Egyptian *tjaty*, which from Dynasty IV designates a new senior official, who effectively functioned as Prime Minister, is usually referred to as the 'Vizier'. During Dynasty XVIII, the post of vizier was split equally into two, with two officials, each being responsible for one half of Egypt.

This duality is also seen with other posts, although some which have been traditionally translated as denoting a 'northern' or 'southern' official, may not be. Connected with this is the point noted earlier on that the royal title *nesu-bity* may not actually mean 'King of Upper and Lower Egypt' as was formerly assumed. One issue concerns the aforementioned title, *sedjawty-bity*; this is often translated as 'Seal-Bearer of the King of Lower Egypt', but there was no corresponding *sedjawty nesu*, 'Seal-Bearer of the King of Upper Egypt'. It now seems clear that this title refers purely to 'the King' *per se*, without any geographical implications.

Many titles refer to the administration of agriculture in Egypt. The farmland of Egypt, and the surpluses it produced provided the bedrock upon which the civilization's achievements depended. Theoretically, the whole of Egypt's land belonged to the king, but in practice most of it was administered by private individuals or religious bodies. Two main areas came under the authority of religious institutions: funerary domains, where land was assigned by a dead person to provide for offerings in his tomb, and a priest to attend to it; and temples, which required land to fund offerings and the priesthood, as well as building works and maintenance. As such, the temple domains were key engines of the economy, giving a livelihood to a wide variety of agricultural, artistic, architectural and sacerdotal personnel, and producing many of the most splendid works of art of the time.

The Priesthood

The basic title that we translate as 'priest', *hem-netjer*, effectively means 'god's servant', and reminds us that the temple was regarded as the home of the god, with a 'household' like any other high-status owner-occupier. The size of that household varied greatly, depending on the deity's resources. The god of a small provincial temple might not have had any full-time priests, leading members of the local community taking it in turns to serve the god for a set period of time; in general, they held the basic priestly title, *waab*, literally 'pure'. At the other extreme, great state gods, such as Amun-Re at Thebes, had large, full-time staffs. At Karnak, the principal seat of the Amun-cult, there were no fewer than four principal priests with the title of *hem-netjer*, and numbered from 1 to 4, the first of whom we normally call the High Priest. There were also many junior members of the clergy, with such titles as the aforementioned *waab* and *hery-khebet* ('Lector Priest', responsible for the divine liturgy). From the New Kingdom onwards, the High Priest of Amun-Re had a female counterpart, known as the God's Wife. At first she was frequently also the Queen, but by the Third Intermediate Period she seems to have remained without an earthly spouse, and by the end of that period was the dominant figure at Thebes.

The High Priests of some of the other major gods had special traditional titles; for example, that of Re at Heliopolis was 'Greatest of Seers' (*wer-maau*), and that of Ptah of Memphis 'Greatest of Craftsmen' (*wer-kherp*), referring to Ptah's patronage of such individuals. There were, of course other local variations, reflecting the fact that Egyptian religion was not a co-ordinated whole, but a loose confederation of separate, often blatantly contradictory, doctrines and practices. Alongside the Egyptian willingness to embrace foreign cults, the religious picture in the Nile valley was far removed from the rigid cultic structures found elsewhere, in the ancient, medieval and modern world.

Everyday Names

By tradition, an ancient Egyptian's name was supposed to have been chosen from his or her mother's words at the time of delivery. Some do indeed seem to fit with such a mode of choice, an example being Iufeni ('He is Mine', as well as such names as Nefret ('The Beautiful'). On the other hand, many names existed that are unlikely to have been chosen in quite such a way, and reflected a considered decision – particularly when, as was common, a child was named after a grandparent. Many names associated the bearer with some deity – Ramose ('Born of Re'), Siamun ('Son of Amun'), Ptahemheb ('Ptah in Festival'), Djedmutiusankh ('Mut decrees that she live') and Hori ('The One of Horus'). Others described qualities – e.g. Qen ('The Brave'), Nakht ('The Strong'), Nedjmet ('The Sweet') – or named a profession – e.g. Pahemnetjer

Above: *Paser, who held the post of vizier during the reign of Rameses II (Dynasty XIX). The vizier was the head of the pharaonic government.*

THE GREAT HOUSE

THE DESIGNATION OF 'PHARAOH', applied so generally today to the ancient Egyptian kings is actually a late addition to their range of titles. The word as used today derives from the Bible, but is ultimately based on the Egyptian *per-aa*, meaning 'the Great House'. It referred to the palace, and its use to mean the ruler or government clearly parallels the modern use of 'No 10 Downing Street' to refer to the Prime Minister of Britain, 'Buckingham Palace' to Britain's monarch, 'The White House' to the President of the USA, and 'The Kremlin' to the President of Russia. It is first found as an actual royal title in late New Kingdom times, and is common by the Late Period. In Roman times during the decorative period, 'pharaoh' appears on its own, within a cartouche, in temples when the identity of the Emperor was uncertain.

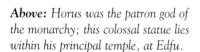

Above: *Horus was the patron god of the monarchy; this colossal statue lies within his principal temple, at Edfu.*

Right: *Although a woman, the female pharaoh Hatshepsut is here shown in ordinary kingly dress, with a false beard, a kilt and a bull's tail.*

('The Priest'). Another category were 'loyalist', coupling the name of the ruling king with a favourable epithet – e.g. Menkheperre-sonbe ('Health to Menkheperre [Thutmose III]') and Rameses-nakhte ('Rameses is Strong'). A number of individuals added such a name to their birth name, this kind of dual naming being particularly common in Dynasty XXVI.

Fashions in names changed over time, and fairly few were current throughout Egyptian history. This applied both to styles of name and the gods invoked, and it is frequently possible roughly to date an individual purely on the basis of his/her name alone. For example, those of the form 'Djed-X-iuf/ius-ankh' were popular in the Third Intermediate Period, while those invoking Sobek are frequently found in the latter part of the Middle Kingdom.

Clearly, many of these names were too clumsy for day-to-day use, and short forms were common. Some took on the standing of official alternate names, and appeared on monuments alongside the 'real' name. While certain short forms were specific to their bearer, there were others that regularly went with a 'real' one. At the simplest, Amenemhat became 'Ameny', but rather further removed from their roots were 'Mahu' for Amenemheb and 'Huy' for Amenhotep. Likewise, the Biblical figure 'Moses' is almost certainly a short-ened version of a name such as 'Ramose' or 'Amunmose'.

Above: *Funerary masks of two prominent figures at the court of Amenhotep III, the 'Chief of Chariots' (Cavalry General – right), Yuya, and his wife, the 'Royal Ornament' (Lady in Waiting – left), Tjuiu. Their daughter became the king's Chief Wife, the famous Queen Tiye, grandmother to Tutankhamun.*

Overleaf: *Procession from the temple of Rameses II at Abydos. Egyptian art included 'personifications', the representation of a place by a human figure or figures. They are usually shown as fairly fat, showing abundant food, and carrying the produce of their area.*

THE ANCIENT EGYPTIAN LANGUAGE

The Tongue of the Pharaohs

Above: *The entrance pylon of the New Kingdom temple of Luxor. 'Hieroglyphs' means 'sacred writing', and the script was most at home in a religious context.*

Opposite: *Rameses I before the god Anubis in his tomb in the Valley of the Kings. The cartouches above him spell out his two principal names.*

THE EGYPTIAN LANGUAGE, the tongue of the pharaohs, is now to all intents and purposes, dead. The only place where it may be heard today, outside Egyptology classes, is in a handful of the most traditionalist of Egyptian churches. There, Coptic, the very late version of Egyptian that used Greek letters, may be found in fragments of the liturgy. Coptic ceased to be an everyday tongue in the Middle Ages and is now fully understood by only a handful of scholars. The modern inhabitants of the Nile valley speak Arabic, a completely different language, originating far outside Egypt's borders.

However, there is a relationship between Arabic and ancient Egyptian. Both belong to the afro-asiatic family of languages, which covers large areas of the Levant and the northern part of Africa. Arabic belongs to the Semitic part of the group (along with Hebrew and Akkadian, the ancient language of Mesopotamia). Afro-asiatic languages have a number of features in common, including the relative importance of consonants over vowels, and the use of the same suffixes for certain parts of speech. Thus, ancient Egyptian is best explored with reference to the grammar of modern Arabic or oriental languages, rather than trying to make it work within the structural context of western languages. As we shall see, the man who deciphered hieroglyphs in modern times had purposefully immersed himself in modern oriental tongues in preparation for the task.

DEVELOPMENT OF EGYPTIAN LANGUAGE

ARCHAIC PERIOD

Dynasties I–II
3050–2660 BC
Earliest script

STELA FROM THE
TOMB OF DJET

OLD KINGDOM

Dynasties III–VI
2660–2200 BC
Old Egyptian

FIRST INTERMEDIATE PERIOD

Dynasties VII–XIa
2200–2070 BC
Transition to Middle Egyptian, which lasts through the Middle Kingdom, Dynasties XIb–XIII

**SECOND INTER-
MEDIATE PERIOD**

Dynasties XIV–XVII
1650–1550 BC
*Middle
Egyptian*

NEW KINGDOM

Dynasties XVIII–XX
1550–1070 BC
*Middle Egyptian
Transition to Late Egyptian*

SPHINX OF AMENEMHAT II

THIRD INTERMEDIATE PERIOD	LATE PERIOD	GRAECO-ROMAN PERIOD	COPTIC PERIOD	
Dynasties XXI–XXV	Dynasties XXVII–XXXI	Ptolemies	Romans	Byzantines
1070–664 BC	664–332 BC	332–30 BC	30 BC–AD 395	AD 395–640
Late Egyptian	*Late Egyptian*	*Demotic*	*Demotic*	*Coptic*
Demotic				*Demotic*

Middle/Late Egyption continue to be used for monumental texts into the Roman Period

FUNERARY STELA
IN COPTIC SCRIPT

THE EGYPTIAN ALPHABET

ANCIENT EGYPTIAN WAS BASED ON an alphabet of 24 consonants. Not all of these correspond directly with those found in the English alphabet, although all are present in that of such a Semitic language as Arabic. The conventional order of the signs is therefore based on that used in Semitics, as given below.

None of the signs below are true vowels. In common with modern printed Arabic and Hebrew, vowels were not written down, and had to be supplied by the reader using his or her own knowledge of the language. The sounds often transcribed today with the letters a, i and u are actually regarded as only semi-vowels, and also

HIEROGLYPH	ACADEMIC TRANSLITERATION[1]	ENGLISH EQUIVALENT	COMMENT
	3	a	
	i, j	a, i	
or	y, jj	y	
	ʿ	a	*ʿayin*, a gutteral sound not found in English
or	w	w, u	
	b	b	
	p	p	
	f	f	
or	m	m	
or	n	n	
	r	r	
	h	h	
	ḥ	h	An emphatic h
	ḫ	kh	
	ẖ	kh	A softer sound, perhaps closer to 'ch' or 'sh'
or	s	s	
	š	sh	
	q	q	
	k	k	
	g	g	
	t	t	
	ṯ	tj	
	d	d	
	ḏ	dj, z	

[1] As described in Chapter V, this method of transcription has been largely standard since the early part of the twentieth century. However, other conventions have existed in the past, most commonly that used by the much-reprinted Wallis Budge. The latter used various accented 'a's for , and and 'th' 't', and 'tch' for , and .

feature in the Arabic script, unlike the true vowels. This, of course, leads to problems when one attempts to vocalize a set of Egyptian words, either while reading in class, or producing versions of personal names that are acceptable to the non-specialist reader – twt-ʿnḫ-imn is clearly far less palatable than Tutankhamun!

The rule generally used by Egyptologists is that if there are any clues as to the vowelling from texts in scripts that do use vowels (e.g. Akkadian, and Coptic, the very late version of Egyptian that used Greek letters), these will be used, but otherwise 'e's are added until something pronounceable is arrived at. This explains the wide variation in transcriptions of pharaohs' names found in different modern works.

Above: *A door-jamb in the tomb of Rameses VI in the Valley of the Kings. The king's prenomen and titles can clearly be seen.*

THE ENGLISH ALPHABET IN HIEROGLYPHICS

	HIEROGLYPH	TRANSLITERATION
a		3
a		i
b		b
ch		ḥ
d		d
f		f
g		g
h		h
i		i
k		k
kh		ḫ
m	or	m
n	or	n
p		p
q		q
r		r
s	or	s
sh		š
t		t
u, w	or	w
y	or	y
z		ḏ

These equivalents are only approximate.

Hierogl.	Abusir	Elephantine	Hatnub	Prisse	Illahun	Sinuhe	Math.	Westcar	Golen.	Ebers
Dyn. 5.	Dyn. 6.	Dyn. 10/11.	Dyn. 11/12	Dyn. 12	Dyn. 12/13.			Hyksoszeit b. Anfang d. Dyn. 18.		

Above and opposite: Some hieroglyphs and their hieratic equivalents

Hierogl.	Louvre 3226	Lederhs.	Guröb	Ennene	Pentoere	Harris Th.	Harris H. M.	P. Abbott	Ndm-t
22 Dyn.18	Bæk.P10621,11	c3 B.N. 202,6.		Orb 9,1 it.6.	II S. 2,6 it. 2,8	9,4	25,10 H. 47,2 m		
23 Dyn.18.					I S.8,11.				
26 Dyn.18.		a 2,3.		Orb 12,3 it.18,4 it.19,1 19,2	I S.2,3.	3,11	42,8 46,8 H. m	4,3 9,1 3,15	4,2
30 18 Dyn	Medum V,12	a1,10 a1,11		N.A. 8,7 Orb 3,2	III S.1,4	5,9	26,11 H. 56 b3 m	4,11	4,7
31 Dyn.18.		a1,2	P9785,4	N.A. 12,5 Orb 12,9	III S6,4	3,9	78,8 hiet.		But.4,7.
32 Dyn.18.		a 2,10		N.A. 5,4 14,2.	III S3,10 II S5, 1S6,7	5,1			13,10.
33 B Dyn.18.	10,2 it. 4,1. 4,9 6,1.	a1,2 it.6 it.8 it.10	P9784,10 it.6 Guro I,1 P9785,10.	N.A.7,8 N a 10,6 II a 52	III S.2,4 I S 3,2	18,4. 10,11 H. 9,8	25,9 H. 51 a6 m	2,1 6,5 1,14 5,19	9,11. 8,20. 13,4
35 Dyn.18	28,4 Bæk.P10621,4	a1,1	I,1,1 P9785,16 P9784,26	N.A.4,8 Orb 18,9	I S.2,2 III S.1,10	4,9	46,4 m 25,1 H.	2,4.	4 17.
B Dasselbe Zeichen, abgekürzte Form	34,4 56,9 54,3		P9785,16 it.19.					5,7 1.15	5,12
36 Dyn.18				II S.10,2					
	Thutmosis III.	Amenophis II.	Amenoph.III/IV	Menephtah/Sethos II.		Ramses IV.		Ramses IX.	21. Dynastie

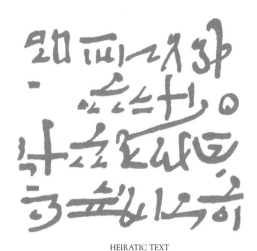

HEIRATIC TEXT

*Year 27, month 4 of Peret,
day 11. The king's daughter
Nebetia, daughter of the king's
son, Siatum.*

HEIROGLYPHIC TRANSCRIPTION

rnpt 27, 3bd 4 Prt
hrw 11, S3t-nsw
Nbti3 S3t
S3-nsw S3-'Itm

Above: *A hieratic text, its
transcription and translation.
This item comes from the
label attached to the mummy
of a Dynasty XVIII princess
during her re-interment,
following robbery, in Year 27
of King Pasebkhanu I of
Dynasty XXI. To study a
hieratic text, scholars usually
convert it it into hieroglyphs.*

THE HIEROGLYPHIC WRITING SYSTEM

Although almost all hieroglyphs represent an animate or inanimate object, they were not 'picture writing' in its crudest sense. Certain signs function as pictures of the things to which they refer, but the vast majority do not, or if they do, only do so indirectly. Their essential purpose is to represent the 24 letters of the Egyptian alphabet in all the combinations necessary to write the Egyptian language.

Determinatives and multitaterals

All ancient Egyptian words are made up of the sounds listed in the table and thus, in theory, any word could be written using the signs shown there. However, in practice this was not the case, and there are many hundreds of other signs which were regularly used in writing.

The first are **determinatives**. Written ancient Egyptian omitted vowels, which meant that more than one word could have exactly the same consonantal structure. An English example could be the words 'shape', 'ship', 'sheep' and 'shop'. Stripped of their vowels, they are reduced to the consonants 'SH' and 'P'. Though it might be possible to guess at which word was meant from the context or grammar, there would clearly be a problem with correctly determining the meaning. A solution might be to add a further character to hint at the meaning of the word – perhaps a picture of the item, or something which might also show what kind of word was meant. This is precisely what the Egyptians did; in our example, SH+P would be followed by 🐑 for 'sheep', ⚓ for 'ship' and ⊓ (the plan of a building) for 'shop'. 'Shape' is more tricky; the noun might have a roll of papyrus (⎯) to indicate an abstract, while the verb could have 🏃, to indicate a physical action.

Opposite: *Extract from the
text found in the pyramid of
Teti at Saqqara. The Pyramid
Texts are amongst the earliest
known examples of Egyptian
religious writings.*

Unluckily for the modern (and ancient) learner, however, there was rather more to the hieroglyphic script than simply the alphabetic signs and determinatives. For alongside these were signs which could write two consonants, three consonants, or even a whole word (known as **biliteral, triliteral** and **word** signs).

BILITERAL SIGN	TRANSLITERATION	BILITERAL SIGN	TRANSLITERATION
	ir		s3
	ꜥ3		sw
	wp		sn
	wn		š3
	b3		k3
	p3		tp
	pr		t3
	mi		ḏd
	mn	TRILITERAL SIGNS	
	mr		ꜥnḫ
	ms		ꜥḥꜥ
	nb		nfr
	ḥr		nṯr
	ḥs		ḥtp
	ḫꜥ		ḫpr
	ḫn		sḏm

Below: Fragment from the tomb of Sethy I, Valley of Kings. In their most elaborate forms, hieroglyphs were intricately detailed representations of the creatures or things they depicted. The falcon stands for the god Horus; the disk may represent a ball of string, and has the phonetic value 'ḥ'. The final arm, holding a flail reads 'ḫw', whose reading the preceding sign reinforces. The whole fragment thus reads 'Horus, protector (of ...)'.

The line between multiliterals and word signs is a fine one; indeed, some signs can fall into both camps, depending on the context within which they are used. One way of spotting a word-sign is if it is followed by a single stroke, although this does not universally hold true. A useful guideline to classification is provided by a peculiarity in the usage of the biliterals and triliterals. These signs, although containing in themselves two or three clear consonants, are usually 'reinforced' by writing after them the alphabetic signs for their own last sounds. For example, **nfr** ('good/beautiful') is perfectly capable of being written with ⌶ on its own – as it is in some instances, particularly where space is limited. However, usually it is written as ⌶⌐; at face value, this appears to read 'nfrfr', but in fact the ⌐ and ⌐ are both what are known as 'phonetic complements'. This means that they are not read, but merely 'reinforce' the main sign. There are, however, few solid rules as to exactly how these complements are used with individual signs in individual circumstances: some triliterals occur only using one complement (e.g. ⌀, sḏm, 'to hear'), and some biliterals may be used with both their sounds written out (e.g. , b3t, 'bush').

Left: Legal document of Year 35 of King Ahmose II written on papyrus. Demotic became the script most used for administrative records during Dynasty XXVI.

Right: Palette belonging to the Royal Scribe Djhutmose. The two cavities at the top held respectively black and red pigment, mixed with water to make ink, much like water colours. The central groove held a selection of pens. Hieratic and demotic were normally written with a reed pen and ink.

HANDWRITTEN HIEROGLYPHS AND THEIR DERIVATIVES

Heiroglyphs were ideal for monumental and decorative purposes, as super-detailing with the chisel and paintbrush could be carried out if required, but they were less useful for day-to-day purposes. While the practised hand can produce a basic hiero-glyph in little more time than it takes to write a modern roman capital letter, their use would make the production of lengthy handwritten documents a laborious task. Accordingly, from early on in Egyptian history, a distinct handwritten version of the hieroglyphic script developed, known today as **hieratic**.

In its early phases, hieratic was little more than a simplification of the underlying signs, but by the Middle and New Kingdoms, it took on various distinctive attributes. The relationship between many hieratic signs and their prototypes is then far less easy to discern. The script takes on various distinctive ways of writing words, which do not mirror those found in hiero-glyphic. Hieratic script was used for a vast range of religious and domestic purposes. It was mostly used on papyri; fragments of stone or pottery, known as ostraka, were used for casual jottings.

Left: Stela from Asyut. The Greek and Roman control of Egypt after 332 BC meant that Greek rapidly came into use alongside Egyptian scripts. Many members of the Greek community adopted Egyptian mortuary customs, and hence we find many combinations of representations and language. Here, a 21-year-old named Apollonios stands before Osiris, with the Egyptian winged sun-disk above him; however, the text below is purely in Greek.

Above: *Coptic relief slab of the 6th/7th century* AD. *It shows
two strangely-shaped fishes (the symbol of Christianity)
and was perhaps used as a wall decoration or grave-stone in
a building erected in the area of the temple of Luxor.*

Hieratic remained the principal script for religious purposes in particular the funerary books such as the Book of the Dead — down to the latest parts of ancient Egyptian history. However, for domestic uses, the handwritten script continued to develop, and around Dynasty XXV a fully distinct variety, demotic, came into use. Although fully developed hieratic is far removed from the traditional hieroglyphs, the origins of many signs are still more or less visible. In contrast, **demotic** script is unrecognizable as a derivative of hiero-glyphs, and has been described as resembling 'a set of agitated commas'.

Demotic script was primarily employed for administrative purposes, although some funerary books were prepared using it. It was designed to be written with a pen on papyrus, but there are quite a few examples of carved versions, particularly in the Ptolemaic and Roman Periods. Amongst the best known examples are certain Ptolemaic decrees which were inscribed in both hieroglyphs and demotic within temples. Some 'editions' coupled these two Egyptian versions with a Greek translation; it was one of these, the famous Rosetta Stone (*see pages 231–4*), that provided the key to the decipherment of the ancient Egyptian scripts.

The last script used to write Egyptian was **coptic**. This was based on the Greek alphabet, with the addition of certain signs from demotic to write sounds

Above: *Fragment from a wall of the tomb of Sethy I. The contrast between hieroglyphs and hieratic is shown neatly by the short ink graffito, just in front of goddess's arm on the left, which contrasts strongly with the elaborate hieroglyphs.*

Left: *Funerary stela from Sheikh Ibada (Antinoë) dating to AD 611. It shows the last phase of the ancient tongue, known as Coptic, and was particularly used for the purposes of the Egyptian church. The script used a mixture of greek letters with a few extra signs taken from demotic.*

ANCIENT EGYPTIAN GRAMMAR

A DETAILED ACCOUNT of the grammar of the various stages of the Egyptian language is beyond the scope of this book; there are many books which deal with the subject, and a number are listed in the bibliography. However, to fully understand how hieroglyphs work, one needs to understand something of the flavour of Middle Egyptian.

Sentence Structure

It is important to remember that the basic form of Egyptian is very different from that of English and most other European languages and, as already noted, is far closer to Arabic and Hebrew. The basic word order of a Middle Egyptian sentence is Verb-Subject-Object; another important feature is the frequent use of suffixes to denote pronouns.

For example,

reads rdi s mw n ḥmt.f and means 'the man gives water to his wife'. ⬭ is the verb rdi, 'to give', made up of the alphabetic sign r, together with the biliteral ⬭; s, 'man', is written

with 🧍, being used as a word sign, this being indicated by the single stroke that follows it. The seated man glyph can also be used as a determinative of various male occupations, or proper names. The next signs show how the use of a hieroglyph can vary depending on context. Of the four ⁓⁓⁓⁓-signs, only the last is the simple alphabetic n, the preposition 'to'. The sign actually represents water, and when three are grouped together they can act as a word-sign for 'water', reading mw. The following group comprises the biliteral ḥm, with an alphabetic t, and a seated woman as a determinative. The t is the feminine ending in Egyptian. Finally, the ⁓, f, is the third person masculine suffix pronoun, 'his'.

Tenses

In Egyptian, tenses are quite complex and do not correspond precisely to those of English. Rather than present and past, the concepts of incomplete and complete action were applied. In most cases, this does not affect the translation, but can make a difference on some occasions. Thus, the basic verb alone denotes the present; the past is indicated by the addition of an n. Thus, sḏm.f means

'he hears', and sḏm.n.f 'he heard'. In these examples, the f is the pronoun 'he'. In Egyptian, the pronoun is usually written after the verb or noun to which it refers (so we also have s3.f, 'his son', and so on). Negation is provided by placing ⁓ (n) in front of the verb, although it is interesting that (e.g.) 'he does not hear' is written n sḏm.n.f and 'he did not hear' as n sḏm.f, the opposite way round from what one might have expected.

Nouns

In Middle Egyptian, nouns usually go without a definite article (an equivalent of the English a or the) although this feature is to be seen in Late Egyptian. Given that the verb to be is only used in certain circumstances, some sentences can look extremely bare. For example, 'the sun is in the sky' can appear as simply 🌞, rꜥ (sun) m (in) pt (sky). Plurals (with the ending w) are indicated by either repeating a word-sign three times, or following the word with three strokes. Thus 'beauties' (nfrw) can be written either

or.

Pronouns

He, she, it, they and other pronouns are normally written as suffixes in Egyptian, although there are other types used in certain circumstances. The suffix-pronouns are as follows:

🧍,𓏺	.i	I, me, my
⌣	.k	you, your (masculine)
⌇	.t	you, your (feminine)
⁓	.f	he, him, his, it, its
⌐	.s	she, her, it, its
⁓ 𓏼	.n	we, us, our
⌇𓏼	.tn	you, your
⌐⁓𓏼	.sn	they, them, their

Adjectives

Words describing nouns are placed after them, and have the same marks of number and gender. For example

, pr wr ('the big house' – masculine singular),

, ḥwt nfrt ('the beautiful castle' – feminine singular).

Left: *Funerary stela of Hor, son of Pedimut, from the Ramesseum at Thebes. The text spells out a prayer by the deceased to the sun-god Re-Harakhty.*

Below: *'Ancient' texts were sometimes 'forged' by later pharaohs. The Memphite Theology claims to be a copy of an Old Kingdom work, but study of the grammar suggests it was written in the seventh century* BC.

not found in the Greek language. Its adoption accompanied the spread of Christianity through Egypt, and progressively replaced demotic in regular use. It was gradually superceded by the Arabic script and language from the seventh century AD onwards, and went out of daily use around the sixteenth century, although surviving in some church liturgy.

THE COPTIC PERIOD

The version of Egyptian written with this coptic script (and known as Coptic) was the very last stage of the language, the result of three millennia of development. It was far removed from the classical forms of the language; it bears the same relationship to them as modern French does to Latin.

Part of this gulf derives from the fact that for much of Egyptian history, the written forms of the language reflected the vernacular of many centuries earlier. This was particularly the case with monumental and religious texts: some Roman period buildings were adorned with texts written in a version of the language which had gone out of daily use nearly two millennia earlier.

Above and opposite:
Wall reliefs from the Tomb of Kaemrehu at Saqqara. Writing was the key to the administration of Egypt. These Old Kingdom scribes record the output of the workshop.

Nevertheless, four distinct phases of linguistic development, prior to Coptic, have been identified:

Old Egyptian Found in documents of the Old Kingdom. It has some distinctive features, but is essentially an early version of the next, classic, phase of the language.

Middle Egyptian Although probably no longer the vernacular by the Middle Kingdom, Middle Egyptian was the standard employed for almost all monuments and documents down into Dynasty XVIII. It remained in use for religious purposes until Roman times, with a slightly modified version also still used for certain literary and monumental purposes.

Late Egyptian The New Kingdom-Third Intermediate Period vernacular, elements of which begin to be found in monumental contexts at the end of Dynasty XVIII. There are changes in word order, and the addition of some foreign words, although most texts retain a heavy overlay of Middle Egyptian conventions.

Demotic The form of the language used by scribes of the Late Period. It mixes a range of idioms, running from Middle Egyptian to the Late/Ptolemaic/Roman Period vernacular.

DATES AND NUMBERS

MANY TEXTS ARE DATED, with the date being the first thing mentioned. Obviously, the era dating that places us in a particular numbered year since the supposed birth of Christ was not employed in ancient times. Instead, it was the reigning king's reign that was used to provide a time structure. An Egyptian date line might run: 'year 15, under the person of the Lord of the Two Lands, Menkheperre (Thutmose III) ...'; this corresponds approximately to 1464 BC.

The hieroglyphs for 'royal year'

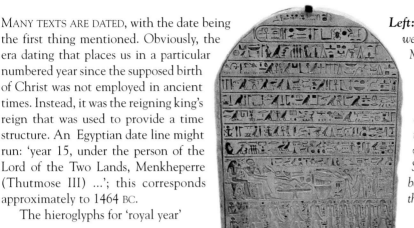

Left: *Stela of Sisepdu. At the very top we find its date, day 20 of the 1st Month of Akhet in Year 17 of Senwosret I. The latter's titles, prenomen and nomen are all unusually enclosed in a single cartouche directly below. The main text is a standard offering formula, while at the bottom of the stela Sisepdu himself and his wife stand before an offering table, and receive the homage of their children.*

are ⌐⊙ , reading rnpt(-sp). Up to the Old Kingdom, this term actually referred to the census of cattle that usually occurred every other year; thus, a year number 10 would actually refer to the twentieth year of the reign. For most of Egyptian history, however, it referred simply to the number of years since the king came to the throne. One slight problem is that during some periods the reign was counted from New Year's day (i.e. the first day of the first month of the official first season of the year), while during others, counting began on the king's actual date of accession. In the latter case this meant that if a pharaoh had come to the throne on (e.g.) 14 June , then 12 June Year 10 and 19 June Year 10 would be not a week apart, but 358 days.

The Egyptian year was divided into three seasons, each of which had four months of 30 days. The full 365-day year was made up by five special festival days.

The seasons were named ⊙△, 3ḫt (Inundation) ⊡⊙ prt, (Winter) and ▭〰〰⊙ šmw (Summer), but because the Egyptians lacked a leap-year, to take into account the 365.25-day solar year, the calendar gradually slipped until the season-names bore no relation to the agricultural cycle; only after 1,460 years did the seasons and calendar synchronize once again. A full Egyptian dateline might thus run as follows:

ⵔⵔ

rnpt 12 3bd 1 prt hrw 6 ḥr ḥm n nsw-bity nbw-k3w-r' (Year 12, month 1 of Winter, day 6, under the person of the Dual King Nubkaure [Amenemhat II]).

Numbers

A few numbers have been mentioned just above. The hieroglyphic script used a decimal system as follows:

𒑡	1
∩	10
ၡ	100
𖠿	1,000
⌇	10,000
𓆉	100,000
𓁨	1,000,000

The signs were used in descending order; thus, 1,732,527 was written:

Below: *Tomb relief from the Mastaba of Ti at Saqqara showing farmers at work. The Egyptian year was built around the agricultural cycle, the beginning of the year nominally coinciding with the rise of the floodwaters of the Nile. There were three seasons: Inundation, Summer and Winter, each lasting 120 days.*

Above: *The Administrator of the Eastern Desert, Khnumhetep trapping birds in a clap-net, from Beni Hasan tomb 3, Dynasty XII. Nobility were frequently shown in their tombs hunting wild animals and birds, pursuing in death what they had done in life.*

Right: *In the same tomb, we see two workers picking and packing fruit in the great man's orchard.*

THE WORDS OF A PHARAOH

HIEROGLYPHS CAN BE READ FROM LEFT TO RIGHT, right to left, or in columns, from top to bottom. Right to left was the most usual, but this was adjusted to cope with location and decorative requirements. The orientation of the animal and bird signs indicate which way a text should be read. This stela, set up to mark the southern border of Egypt as established in Dynasty XII by Senwosret III, begins with the names and titles of the king.

Introduction to text

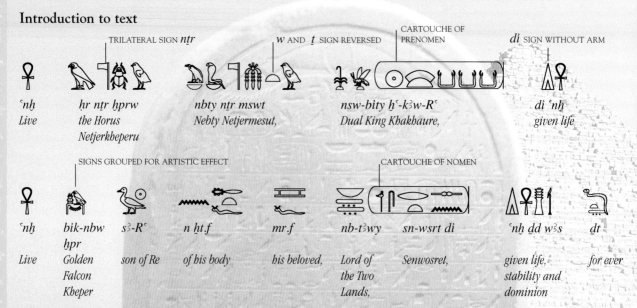

TRILATERAL SIGN *ntr* — *w* AND *t* SIGN REVERSED — CARTOUCHE OF PRENOMEN — *di* SIGN WITHOUT ARM

ꜥnḥ	ḥr nṯr ḫprw	nbty nṯr mswt	nsw-bỉty ḫꜥ-kꜣw-Rꜥ	di ꜥnḫ
Live	the Horus Netjerkheperu	Nebty Netjermesut,	Dual King Khakhaure,	given life

SIGNS GROUPED FOR ARTISTIC EFFECT — CARTOUCHE OF NOMEN

ꜥnḫ	bik-nbw ḫpr	sꜣ-Rꜥ	n ḥt.f	mr.f	nb-tꜣwy	sn-wsrt di	ꜥnḫ ḏd wꜣs	dt
Live	Golden Falcon Kheper	son of Re	of his body	his beloved,	Lord of the Two Lands,	Senwosret,	given life, stability and dominion	for ever

The signs are generally read as written, except for in the first cartouche, where the god's name, Ra, is written first, but read last; in the Golden Falcon name, where the scarab is written, for artistic impression, before the hawk; and in the second cartouche, where the first signs, *wśrt*, refer to a goddess, so are written first, but read last.

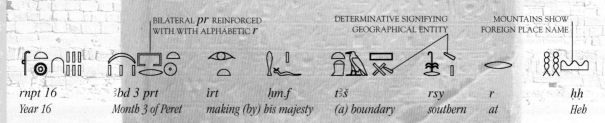

BILATERAL *pr* REINFORCED WITH WITH ALPHABETIC *r* — DETERMINATIVE SIGNIFYING GEOGRAPHICAL ENTITY — MOUNTAINS SHOW FOREIGN PLACE NAME

rnpt 16	ꜣbd 3 prt	irt	ḥm.f	tꜣš	rsy	r	ḥḥ
Year 16	Month 3 of Peret	making (by) his majesty		(a) boundary	southern	at	Heh

Beginning with the date, the name of the month ends with a 'sun' sign, showing that the word refers to time. 'Boundary' is spelled out with a mixture of alphabetic signs (the first, third and fourth), reinforcing the second, which is the biliteral *tꜣ*. The last two signs are determinatives, the first of uncertain meaning, the second being a tongue of land, showing that the word is a geographical term. It is also seen in the word for 'southern', placed after its noun, as usual in Egyptian. The final sign represents mountains, and signifies a foreign place-name.

The Royal Proclamation

Where a sentence wishes to make an emphasis, it begins with a line particle i.e. derived from the verb 'to be'. The sentence is fairly simply written, except for the final word, where 'father' includes the apparent *f* sign, the snake. This is not read, being a determinative with some obscure symbolic meaning. The seated-king determinative shows that the implication of the whole group is 'royal forefathers'.

n SIGNIFYING COMPLETED ACTION

BOAT DETERMINATIVE AS TRAVEL IN THE SOUTH WAS BY BOAT

iw	*ir.n.i*	*tꜣš.i*	*ḫnt.i*	*itw.i*
it is the case that	I made	my boundary	I going further south	(than) my fathers

di SIGN WITH ARM

PAPYRUS ROLL SIGNIFYING ABSTRACT

iw	*rdi.n.i*	*hꜣw*	*ḥr*	*swdt*	*n.i*
it is the case that	I made	an increase	upon	what was ordained	for me

Again a simple sentence, all but the first and last groups combine bilateral signs with reinforcing alphabets.

The future

BILATERAL *sꜣ*

SEATED MAN DETERMINATIVE SHOWING THAT READING IS 'SON'

SEATED MAN MEANING 'I'

ir	*grt*	*sꜣ.i*	*nb*	*srwdty.fy*	*tꜣš*	*pn*
Now	as for	son of mine	any	who shall maintain	border	this

The third group shows how the same sign can have two usages; the first seated man determines the word 'son', the second is the masculine pronoun 'I'. The fifth group of this line is a fairly unusual form of the verb that refers to the future: if it is spelled alphabetically, determined by a bow string and the papyrus roll, the latter showing it to be an abstract idea. Both adjectives and demonstratives (e.g. 'this') are placed after their nouns.

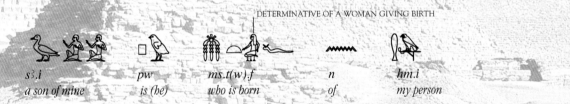

DETERMINATIVE OF A WOMAN GIVING BIRTH

sꜣ.i	*pw*	*ms.t(w).f*	*n*	*ḥm.i*
a son of mine	is (he)	who is born	of	my person

The third group shows how the passive is written in Egyptian with it inserted into the middle of the verb the *vvv* is frequently left uncertain. The last group writes the first person with the sign of a hawk on a perch, in contrast to the seated man used elsewhere. This is because the king was an incarnation of the hawk god Horus and the term *ff* was a specific designation of the king himself.

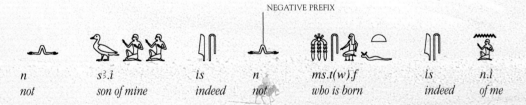

NEGATIVE PREFIX

n	*sꜣ.i*	*is*	*n*	*ms.t(w).f*	*is*	*n.i*
not	son of mine	indeed	not	who is born	indeed	of me

The same 'prospective' verb form mentioned above again appears in the third and fifth groups of hieroglyphs in this line. The latter is interesting in that the verb 'tm' means 'to not', a concept alien to English language structure. A more normal negation, using the prefix *n*, is found in this final line.

THREE MILLENNIA OF WRITING

Lists, Stories and Inscriptions

Hieroglyphic script and its direct derivatives were in use on the banks of the Nile for more than 3000 years. During this time they were employed for a wide variety of purposes, ranging from monumental inscription of the most sacred religious import to laundry-lists and tourist graffiti.

Many different materials were used as writing surfaces. The most permanent documents were carved into stone, the walls of buildings, free-standing slabs known as stelae, or the living rock. Almost all such compositions used the formal hieroglyphic script, except in very late times, when carved examples of both hieratic and demotic are to be found. Hieroglyphs were also widely used on painted surfaces, such as plastered walls and items of funerary equipment. In some cases, however, long religious texts might be written out in hieratic, using a pen, rather than a paintbrush. A particular example of this is the so-called 'Coffin Texts' of the Middle Kingdom. Most of the written decoration of the coffins of this period is properly painted in often extremely detailed hieroglyphs, but the interiors frequently feature areas in which a particular, extensive, collection of religious spells (the Coffin Texts) is added in hieratic in ink, using a reed pen. Hieratic was the script used for most everyday purposes, the principal media being ostraka (fragments of pottery or limestone), white-washed wooden writing-boards and papyrus.

A CHRONOLOGY OF LITERATURE

ARCHAIC PERIOD	OLD KINGDOM	FIRST INTERMEDIATE PERIOD
Dynasties I–II	Dynasties III–V	Dynasties VII–XIa
3050–2660 BC	2660–2200 BC	2200–2070 BC
Labels; short inscriptions only	*Pyramid Texts First biographies*	*Decrees Biographies*

Above: *Djoser's Step Pyramid at Saqqara, the ancestor of all pyramids, signalled the birth of monumental stone architecture in Egypt. The reign of King Djoser marked a* *major technological and political step forward for Egypt. The end of years of civil war allowed rapid progress, made manifest by the beginning of the large-scale use of stone.*

MIDDLE KINGDOM	NEW KINGDOM	THIRD INTER-MEDIATE PERIOD	GRAECO-ROMAN PERIOD	
Dynasties XIb–XIII 2070–1650 BC *Coffin Texts, Stories, Wisdom texts*	Dynasties XVIII–XX 1550–1070 BC *Book of the Dead; 'Historical' texts*	Dynasties XXI–XXV 1070–664 BC *Major mythological texts: continue through Late Period, Dynasties XXVI–XXXI.*	Ptolemies 332–30 BC *Increasing Greek influence*	Romans 30 BC–AD 395

COFFIN OF MENKABU

ROMAN MUMMY MASK

Above: *The sanctuary of Sobk and Haroueris at Kom Ombo, completed by Ptolemy XII, father of the last Greek ruler of Egypt, Kleopatra VII. After the decline of the New Kingdom, the history of Egypt was marked by her increasing subjection to foreign powers. Ultimately, the country was taken over by the Greeks, and then was incorporated into the Roman Empire. Nevertheless, traditional temples to the old gods, such as this one, continued to be built.*

As we have already seen (*see page 145*) the first examples of what might be termed 'proper' Egyptian texts come in Dynasty III, coinciding with the introduction of monumental stone buildings into the archaeological record. By the foundation of Dynasty IV, around a century later, the written language was approaching maturity, with much more extensive narratives being written and, more importantly, surviving to the present day. At the same time, other manifestations of Egypt's culture were reaching their first high spots. Thus, the Old Kingdom (Dynasties III–VI) witnessed the building of the vast pyramids at Dahshur and Giza and their smaller, but brilliantly decorated, successors at Abusir and Saqqara, together with sculptures that remain amongst the masterworks of Egyptian art.

INSCRIPTIONS FOR THE GODS

Examples of the various uses to which the hieroglyphic script was put first appear in the Old Kingdom. Perhaps the most common function of hieroglyphs was to act as captions to scenes in tombs and temples. These are usually straightforward, stating what activity is being carried out, or giving snatches of the dialogue between the protagonists. In temples, these are likely to be the flowery speeches of kings and gods. However, in scenes from private tomb-chapels, which usually depict activities from daily life, in particular agricultural work, the banal chit-chat of workmen may be recorded.

PAPER FROM PLANTS

PAPYRUS IS A PAPER produced from the fibrous stem of the papyrus plant (*Cyperus papyrus*), a member of the sedge family. The long stems are sliced up, then the slices are laid across each other to form a mat, and placed in a press to produce a highly serviceable writing material. The earliest (uninscribed) example of a papyrus roll comes from the Dynasty I tomb of Hemaka at Saqqara; the material remained in use until Arab times, but then disappeared with the extinction of the papyrus plant in Egypt. However, it survived in the Sudan and elsewhere in the Mediterranean, and is now grown commercially in Egypt to provide paper for the tourist market.

Above: *Detail from the Botanical Temple within the Great Temple of Amun, Karnak. Birds roost in a papyrus thicket.*

Left: *Sphinx of Amenemhat II. After a century or more of civil war, the Middle Kingdom (Dynasties XIb–XIII) marked a restoration of central power, and a second flowering of Egypt's civilization. This sphinx had a chequered history, being inscribed both for its maker and three much later kings. Egyptian rulers often usurped their predecessors' monuments, and thus an inscribed name upon an object does not guarantee its date.*

Above: *The pylon-gateway of the temple of Luxor. It was adorned by a pair of obelisks (one of which is now in Paris) and an account of Rameses II's battle of Qadesh, in Syria.*

Above: *Scene from the Hypostyle Hall, Karnak. Hieroglyphs served as captions for a temple scene, in this case with the king making an offering to Amun-Re, King of the Gods. The hieroglyphs give the names and titles of the protagonists. The king was originally labelled as Sethy I, but his cartouches were later changed to those of his son, Rameses II.*

Below: *The tomb of Rameses VI. For many centuries, the interiors of royal tombs were simple, and largely unadorned. However, they had developed into complex series of elaborately decorated corridors and chambers by Dynasties XIX–XX.*

Temples normally featured two kinds of scenes and texts. One showed the king displaying his prowess against Egypt's enemies; the other depicted the monarch making offerings to the temple gods, accompanied by texts describing the rituals, and sometimes lengthy mythological inscriptions, including hymns and narratives relating to the relevant deities. Such texts are particularly common in temples of the Graeco-Roman Period. One example, in the temple of Horus at Edfu, gives a lengthy account of the war between Horus and his uncle, Seth; the inscription, carved in the second century BC, contains echoes of a civil war in Dynasty II, 3,000 years earlier.

The majority of temple-carvings relate to the daily cult of the god, in which the king is shown as principal officiant, although in practice a high priest would have taken his place. From these, it is possible to reconstruct much of the 'daily life' of a god in his temple – dressed and fed regularly, and carried in procession on great feast-days.

Above: Scene from the funerary chapel of the Vizier Ramose, who flourished in the reign of Amenhotep III. It shows a nobleman's funeral, with servants carrying his possessions and a crowd of professional female mourners. Once again, the hieroglyphs provide captions to the events.

Left: The stela of Sennefer of Dynasty XVIII. The focal point of a chapel was its stela – indeed, for middle class individuals, their chapel may have been no more than a shelter for the stela. This usually featured the deceased in front of a table of offerings, sometimes accompanied by members of their family; the belief was that by being depicted, everything would magically be supplied to the deceased in the next world.

THE TEXTS OF BURIAL

ALONGSIDE THOSE from the temples of the gods, texts from funerary contexts are amongst our most numerous survivals of Egyptian texts. Ideally, an Egyptian tomb comprised an above-ground offering-place and a subterranean burial chamber. The former range from a bare stela to complexes of rooms, either built into the core of a mastaba (bench-shaped tomb), or carved into a rock escarpment. Culminating in the stela, sometimes in the form of a 'false door', that served as the point of interface between this world and the next, these chapels were decorated with a wide range of scenes showing the agricultural and industrial life of the country. The stela and these scenes also bore texts in hieroglyphs, that act either as direct captions on the activities depicted, or supplying magic formulae to ensure the safe passage to, and existence in, the world beyond.

These beautifully decorated chapels, and their royal equivalents, the temple-complexes that stood before the

pyramids, formed only part of the whole magical machine that was the Egyptian tomb. Far below ground was the burial chamber in which the embalmed body was to sleep out eternity. In only a few cases was this room decorated, usually with lists of offerings to sustain the dead. Late in the Old Kingdom, such lists begin to appear inside the rectangular wooden coffins that housed the body. In addition, coffins bore the earliest versions of a standard offering formula that was to become ubiquitous in Egyptian funerary contexts. This is the ḥtp di nsw, which magically provided the dead with eternal sustenance. Found throughout Egyptian history, it has a number of variants, but a typical example runs as follows:

'Royal offering to [the god] Osiris … that he may give offerings consisting of bread and beer, oxen and fowl, alabaster and clothing, all things good and pure on which a god lives, to the spirit of the deceased NAME'.

During the Middle Kingdom, more extensive funerary inscriptions begin to be found, beginning with the 'Coffin Texts', written on the interiors of wooden coffins and designed to aid the dead person's journey into the next world. This was envisaged as being to the west of the world of the living, and to reach it the dead had to endure many dangers. By the time of the New Kingdom, a complete guidebook to the journey had been prepared. This was referred to as the 'Book of Coming Forth by Day', better known today as the 'Book of the Dead'. It was usually inscribed on an illustrated papyrus

Top: *Thutmose IV offered the sign of life by the goddess of the West. The scene forms part of the extensive decoration of the king's tomb in the Valley of the Kings, where the time-hallowed pyramid was discarded in favour of concealment.*

Below: *Coffin of Pasherhorawesheb (Dynasty XXII), covered with divine images and hieroglyphs. The latter spelled out the magic formulae that ensured that the dead would go safely and well-nourished into the afterlife.*

Right: *The pyramid of Khaefre at Giza. Funerary chapels could either be cut in the rock escarpment, built into a bench-shaped structure known as a mastaba, or be completely free standing. The first two types can be seen here, on the south-east of the pyramid. During the Old and Middle Kingdoms, kings differed from their subjects in being buried under such great monuments. The remains of the pyramid's chapel may be seen against its east face.*

roll, but was also found on coffins and the walls of the tomb. It led the dead through the journey west, giving the correct response to those who guarded the gates along the way, and culminated in the deceased's trial before Osiris, King of the Dead.

Only those who had led a good life would be allowed into the world of eternity. The heart was regarded as the seat of memory and intelligence, and to test the dead person it was weighed against a feather – the hieroglyphic symbol of Maat, goddess of truth. If the scales balanced, all was well; if not, the heart was thrown to a monster, which ate it and condemned the soul to wander for eternity. But this would never happen: the illustrations in the Book of the Dead showed success, and according to Egyptian belief, if something was shown happening, by magic it did happen. This idea lies behind many images in both tombs and temples, guaranteeing continuity for ever. The written word had similar importance: as long as a person's name survived in writing, they too survived. To be utterly forgotten was a person's real death.

During the New Kingdom and later, many other funerary 'books' grew up, with different themes, but still with the intention of easing the transition between the two worlds. Most books first appeared in the tombs of the kings, and only later spread to their subjects at all levels of society.

Left: *New Kingdom papyrus of Amenemsaf. From the New Kingdom onwards, the mummy was usually equipped with an illustrated papyrus roll known as the Book of the Dead. This was a 'guidebook' for reaching the next world, normally written in hieratic. This detail shows four guardians of the dead, known as the Four Sons of Horus, from the right Imseti, Hapy, Duamutef and Qebehsenuef.*

Demetrios

Above: *Thutmose III.
During the New Kingdom
(Dynasties XVIII–XX),
Egypt became a world power.
Under Thutmose III, her
empire and collection of
satellite states extended from
northern Syria to the heart of
the Sudan.*

Previous pages: *Wall
bearing the autobiography of
Ahmose-si-Ibana at El-Kab.
It recounts his role in the
wars of liberation at the
beginning of the New
Kingdom, in which the
Palestinian Hyksos kings
were expelled from Egypt.*

AUTOBIOGRAPHIES

Besides material relating to the afterlife, burial-places also contained some of
the earliest lengthy secular compositions. These are the autobiographies sometimes included by officials in their tomb-chapels. Their primary purpose is to
glorify the author, particularly from the point of view of emphasizing his close-
ness to the king, the lynchpin of Egyptian society. In spite of this
less-than-objective approach, useful factual material can often be gleaned.
One of the most important of the earliest such compositions, that of Uni,
from Abydos, speaks tantalizingly of his having presided over the trial of one
of the wives of King Pepy I (Dynasty VI). However, nothing is said of the
nature of the charges, nor the outcome, so that we can only speculate on what
dynastic intrigues may have lain behind Uni's bland statements.

Some of the most fascinating texts of the Old Kingdom are the autobiographies of the governors of the southern city of Aswan. Amongst their duties
were the conduct of trading expeditions into eastern and central Africa. In
the text of Harkhuf, we read of a dancing dwarf being acquired somewhere
in the south, the news of whom delighted his young king, Pepy II. The king's
letter is quoted verbatim by Harkhuf, emphasizing his intimacy with his
monarch. Yet another deals with a mission by Sabni, to recover the body of
his father Mekhu, killed by bandits while on an expedition into the Eastern
Desert to build a ship for a voyage down the Red Sea coast.

Autobiographies are found throughout Egyptian history. One, from the
Middle Kingdom, gives us one of our most comprehensive accounts of the
kind of 'passion play' that formed part of some religious festivals. Written by
Ikhernofret, and found on a stela from his tomb, it gives an account of the
annual festival of Osiris at Abydos. In it, the story of the life, death, resurrection and vindication of the god was re-enacted, with Ikhernofret playing
important parts:

[Ikhernofret has been sent to Abydos by King Senwosret III to oversee the
festival, and also renew the god's cult-image]:

*I did everything that His Person commanded, putting into effect my lord's command
for his father, Osiris, Lord of Abydos, great of power, who is in the Thinite nome.
I acted as beloved son of Osiris. I embellished his great barque of eternity; I made
for it a shrine which displays the beauties of Khentyamentiu, in gold, silver, lapis-
lazuli, bronze and wood. I fashioned the gods in his train. I made their shrines anew.
I caused the temple-priesthood to do their duties, I caused them to know the custom
of every day, the festival of the Head-of-the-Year. I controlled work on the neshmet-
barque; I fashioned the shrine and adorned the breast of the Lord of Abydos with
lapis-lazuli and turquoise, electrum and every precious stone, as an adornment of
the divine limbs. I changed the clothes of the god at his appearance, in the office of
Master of Secrets and in my job as sem-priest. I was clean of arm in adoring the
god, a sem clean of fingers.
I organized the going-forth of Wepwawet when he proceeded to avenge his father;
I drove-away the rebels from the neshmet-barque; I overthrew the enemies of*

Osiris; I celebrated the great going-forth. I followed the god at his going, and caused the ship to sail, Thoth steering the sailing. I equipped the barque with a chapel and affixed (Osiris)'s beautiful adornments when he proceeded to the district of Peqer. I cleared the ways of the god to his tomb before Peqer. I avenged Wennefer that day of the great fight; I overthrew all his enemies upon the sandbanks of Nedyt: I caused him to proceed into the great barque. It raised up his beauties, I making glad the people/tomb-owners of the Eastern Desert, creating joy amongst the people/tomb-owners of the Western Desert; they saw the beauties of the god's barque when it touched land at Abydos, when it brought Osiris-Khentyamentiu to his palace; I followed the god to his house, I carried out his purification and extended his seat and solved the problems of his residence [... and amongst] his entourage.

Works of Faction?

Another autobiography of this general period, now lost, may have formed the basis for the 'Story of Sinuhe', one of the classics of Egyptian literature. The exiled Sinuhe, a courtier of Amenemhat I, wanders the desert, is befriended by Bedouins, has many adventures, is finally pardoned when a new king, Senwosret I, comes to the throne, and returns to his beloved homeland. In its vivid detail and general 'feel' it clearly diverges from standard tomb autobiographies, yet it follows their basic structure and is either a pure romance using the traditional autobiography as a literary device, or Sinuhe's genuine tomb inscription greatly elaborated – either as a work of 'faction', or a genuine narrative from which a tomb inscription might have been edited down.

A similar example, from the reign of Thutmose III (Dynasty XVIII), describes the capture of the Palestinian town of Joppa by General Djehuty, whose tomb (now lost) seems to have been at Saqqara. His stratagem of smuggling his soldiers into the city, hidden in baskets carried by porters, survives in a folk-tale, but is probably based upon an original tomb inscription.

Above: *The dramatically-located tombs of Mekhu and Sabni at Aswan. Biographical inscriptions in private tombs are often banal, but a few are of considerable interest and this one contains the account of how Sabni journeyed into the Eastern Desert to retrieve the body of his dead father and punish his murderers.*

Below: *Abydos, the scene of the 'passion play' described in Ikhernofret's autobiography. The great brick mortuary enclosure of Khasekhemwy (Dynasty II), stands above the wadi in which most of the action occurred.*

Soldiers' Tales

Warriors' autobiographies from the early years of Dynasty XVIII provide much useful detail. In particular, texts in the tombs of an army officer, Ahmose-Pennekhbet, and a naval officer, Ahmose-si-Ibana, at El-Kab relate to their service in the wars of Kamose and Ahmose I that liberated northern Egypt from Palestinian rule. General Amenemhab, in his tomb at Thebes, provides details of incidents from the campaigns of Thutmose III, including one when he saved the king from a charging elephant while out hunting in north Syria.

Such informative autobiographies become less common in later times, most examples being more concerned with the offices held by the author, and how high he stood in the favour of the king and the gods. Their historical importance is often incidental, for example where the order of kings is mentioned. Similarly, officials with a royal ancestor may trace their line of descent back far enough to inform us of the names of some otherwise unknown kings and queens. One important exception is the inscription on a statue of one Udjahorresnet (now in the Vatican Museum), whose owner began his career at the end of Dynasty XXVI, and whose tomb was found at Abusir in 1980. He subsequently served the Persian kings who invaded Egypt in 525 BC, was responsible for the formulation of Egyptian titulary for the Persian ruler Kambyses (*d.* 522 BC) and undertook various activities relating to temple administration for his foreign masters.

Below: Scene from the first pylon of Rameses III's mortuary temple at Medinet Habu. Rameses III smites his enemies before the god Amun. They are held together by their hair, while the king raises his mace above his head. The king's cartouches are particularly deeply carved, perhaps as a defence against those who might wish to usurp the relief in the future!

Above: Fight scene from a tomb at Saqqara. A number of Old Kingdom tombs are decorated with scenes of boatmen carrying out mock battles, presumably for the entertainment of the resident of the tomb.

Left: A model army of Egyptian spearmen found in the tomb of Mesehti, a Governor of Asyut during Dynasty XI. The tomb also contained a troop of Nubian soldiers. The Governors of the nomes (provinces) of Middle Egypt were heavily involved in the civil wars that waged during the First Intermediate Period.

HISTORICAL INSCRIPTIONS

Above: *The tomb of the nobleman Rekhmire at Luxor. A procession of people bring apes, ivory and leopards, possible tributes from Egypt's lesser neighbours.*

Below: *Thutmose III smiting his enemies, from the temple of Amun-Re at Karnak. All Egyptian 'historical' texts had a propaganda role, and the intention here was to show the king's dominion over both Egypt and the outside world.*

Lengthy royal 'historical' texts seldom survive from the early periods of Egyptian history. The term 'historical' is used advisedly, since it is important to understand that kings did not leave records of their deeds as records for posterity. Rather, monarchs commissioned texts that demonstrated how they had fulfilled the cosmic role of the king: to maintain cosmic order, defeat Egypt's enemies and provide for the cult of the gods, to name but a few of the more important royal tasks. These inscriptions often described a king's activities as an illustration of how he carried out his role, and are thus often labelled as 'historical' documents; nevertheless, they have an explicit propagandistic purpose, and accordingly must be used with great care.

One particular cautionary tale underlines this point. In the mortuary temple of Pepy II of Dynasty VI at Saqqara there is a relief of the king smiting a Libyan chieftain, while the latter's family look on. The chief and his family are all named, apparently indicating that the scene records a genuine campaign by King Pepy. However, the same scene occurs in the earlier Dynasty V temple of Sahure at Abusir – including the same names for the chief and his family. Not only this, but nearly 2,000 years later, in Dynasty XXV, King Taharqa is shown at Karnak, smiting the self-same chief, while the very same members of his family look on.

The largest body of 'historical' texts comes from the New Kingdom, when the kings of Dynasty XVIII extended Egyptian overlordship into the heart of the Sudan, and as far as the Euphrates in Syria. Many were set up in the gigantic temple of Amun-Re, King of the Gods, at Karnak, either on the walls of the temple, or on free-standing round-topped stelae. Among the most informative are those of Thutmose III, under whom the Egyptian 'Empire' reached its greatest extent. His inscriptions are less smothered in the elaborate rhetorical flourishes that frequently hinder the understanding of other examples, and they allow us to trace the progress of his military campaigns in some detail. Nevertheless, poetry was

used within one of his stelae from Karnak. The text is couched in the form of a speech to the king by Amun-Re, and after a dozen lines of plain prose the next ten lines take a clear metrical form; four of these illustrate the pattern:

I have come that I may cause you to trample the chiefs of the Lebanon when I spread them under your feet throughout their lands;

I cause them to see Your Majesty as lord of sunshine as you shine in their faces in my likeness.

I have come that I may cause you to trample those of Asia, when you smite the heads of the Asiatics of Palestine;

I cause them to see Your Majesty equipped with your ornaments as you brandish weapons to fight upon the chariot ....

Extensive texts survive relating to the campaigns of Rameses II (Dynasty XIX), in particular that which culminated in the Battle of Qadesh (*c.*1285 BC) against the Hittites in Syria. Two basic versions of the narrative exist, one couched in a 'poetic' form, and they can be found on the walls of at least five temples, and on papyrus. Although the battle nearly ended in disaster for the Egyptians, the inscriptions' purpose is made clear by the superhuman strength and skill attributed to the king, who is credited with single-handedly turning the tide of the battle.

Amongst later royal texts, the stela of the Nubian king Piye (Dynasty XXV), from Napata in the Sudan, stands out. It relates the conquest of Egypt by the ruler of Nubia, reversing the trend of history, which had normally seen the southern country subjugated by Egypt. Its inhabitants were not well regarded by their northern neighbours, a stela of Senwosret III (Dynasty XII) from Semna (*see also pages 180–1*), then the Egypto-Nubian border, and now in Berlin, states that a Nubian

.... listens, to fall at a word:
To answer him is to make him retreat;
Attack him: he will turn his back;
Retreat: he will start attacking.
They are not people worthy of respect,
They are wretches, craven-hearted!
My person has seen it: it is not a lie!

However, during Dynasties XXII–XXIII, Egypt had gradually fallen into a number of separate petty polities, the southernmost of which, centred on Thebes, had come under the effective control of the kings of Nubia. In response to the expansionist plans of one of the rulers of the far north (Tefnakhte, of Dynasty XXIV), Piye had marched into Lower Egypt, and succeeded in forcing the various local potentates, including four 'pharaohs' to accept him as paramount ruler. The language used in the stela is unusually straightforward, and allows us to follow the events of this historic event in more detail than is often possible.

Above: *Pylon VIII of the Karnak temple, dating to Dynasty XVIII. The pylon gateways of the principal temples were prime sites for propagandist inscriptions.*

Below: *The 'poetic' stela of Thutmose III, from Karnak. Most 'historical' inscriptions were to be found on large stelae, placed around the main temples.*

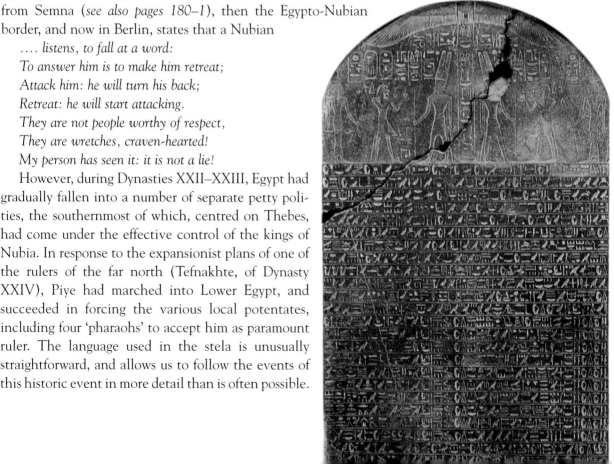

CHRONICLES

Above: A basalt slab recycled as the lid of the sarcophagus of Ankhnespepy a late Dynasty VI queen. It had once been covered with a chronicle, listing accounts of each year of the reigns of earlier kings.

Below: The Turin Canon of Kings. Although it is the most comprehensive chronicle document known to date, severe damage has left it with many frustrating gaps.

An exception to such highly partial 'historical' texts are a small group of items which, at first sight at least, may represent an attempt at a basic recording of historical data. The best known is a slab of basalt, now known as the Palermo Stone because it is in the museum at Palermo. Now damaged, when complete, it appears to have provided a year-by-year chronicle of Egypt, from the unification of Egypt down to the middle of Dynasty V, together with a list of the preceding rulers of the separate Upper and Lower Egyptian polities. Unfortunately, the vast majority is missing, while a second copy, mainly in Cairo, is even less complete. A document of similar format was identified in the 1990s, which seems to have carried on the chronicle into Dynasty VI. Regrettably, it had been re-used as a sarcophagus lid at the very end of that dynasty, and almost all the text has been worn away.

A much later document of a similar kind is the papyrus now in the Turin Egyptian Museum. Written early in Dynasty XIX, it contains a complete list of kings, from the rule of the gods onwards, with each monarch's reign-length recorded, down to the nearest day. Unfortunately, it has been very severely damaged, and only a small proportion of its priceless information is preserved.

Often bracketed with these documents are the so-called 'king-lists', which were found in the temples of Karnak and Abydos, and a tomb at Saqqara. Dating from Dynasty XVIII and XIX, they are actually lists of deceased kings to whom a prayer is offered. On all but one of these monuments, the kings are listed in chronological order, but this is clearly for the convenience of the scribe who laid out the texts. The lists have also been edited to fit the available wall space, with obscure or proscribed kings omitted. The 'historical' value of these lists is thus incidental – although very real in establishing the order of certain obscure rulers.

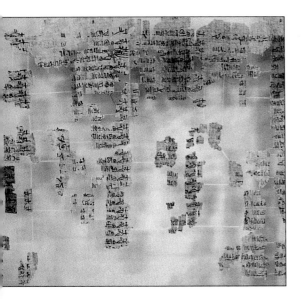

Left: *The temple of Sethy I, one of the best preserved in Egypt. Its king list lies in one of the rear corridors of the building.*

Above: *Sethy I and his son, Crown Prince Rameses (later II), seen to the left of the list in Sethy's temple. Rameses reads a prayer from a scroll, which is for the benefit of the long list of kings whose cartouches are carved in front of him. Although generally accurate, many kings are omitted. Some, including the whole of Dynasties XIII–XVII, seem to have been missed out for reasons of space, while others, such as Tutankhamun, had been wiped from history for political reasons.*

Opposite: *The temple of Sethy I at Abydos. A list of recipients of temple offerings found here conveniently places ancient kings in their historical order.*

Right: *The Temple of Rameses II at Abydos. Another chronological 'king list' was found here.*

ADMINISTRATIVE DOCUMENTS

Above: The pyramid of Senwosret II at Lahun. It was serviced by Kahun, a 'workmen's settlement' set up in Dynasty XII. Kahun is one of our best sources for administrative documents.

Below: Kahun lay in a now-desolate area alongside the vanished valley temple, 1.6 km (1 mile) to the east. Many papyrus documents were found in and adjacent to the town, and are now in Berlin and London.

Other 'historical' written material includes surviving administrative documents. A wide range exists, generally written on papyrus or ostraka, in cursive forms of the hieroglyphic script. The workmen of the Theban village of Deir el-Medina, who built the tombs of the pharaohs, have left behind material that both explains the way in which work was organized, and illuminates the lives of the workers themselves and their families. The joys and tribulations of family life are well illustrated, including some choice scandals and even acts of homicide. In addition, the records include those of the first known strike and sit-in.

The work journals from Deir el-Medina are also useful in reconstructing the chronology of Dynasties XIX–XX, because almost every year of every king is recorded. From a 'missing' four years in the middle of the reign of Sethy II, it can be inferred that his reign in the south was interrupted by that of a usurper named Amenmesse – whose four years are included in the community records.

Another group of material from the archives of the Theban necropolis includes the records of the investigation under Rameses IX (Dynasty XX) of a series of major tomb robberies. These culminate in the minutes of the court proceedings against the culprits. Another set of judicial records cover the trial of individuals accused of the murder of Rameses III, a conspiracy that seems to have included attempts to use 'voodoo' dolls.

Most of these documents come from Thebes; the wetter conditions in the north of the country detracted from the preservation of papyrus and ink. Nevertheless, papyri have come to light from temple archives found at Abusir (Dynasty V) and also at the Dynasty XII site, Lahun/Kahun. A lot can be learned about temple administration from the accounts and priestly duty rosters found there. The rosters show that smaller sanctuaries lacked a full-time staff, and relied on local administrators, farmers and soldiers, who served as priests on a rota basis. Medical and veterinary treatises and the wills of members of the temple-community were also found.

Above: *The mortuary temple complex of Rameses III at Medinet Habu, which served as the headquarters of the administration of the huge necropolis, or cemetery area, at Thebes during Dynasties XX–XXI. It is an important source of documents, most of which were found in the early years of the nineteenth century. From here came the trial records of those accused of robbing some of the royal tombs.*

Below: *Village of Deir el-Medina. Dating from the New Kingdom, it was the home of the workmen and artists responsible for building the royal tombs in the Valley of the Kings. A vast range of documents has been recovered from the area. The village is in the foreground, while on the incline opposite were built the workers' own tombs, decorated with the same care and attention that they lavished on the pharaohs' sepulchres.*

Above: *Ostrakon from Thebes. Many administrative documents were written on papyrus, but slivers of limestone, known as ostraka, were also used, usually inscribed in hieratic script.*

EXPEDITION RECORDS

Above: The tombs of the governors of Aswan on the hill of Qubbet el-Hawa opposite their city. The governors were the greatest explorers of their day, and their tombs contain accounts of many of their journeys into the heart of Africa.

A lot of the state's energy and resources was devoted to expeditions into the desert regions of Egypt. When their expedition was completed, leaders would leave behind inscribed records of their activities at the site. A particularly frequent destination was the Wadi Hammamat, in the Eastern Desert, from which greywacke, a stone much used for statuary and sarcophagi, was quarried. In the reign of Montjuhotpe IV (end of Dynasty XI), the Vizier Amenemhat was sent there to procure stone for the royal sarcophagus; his inscription relates that:

> There came a gazelle great with young, going with her face before her, while her eyes looked backwards. She did not turn back, and arrived at this august moment, at this block, still in its place, that was intended to be the lid of the sarcophagus. She dropped her young upon it while the army of the king looked on. They sacrificed her upon the block, and made a fire.

With the encouragement of this omen, the block was safely quarried for its journey to Thebes.

Quarry texts are found around the many locations in which the Egyptians obtained stones, ores and other precious materials. Many such texts can be found in the Sinai Peninsula, where copper and turquoise were mined. The earliest texts there date to the beginning of Dynasty III, the latest to Dynasty XX, and follow the usual kinds of patterns of royal names, offering scenes and

Below: The Tomb of Harkhuf, one of Aswan's governors. Included on its facade is a copy of a letter he received from his young king.

Above: Inscription from the Wadi Maghara. Another kind of expedition record is provided by the graffiti left by various quarrying expeditions. Some of the earliest examples are in the Sinai, where turquoise was mined; this one shows Seneferu slaying an enemy.

other records of the quarry workers. However, from the Second Intermediate Period come some extremely strange texts. Known as 'Protosinaitic', they comprise signs that appear at first sight to be hieroglyphs, but do not, in fact, belong to the Egyptian corpus. Their limited number suggests a true alphabetic script, with the forms of the signs derived from certain Egyptian hieroglyphs, but with different meanings. It has been argued that they form the direct ancestors of the later Phoenician/Canaanite alphabet, but although some words have been read plausibly, confirmation is yet lacking.

Examples have also been found in Palestine, but recent work by John and Deborah Darnell has now brought to light examples of the script much further south, in the Wadi el-Hol, part of a desert caravan track north-west of Luxor. These also date to Middle Kingdom times, and raise further questions as to the origins and purpose of these mysterious inscriptions.

Above: The necropolis at Thebes, intended destination of Montjuhotpe IV's sarcophagus. The Deir el-Bahari temples are towards the right, with private tomb chapels of the New Kingdom in the centre.

Below: Wadi Hammamat, a major quarrying area, whose stone was particularly popular for the manufacture of sarcophagi. This ram was carved by quarrymen working in Year 3 of Psametik II.

WISDOM AND PHILOSOPHY

A type of text related to autobiography is 'wisdom literature', in which the author gives advice to his descendants. These texts are found throughout Egyptian history, the earliest surviving example probably dating to Dynasty V, but attributed to the Dynasty IV Prince Hordjedef, son of Khufu, builder of the Great Pyramid. They advise 'proper' behaviour towards one's fellow citizens, and respect for all. Gluttony and arrogance are abhorred; modesty and charity are recommended; sexual temptation is warned against.

As time went by, these compositions become less idealistic and more utilitarian. One of the latest examples, the 'Instructions of Ankhshoshenqy' (Ptolemaic Period) replaces the elegant stanzas of the earliest works with one-line sayings, some of which are of a distinctly misogynistic flavour; contrast advice of the Dynasty XIX scribe, Any, to *'not control your wife in your house … recognize her skill'*, with Ankhshoshenqy's claim that *'[i]nstructing a woman is like having a sack of sand whose side is split open'*.

A curious genre of 'philosophical' literature that was particularly popular in the Middle Kingdom is the so-called 'pessimistic literature', where an author laments the condition of the world. The meaning of such texts has been much debated, the main question being how far they are a literary device, and how much a reflection of events that had accompanied the civil wars of the preceding First Intermediate Period. Either way, the 'Lamentation of Ipuwer' paints a lurid picture of the country:

> *Lo, the face is pale, the bowmen ready,*
> *Crime is everywhere, there is no man of yesterday …*
> *Lo, Hapy inundates and none plough for him,*
> *All say, "We know not what has happened to the land" …*
> *Lo, poor men have become men of wealth,*
> *He who could not buy sandals now owns riches …*
> *Lo, hearts are violent, a storm sweeps the land,*
> *Blood is everywhere, there is no shortage of dead …*
> *Lo, many dead are buried in the river,*
> *The stream is the grave, the grave is the stream,*
> *Lo, nobles lament, the poor rejoice,*
> *Every town says, "Let us expel our rulers" …*
> *See now, men rebel against the Serpent,*
> *Stolen is the crown of Re, who pacifies the Two Lands …*
> *See the royal residence is fearful from want …*
> *The troops we raised for ourselves have become Bowmen, bent on destroying!*

A similar tone pervades a number of other types of text, for example the 'Harpers Songs', which cast a jaundiced eye upon life and death. One seems

Above: *King Khufu, the builder of the Great Pyramid at Giza and second ruler of Dynasty IV. In his reign lived one of the earliest known authors of 'wisdom literature', Prince Djedefhor.*

Above: *A scribe of Dynasty V, one of the periods when 'wisdom literature' flourished.*

to even doubt the belief in eternal life that so characterizes the ancient Egyptians, and adopts the philosophy of 'eat, drink and be merry, for tomorrow we die':

The nobles and spirits are entombed in their pyramids,
They built chapels, but their shrines are no more: what has become of them?
I have heard the sayings of [wise men], which are quoted to this day:
Where are their shrines? Their walls have fallen and their shrines are gone.
There is no one who can come back from [the next world] to tell us how they fare,
To comfort us until we reach the place where they have gone.
So ... follow your desires while you live;
Place myrrh on your head, cloth yourself in fine linen ...
Remember, one cannot take his goods with him;
None goes away and then comes back.

Following pages: *Detail of wall painting from the tombs of the workmen. A harper plays for the Foreman of the Royal Tomb workmen, Anhurkhau, and his wife, Waab, in their burial chamber at Deir el-Medina.*

Below: *Scenes of celebration on the 'Red Chapel' erected by Hatshepsut at Karnak.*

HUMAN RELATIONSHIPS

Below: *The Overseers of the Manicurists Niankhkhnum and Khnumhetep, from their joint tomb at Saqqara. The nature of their relationship is uncertain, but their unusual intimacy has been interpreted variously as that of twins, siamese twins and homosexual lovers.*

In contrast to these gloomy thoughts, Egyptian love songs and poetry celebrate the here and now. Egyptian marriages were arranged between parents while the couple were still children, but love-matches were still idealized.

'He stares me out when I walk by, and all alone I cry for joy; how happy is my delight with the lover in my sight ...'; 'Hearing your voice is pomegranate wine, for I live to hear it; every glance (of yours) which rests on me means more to me than food and drink ...'.

There are many documents of this kind, some of which are riddled with double-entendres, particularly with references to ladies' 'grottos'. Rather more prosaic are documents relating to the details of relationships. There seems to have been no 'marriage ceremony' as such: the woman simply moved into

Right: *Letters from the Dynasty XI mortuary-priest Heqanakhte. The papyri are written in hieratic, in columns. Soon afterwards, this practice ceased for day-to-day documents, in favour of horizontal lines.*

her husband's house. However, wills and adoptions can be traced through documents from towns such as Deir el-Medina and Kahun. One interesting set relates how a childless couple purchased a slave, with whom the husband fathered a number of children, who then became his heirs. There are also the usual small-town stories of domestic scandals that allow us to know more about the citizens of Deir el-Medina than those of any other settlement of early antiquity. Some individuals are so well known that their handwriting alone is enough to identify a document: the Dynasty XX scribe Djhutmose and his son Butehamun, for example, and the rather earlier Qenhirkopshef, who is easily identified by his atrocious script!

Even earlier is the correspondence sent by the Dynasty XI/XII mortuary priest, Heqanakhte, to his son, covering aspects of running the family farm and other domestic issues. The situation revealed about the relationships within the household inspired Agatha Christie to use it as the basis for her novel, *Death Comes as an End!*

Below: *The tomb of the Vizier Ipi at Deir el-Bahari, just left of the path. The private archive of his priest Heqanakhte was found in front of the tomb, where it had been discarded for some reason by Heqanakhte's son and deputy.*

STORIES

Above: *The gods Horus, Isis and Osiris from the temple of Sethy I at Abydos. One of the best-known stories from ancient Egypt was the myth of the god of the dead, Osiris, which told of his murder by his brother, Seth, his rescue by his sister-wife, Isis, and the vengeance carried out by his son, Horus.*

Alongside all these written sources is a wide range of stories. Most were doubt-less told by public story-tellers long before being written down. We can often see this from the way that the tales are put together, with frequent repeti-tions, and a more-or-less poetic make-up. Some may be heavily-embroidered accounts of real events (such as the 'Story of Sinuhe', *see page 193*); others contain a kernel of political propaganda.

A good example of the latter is the Westcar Papyrus (named, like many other papyri, after its first modern owner), a Second Intermediate Period copy of what was originally an Old Kingdom story. It is given the form of a cycle of stories of magic told to amuse the bored King Khufu. They are related by his sons, and conclude with one which tells of the birth of triplets, fathered by the sun-god, Re, who will one day be kings. The triplets are actually the

THE STORY OF THE SHIPWRECKED SAILOR

A classic of Egyptian literature is the tale known as the 'Story of the Shipwrecked Sailor'. It opens with a sailor trying to comfort a colleague who has just returned from a disastrous expedition. The sailor tells how his ship was sunk in a storm, with the loss of all of its crew apart from himself. He is washed up on an island where he meets a giant snake. Although terrifying to look at, the snake is friendly, and the sole survivor of his family, the rest of whom had been killed by a falling meteorite. Sympathizing with the sailor for the loss of all his shipmates, he loads him with gifts, and correctly prophesies that a ship will pass and pick up the castaway. The sailor ends up being presented to the king and promoted. Unfortunately, his attempts to show his colleague that 'all's well that ends well' are of no avail: the latter dismisses him with the remark 'Don't try and be clever with me: who gives water to a goose just before it is killed?' He knows that he is to be punished for his failure (the nature of which is not revealed in the surviving copy of the story).

Right: *Model boat from the tomb of the Chancellor Meketre at Thebes. This is one of the finest examples of an artefact that was common placed in Middle Kingdom tombs.*

first rulers of Dynasty V, and the story was clearly composed under the last of them to show that his family was of divine origin.

On the other hand, some stories are simply for entertainment. More than one contains elements found in stories across several continents: princesses locked up in towers, princes in disguise and quests for magical items. Allegories such as 'The Blinding of Truth by Falsehood' and others demonstrate the victory of good over evil. Stories featuring gods are common: more than one tells of the conflict between Horus and his uncle Seth, the murderer of Osiris. Some of these formed the basis for theatrical performances during festivals, such as that related in the autobiography of Ikhernofret (*see page 192–3*).

TEXTS OF MAGIC AND MEDICINE

Opposite: *The temple of Sobk and Harouris at Kom Ombo. This relief shows various medical instruments, from the Ptolemaic Period.*

Below: *Greco-Roman Period mummy. The Egyptians were well known in the ancient world as physicians. The medical papyri include many examples of treatment for trauma. The owner of this mummy had lost an arm early in life, an injury which had clearly been successfully treated. The embalmers had provided him with a prosthetic arm for use in the afterlife.*

In the ancient world, the Egyptians were renowned as physicians, and records exist of Egyptian doctors being sent abroad to treat highly-placed foreigners. Amongst the myriad papyri that have survived are a number which deal with the treatment of disease. These provide a fascinating mixture of what we would regard as proper 'medical' procedures, and those which we would dismiss as 'magic'. However, one must be wary of making such pejorative divisions based on modern scientific knowledge. In an era where the mechanism of disease transmission was unknown, and existence of supernatural beings was regarded as fact, 'magical' practices were perfectly logical. Indeed, given the importance of a patient's attitude to successful treatment, the rituals sometimes carried out may indeed have had a positive result.

The 'real' medicine in the papyri deals with injuries and conditions that clearly had an external cause or manifestation. One of the most important of such documents is the Edwin Smith Surgical Papyrus, now in New York, a systematic guide to the examination and treatment of various conditions. It describes the examination procedures, states whether or not treatment is possible, and then gives instructions as to how to carry out any treatment.

Other papyri have a rather less systematic approach, and are often general compilations of remedies for a range of conditions, although there are a number that concentrate on particular themes, for example gynaecology, or snake bites.

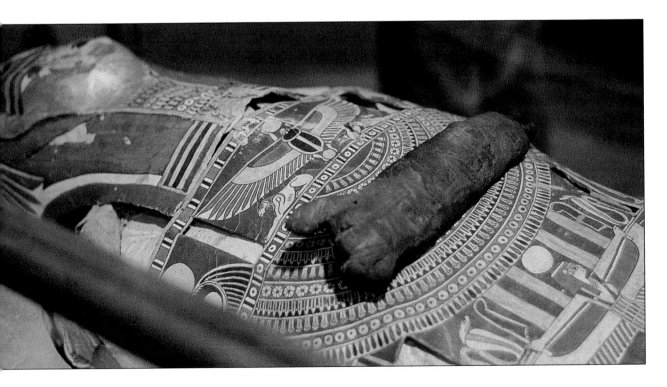

Above: *The tomb of the Steward Kheruef from Dynasty XVIII. The ancient Egyptians were themselves amongst the earliest tourists, and left their graffiti on the ancient monuments they visited. Here an ink-written hieratic graffito has been added to the carved façade of the tomb.*

THE END OF THE ANCIENT LANGUAGE

The various scripts of the Egyptian language remained unchallenged in Egypt until the end of the Late Period, when the country fell under the yoke of foreign empires. Following Alexander the Great's conquest in 332 BC, and the establishment of the Macedonian Greek dynasty of the Ptolemies, there was a steady influx of Greek settlers. With the ruling class composed of Greeks, Greek writing became widely used. It served with demotic as the main administrative medium, and appeared alongside it and hieroglyphic text on a number of monumental decrees, such as the Rosetta Stone and Decree of Canopus.

However, hieroglyphs and hieratic were by now largely restricted to religious uses, and it is clear that knowledge of them became more and more restricted as time went by. Temples continued to be built with the ancient religious images and texts, but they were using a version of the language that was now some 1500 years old, and bore little or no relation to the current speech. All that kept the ancient script alive was the religion whose dogma it was used to enshrine.

Pressure on the ancient script was further increased by the inexorable spread of the Christian religion through the country. The last great stronghold of paganism was the temple-isle of Philae, the cult-centre of the goddess Isis since the Late Period, and it was there, in AD 394, that the last dated hieroglyphic inscription was carved, 82 years after the Empire became Christian. Paganism maintained a tenuous toe-hold at Philae, and at Siwa in the Western Desert until AD 553, when the final sanctuaries were forcibly closed. However,

Above: *Part of the temple of Maharraqa in Nubia. Although temples continued to be built in the ancient style during the Roman Period, knowledge of the ancient scripts gradually declined.*

Left: *The Temple at Philae: the final stronghold of paganism in Egypt.*

by then the last demotic text had also been written, again at Philae, in AD 452. Writing in Egypt was by then either in Greek or Coptic, and within 200 years, increasingly in Arabic as well. Hieroglyphic script now slumbered.

HIEROGLYPHS FOR THE MODERN AGE

It was not until 1,400 years after the last ancient hieroglyphic inscription had been written that knowledge of the script was regained (*see Chapter V*). This knowledge has largely been diverted towards the study of texts written in ancient times, but there have been examples of new texts being composed.

Possibly the earliest of these is to be found at the Great Pyramid at Giza, where a large, well-cut hieroglyphic inscription is to be found to the top right of the entrance to the monument. Rather than King Khufu, the founder of the pyramid, it commemorates the king of Prussia, Friedrich Wilhelm IV (1840–61), and was inscribed by the Prussian Egyptologist Carl Richard Lepsius (*see page 243–4*), who led a great scientific expedition to Egypt from 1842–5.

Since then, such new texts have appeared elsewhere in the world. Most spectacularly, in the 1980s, the zoo in Memphis, Tennessee, USA, built its new gate in the form of a temple pylon in celebration of its namesake, the ancient capital of Egypt. For this, scholars at the University of Memphis translated the zoo's Mission Statement into Middle Egyptian, which was then carved in hieroglyphs onto the façades and architraves of the gateway, a magnificent reminder of the enduring power of ancient Egypt and its age-old script.

Below: *The front façade to Memphis Zoo, Memphis, Tennessee. The zoo's mission statement, translated into Middle Egyptian, is colourfully displayed on the gateway. This is perhaps the most impressive example of the modern use of hieroglyphs.*

Above centre: *Modern cartouche at Giza. Made for King Farouq, the penultimate ruler of modern Egypt, this new cartouche is affixed to the gates of the former royal rest-house, now a cafeteria, just in front of the Great Pyramid.*

Right: *The Penzance Egyptian House, built for John Lavin in 1835, just as interest in ancient Egypt was re-ignited. While the overall arrangement is derived from Egyptian concepts, the female 'deity' busts look rather more akin to ships' figureheads.*

THE MYSTERY OF THE HIEROGLYPHS

Hieroglyphs Eclipsed

Above: *Temple of Isis at Philae. With the victory of Christianity, many pagan temples were converted to churches. Here, the cross has been carved on top of the sacred texts of the cult of Isis.*

GENERAL KNOWLEDGE of the hieroglyphic script contracted rapidly during Roman times. Its use was effectively limited to the walls of temples, and so to the restricted world of the priesthood. In these circumstance, the existing belief held by Greek and Roman writers that hieroglyphs were somehow something more mysterious than simple letters gained further support.

Earlier Classical writers broadly supported the view that hieroglyphs were a true system of writing, and even that they were the ancestors of all alphabets. Plato and others attributed its invention to a 'a certain Theuth' (the ibis-god Thoth). However, they clearly had difficulty in seeing the hieroglyphs as a phonetic script, or in distinguishing actual hieroglyphs from parts of the scenes that they frequently accompany. This was because very few Greeks and Romans, even if living in Egypt, learned the script. Most would simply use Greek, the language of government; a few might venture into demotic, but hieroglyphs lay outside their sphere. Thus, Classical scholars conceived hieroglyphs as symbolic, not

> 'express[ing] the intended concept by means of syllables joined one to another, but by means of the significance of the objects which have been copied, and by its figurative meaning that has been impressed on the memory by practice'.

This view was expressed by the Roman historian Diodorus Siculus, writing in the middle of the first century BC, at a time when temples were still being constructed covered with texts in hieroglyphs. Over subsequent centuries, there was no change in this generally held view.

FROM ALEXANDER TO NAPOLEON

PTOLEMAIC PERIOD

332–30 BC
Egypt ruled by heirs of Alexander the Great

ALEXANDER THE GREAT IN
EGYPTIAN GUISE, KARNAK

ROMAN PERIOD

30 BC–AD 395
Egypt made a Roman Province

HELLENISTIC
SPHINX OF THE 2ND
CENTURY AD

COPTIC PERIOD

AD 395–640
Egypt part of the Eastern Empire, based on Constantinople

Above: Temple at Wadi el-Sebua in Nubia. One of the temples later converted into a church, it had been originally built by Rameses II, who had been shown offering flowers either side of the niche at the back, which had held the divine images.

Right: Detail from Temple at Wadi el-Sebua. When the temple was converted, everything was coated in whitewash, and a figure of St Peter, holding a massive key, painted in the niche. The whitewash has now partly fallen away, leaving the appearance that it is the saint who is the recipient of Rameses' gifts!

ARAB PERIOD

AD 640–1517
The General Amr conquers Egypt for the Kaliphs

INSCRIPTION OF THE KALIPH EL-MUSTANSIR, DATED 1084–5 AD

OTTOMAN PERIOD

AD 1517–1805
The Turkish Sultan Selim I invades and incorporates the country into his Empire

TOMBS OF THE OTTOMAN PERIOD IN CAIRO

Above: *The Christian cathedral at Qasr Ibrim in Nubia. It is the last part of Lower Nubia to remain above the surface of Lake Nasser, and originally towered over the river.*

Above: *Statue of Thoth in his chapel in the catacomb of his sacred animals at Tunah el-Gebel. A lunar god, Thoth was sometimes shown as a baboon with the crescent moon on his head. He was later equated with Hermes.*

There were some honourable exceptions to this state of ignorance. One was Chairemon (*fl.*mid-first century AD) who had lived in Alexandria, and described various signs with meanings that are not too far from the truth, although tied up in a symbolic world view. Clement of Alexandria (*c.*AD 150 – AD 215) seems to have recognized the existence of phonetic signs, although only in an overall symbolic and allegorical context and a translation of the text on an obelisk at Rome (now in the Piazza del Popolo) by a certain Hermapion in the middle of the third century, later quoted by the Roman historian Ammanius Marcellinus (*c.*AD 330–60), is broadly correct. However, by this time, the philosopher Plotinus (AD 205–70) had set out the theory which was to underpin European hieroglyphic studies for one and a half millennia. Plotinus suggested that rather than representing ordinary letters expressing sounds that went on to make up words, hieroglyphs were images from which the initiated could gain a fundamental insight into the very essence of things.

These conceptions became bound up in various allegedly 'Egyptian' philosophical speculations, known as the 'Hermetic Corpus' after the Greek god Hermes who was equated with Thoth. Although purely Greek in origin, these ideas formed the foundation of later work, and were in many ways instrumental in delaying the decipherment of hieroglyphs.

Another hindrance was the survival of a work by Horapollo, an Egyptian, probably written around the fourth century and known as the *Hieroglyphica*. It has 179 chapters, each dealing with a single hieroglyph or concept, and often contains a frustrating mixture of half-truth and non-Egyptian metaphysical speculation. For example, according to Horapollo, the vulture and

the goose are said to mean 'mother' and 'son', respectively. This is quite true, but for purely phonetic reasons, not because 'male vultures do not exist' or 'geese love their offspring more than any other'! There are a fair number of similar examples where a sign's usage is correctly identified, albeit for unlikely reasons, but there are also examples of imaginary signs or completely wrong-headed interpretations. It is clear that Horapollo had access to something akin to contact with those who still understood hieroglyphs, but lacked that understanding himself. His work was a classic example of the kind of account produced by someone with a passing acquaintance with a subject, but without the insight to understand his limitations. Horapollo's work was lost from the end of antiquity down to its rediscovery in the fifteenth century, but was subsequently printed and regarded by almost all scholars as the only 'authentic' account of the hieroglyphs.

Above left: The sarcophagus made for the last native Egyptian pharaoh, Nakhthorheb. Pharaonic monuments became objects of curiosity, to be re-used where appropriate. This sarcophagus was used as part of an ablution fountain in the Attarin Mosque in Alexandria.

THE RENAISSANCE VIEW

During the Middle Ages, interest in hieroglyphs slumbered. In Egypt, the absolute victory of Christianity, and its widespread replacement by Islam after AD 640, meant that the old scripts were utterly obsolete and all knowledge lost. In the west, ancient Egypt and its works were seen only through the fog of the biblical narrative and odd fragments of classical writings. Thus, in the mosaics of St Mark's Cathedral, Venice, built in the late eleventh century, the pyramids are the granaries of Joseph.

However, with the Renaissance, a real interest in the past became manifest, including a desire to reconcile Christian and ancient philosophies. A number of classical texts were rediscovered, including views on Egypt and its hieroglyphs; of particular importance was Plutarch's work on the myth of the god of the dead, Osiris, and his wife, Isis. The work of Horapollo (*see above*) was found on the Greek island of Andros in 1419. Horapollo's view of hieroglyphs thus became central to the learned view of them during the Renaissance and beyond; indeed, 15 editions of Horapollo were to appear during the sixteenth century.

The Horapolloan conception of hieroglyphs became mixed in with the creation of new 'hieroglyphs'. These were intended to provide architectural ornamentation that expressed ideas which be read and understood by initiated scholars. Although they neither copied or were even based upon genuine

Above right: The Rafai Mosque in Cairo. The decisive break with the past came with the Arab invasion of Egypt in AD 640. With the victory of Islam, Arabic gradually replaced Coptic as the general language of the country.

Above: Francesco Colonna's Egyptian fantasy. His invented hieroglyphs were of considerable influence during the sixteenth century, although, as may be clearly seen, they bore no resemblance to the real thing.

POINTING THE WAY

THE OBELISK (from the Greek for 'roasting spit') was the fundamental symbol of the sun, its tip representing the rays of the sun striking down through the clouds. A squat example (known as the *ben-ben* stone) was the focus of devotion in the great temple of the sun-god Re at Heliopolis. However, most obelisks were far more slender, and usually flanked the entrance to a temple.

The earliest known example was erected by Teti (Dynasty VI) at Heliopolis, although the oldest one still standing is that of Senwosret I (Dynasty XII), also at Heliopolis. Most obelisks were quarried from the granite of Aswan, and carried on barges downstream to the temples of Thebes, Memphis, Heliopolis, Pirameses, and other cities further north. The transport of one pair of Karnak obelisks is depicted in the Dynasty XVIII temple of Hatshepsut at Deir el-Bahari. It is generally agreed that the actual erection took place by dragging the obelisk to the top of a ramp, below which was a sand-box. Sand was allowed to escape from the latter, gently lowering the obelisk into place. A televised experiment carried out in the USA has now proved the efficacy of the technique.

Obelisks were generally decorated with the names and titles of the king who ordered them to be erected, together with some statement on his or her dedication of the monument to the gods. The last examples were produced in the Roman Period, during which time many earlier obelisks were transported to Rome for re-erection. There, they played an important role in the early attempts at deciphering the hieroglyphs.

Above: *Rameses II's entrance to the temple of Luxor. The obelisk's associations are reinforced by figures of baboons on the base adoring the rising sun.*

Top right: *Temple at Karnak. The surviving obelisks of Thutmose I and Hatshepsut tower over the central area of the temple.*

Left: *The obelisks of Hatshepsut are amongst the best documented in existence. Their quarrying is recorded in the female king's temple at Deir el-Bahari, while their dedication is commemorated on this quartzite block from her 'Red Chapel' at Karnak.*

Egyptian hieroglyphs, these new signs became intimately mingled with speculations related to the real ancient script. An example of the confusion over what constituted real hieroglyphs is shown by the frequent reproduction of an 'Egyptian text' on a Roman temple frieze from Rome, and a widespread belief that the invented hieroglyphs in an illustrated fantasy by Francesco Colonna (1433–1527) were copies of actual inscriptions!

During the sixteenth century, an increasing number of scholars began to take an interest in hieroglyphs. An important stage was reached with the publication in 1556 of the *Hierogliphica* by Pierius Valerianus (1477–c.1560), a compilation of a series of 58 of his works on the subject, previously produced separately. Each deals with a specific hieroglyph, or group of hieroglyphs, and uses the now-traditional method of allegory to explain them. Explanations were thus far from the mark, yet the erudition displayed in the work, referencing some 200 authors, marks its importance. It was subsequently reprinted in more than one language, and remained a key reference source for a century.

The century also brought to light more genuine Egyptian texts, through the re-erection of a considerable number of obelisks at Rome. These had been brought there by the Roman emperors, overthrown at the end of antiquity, and then rediscovered and re-erected by a succession of Renaissance popes. The process continued into the seventeenth century; one of the men most closely associated with the works, Athanasius Kircher, being perhaps the key figure in the speculations concerning hieroglyphs in this period.

KIRCHER'S FLIGHT OF FANCY

Athanasius Kircher (1601–80) was a polymath, whose interests covered a whole range of scientific and humanist subjects. His interest in Egyptian antiquities was kindled by seeing a book containing pictures of the obelisks in Rome, which inspired him to attempt to decipher their inscriptions. However, his first work on the Egyptian language was focused on Coptic, manuscripts and knowledge of which had begun to come to the west early in the seventeenth century. Kircher had been entrusted with the publication of manuscripts brought back by Pietro della Valle (1582–1652), an Italian nobleman and traveller, and produced an introduction to the Coptic tongue in 1636. Although a number of Kircher's conclusions were incorrect,

Above: Relief from the temple of Sethy I at Abydos. The ibis-headed Thoth, god of writing and wisdom, revivifies the resurrected Osiris.

Below: The Roman 'birth house' temple at Dendara. Emperor Augustus, depicted as a pharaoh, makes offerings to Isis and her son, Horus. Egyptian cults, especially that of Isis, spread to Rome itself.

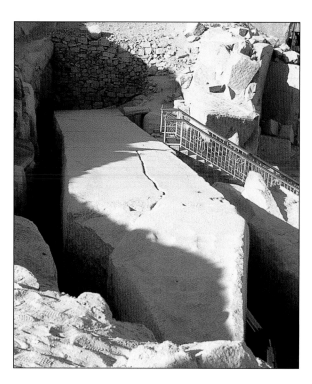

Above: *The intended mate of the Lateran obelisk. It still lies in its quarry at Aswan. A flaw in the rock led to its rejection and abandonment by the ancient craftsmen.*

Above: *Medal made for Sixtus V (1585–90). The obverse shows the monuments placed at the Vatican, Lateran, Piazza Popolo and on the Esquiline in Rome. Interest in the hieroglyphs was re-engendered in the sixteenth and seventeenth centuries, when various popes re-erected a number of the obelisks that had been brought to Rome in Imperial times. Pope Sixtus V was the greatest of the obelisk-pontiffs.*

Above centre: *Obelisk outside the Church of San Giovanni, Lateran, Rome. It is the largest of all the surviving Egyptian obelisks.*

the book contained the fundamental observation that Coptic and ancient Egyptian were the same language. A further volume, published in 1644, provided a far more in-depth account of Coptic, and became the basis for all study of the language in the immediately succeeding decades.

In 1650, Kircher was further entrusted with the publication of a study of the obelisk then being re-erected in the Piazza Navona (*see page 227*), one of the latest known, and (as we now know) carved for the Emperor Domitian (AD 81–96). Kircher also studied other obelisks and Egyptian material in Rome. He began from a belief in the close equivalence between classical and Egyptian mythologies, and that a correct idea of Egyptian philosophical conceptions had been preserved in the works of the classical and other writers. On the basis that the classical sources had also said that the hieroglyphic script contained the esoteric knowledge of the Egyptians, Kircher thus felt that he knew in advance what hieroglyphic texts said, and it was simply a question of determining how the one could be derived from the other.

In doing so, Kircher regarded the hieroglyphs as symbols, yet also believed that there was a parallel 'vulgar' usage, that might be basically alphabetical. While his limited work in this direction was based on wholly-wrong assumptions, there was one flash of insight which allowed him to read the group ≋ as 'm' (actually 'mw' – 'water') – the first time that a hieroglyph had been read for over a thousand years.

Unluckily, the vast majority of Kircher's efforts was directed towards the non-existent 'symbolic' use of hieroglyphs, that based their meaning on allegory, understandable only by initiates. Each hieroglyph was assigned a philosophical concept or demonological manifestation, and then examined within the cosmos that Kircher had constructed out of the material available to him. Thus in his publication of the Navona obelisk, the Emperor's alphabetically-written cartouche was 'translated' as follows: *'The beneficent generative force commanding through supernal and infernal dominion, augments the flow of sacred humour emanating from above. Saturn, the disposer of fleeting time, promotes the fecundity of the soil, commanding humid nature. For by his influence all things have life and force'.*

While to modern eyes absurd, Kircher's conclusions were based on a scholarly method, the pity being that the method was so badly chosen; but Kircher was by no means the last scholar to be led astray.

THE FIRST GLIMMERS OF ENLIGHTENMENT

The philosophic ideas that underpinned Kircher's work were already under attack during his lifetime, principally through demonstrations that the Hermetic works were in no way derived from ancient Egypt. Following on from this came scepticism over whether the hieroglyphs were indeed the esoteric repositories of priestly learning.

Above: *The site of the Lateran Obelisk. Having lain by the Sacred Lake in Karnak temple for nearly 30 years, the Lateran obelisk was finally erected here by Thutmose IV, at the easternmost end of the temple. It stood alone, as a symbol of the sun.*

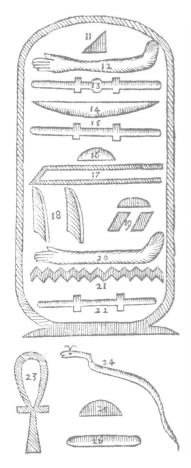

Left: *The title page of Athanasius Kircher's* Obeliscus Pamphilius *(Rome, 1650), which published his conclusions on an obelisk re-erected in the Piazza Navona.*

Right: *Obelisk in the Piazza Navona, Rome. This monument was one of the latest of its type, having been carved and erected for the Roman Emperor Domitian.*

Above: *Kircher's (inaccurate) copy of Domitian's cartouche on the Navona obelisk. This he interpreted as reading:* 'The beneficent generative force commanding through supernal and infernal dominion, augments the flow of sacred humour emanating from above. Saturn, the disposer of fleeting time, promotes the fecundity of the soil, commanding humid nature. For by his influence all things have life and force'. *The cartouche and the signs that follow it actually read:* 'Kasaros Temiytyanos [Caesar Domitianus], who lives for ever'.

Early in the eighteenth century came recognition of the existence of cursive Egyptian scripts, while a conceptual step forward is to be seen in Book IV of *The Divine Legation of Moses* (1740), by William Warburton, later Bishop of Gloucester (1698–1779). In this, he set out the view that scripts developed from pure pictograms to 'contrasted and arbitrarily instituted marks' in a steady manner. The Abbé Jean Jacques Barthélemy (1716–95) took this concept, and demonstrated that some hieroglyphs could indeed be the ancestors of hieratic signs. In a paper published in 1761, the Abbé also observed that cartouches might contain royal and divine names. Warburton also proposed the existence of a number of types of hieroglyph, including ideograms and determinatives, as well as making the case for the script having been designed not for 'sacred secrets', but for day-to-day purposes. Nevertheless, he did not make any attempt to apply his concepts to actual texts.

Alongside these rejections of the stale theories of the Renaissance came other fruitless avenues of speculation. The eighteenth century displayed a further expansion of the literature concerning Egyptian writing, one theme, pursued by the English academic John Needham (1713–81), being the equation of Egyptian and Chinese, based on a so-called 'bust of Isis' that actually bore neither Egyptian nor Chinese characters! A considerable number of others followed a similar route. Joseph de Guignes (1721–1800) made China an Egyptian colony, and their languages originally identical. He dismissed

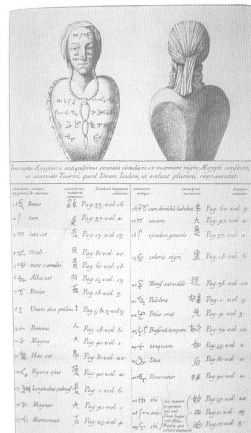

Coptic as so corrupted by its links with Greek as to be useless from the point of view of decipherment. De Guignes' views remained popular throughout the century, one major proponent being the Swedish diplomat Count Nils Gustaf Palin (1765–1842), who wrote several volumes on the subject between 1802 and 1812.

More helpful was the growing corpus of copies of real Egyptian texts, in particular those brought back by travellers to the Near East. Carsten Niebuhr (1733–1815) spent 1761–2 in Egypt and made accurate copies that enabled him to produce a table showing a selection of hieroglyphs, sorted by kind.

Barthélemy's observations on the import of cartouches were reinforced over 35 years later, by the work of the Danish antiquarian Jørgen Zoëga (1755–1809). In 1797, he published a study of the Roman obelisks for Pope Pius VI, a massive tome that included an in-depth discussion of the hieroglyphs. Zoëga recognized the significance of the direction in which a hieroglyph faced to indicate which way a text ran and, most critically, that some signs might be purely phonetic. However, he went too far in suggesting that the final pre-Coptic variant of the script (demotic) might have become alphabetic. In spite of his insights, Zoëga did not actually try to decipher the script; rather, he drew a line under what had come before and provided an intellectual springboard towards true decipherment. Within a year of the publication of his book, the key to the mystery of the hieroglyphs had been found.

Above: *The notorious 'Bust of Isis', in Turin. It had been classified as 'Egyptian' on the grounds that the characters it bore were hieroglyphs; a number of writers, including John Needham, then interpreted them as Chinese, thus proposing identity between the two scripts. In fact, the signs signify the zodiac, there being nothing to even link the image with Egypt!*

DECIPHERMENT OF THE HIEROGLYPHS

The Key is Found

Above: *Napoleon Bonaparte inspecting a mummy during his 1798 Egyptian expedition. Napoleon's military ambitions produced an unexpected result for Egyptology.*

Opposite: *Queen Hatshepsut's obelisk at Karnak. This is part of the dedication inscription, showing the hieroglyphic style of the XVIII Dynasty.*

IN SPITE OF THE MODEST PROGRESS in the study of hieroglyphs during the last part of the eighteenth century, there remained a fundamental problem. There was no way of testing any of the theories or suggestions in a meaningful way. In short, unless one had an inscription or document in which the same material was provided in both hieroglyphs and in a known language written in a known script, there was little more that could be done to expand the field of knowledge.

Just such a pivotal document was ultimately provided during the French occupation of Egypt, begun by General Napoleon Bonaparte (later Emperor Napoleon I) on behalf of the French Republic in 1798. The expedition was primarily aimed against the United Kingdom; it was intended to provide a strategic base for an assault on British possessions in India. However, it also had the alleged 'higher' aim of 'improving the lot of the natives of Egypt', and exploring, mapping and recording the country. In addition to military and naval forces, teams of scientists, scholars and artists were also assembled to follow the advancing armies and capture Egypt for the world of knowledge. Their work was ultimately to be published in the vast, 19-volume *Description de l'Egypte*, which appeared between 1809 and 1822. This immense work provided for the first time a comprehensive, reliable documentation of the land of the Nile, and played an absolutely central role in the development of European interest in ancient Egypt. Together with the political changes that it also ushered into Egypt, the Napoleonic expedition is generally felt to be the first great turning point in the history of Egyptology.

COUNTDOWN TO UNDERSTANDING

AD 394
Last hieroglyphic text

LAST HIEROGLYPHS, PHILAE

AD 452
Last demotic text

1419
Rediscovery of Horapollo's work, lost since the fifth century

1636
Kircher publishes his first work

1740
Warburton writes on hieroglyphs

FRONTISPIECE OF KIRCHER'S FIRST WORK

1761
Barthélemy identifies link between hieratic and hieroglyphs

1798
Discovery of the Rosetta Stone

ROSETTA STONE

1814
Young identifies words within Rosetta Stone

1816
Bankes Obelisk found

BANKES OBELISK

1819
Young publishes first findings

1822
Champollion publishes first conclusions

JEAN-FRANCOIS
CHAMPOLLION

1836–44
Champollion's dictionary and grammar conclusions published

1836
Lepsius publishes conclusions

Above: *The* Description de l'Égypte *was the enduring result of the militarily abortive Egyptian expedition. Bonaparte had brought a large team of scholars with his army, which undertook the first systematic survey of the country and its monuments. The results were published in nine volumes of text, and ten of plates between 1809 and 1822, and formed the springboard from which the subject of Egyptology then developed.*

The French expedition sailed from Toulon on 18 May 1798, captured Malta in June, and arrived near Alexandria at the end of the same month. Egypt's second city was rapidly captured, and within a short time the whole country was under French rule. However, the French were already trapped in Egypt as, on 1 August, a British fleet under Rear-Admiral Horatio Nelson had attacked the French fleet in Abuqir Bay, and destroyed it all except for two frigates.

Only a few days earlier, on 25 July, a slab of granite had been found during work on the construction of Fort Julien, just outside the north Delta town of Rashid. This was the location of one of the mouths of the Nile, and had been known to the Greeks as Rosetta. The slab bore three sets of text, in hieroglyphs, demotic script and Greek respectively. Luckily, its importance was instantly recognized by a French officer of the Engineers, Pierre-François-Xavier Bouchard (1772–1832), and it was sent to the Institute National in Cairo, set up by Bonaparte as part of his plan to transform Egypt into a modern country as the centre for scholarly work. At the Institute, the stone was inspected by the General himself, and copies made for dispatch to the leading scholars of Europe.

The stone was scheduled to be taken to France with the rest of the French expedition's antiquities, and was in the house of General Menou at Alexandria, when the French capitulated to the British forces led by Sir Ralph Abercromby in spring 1801. Ever since Nelson's destruction of the French fleet in 1798, the French position had been increasingly untenable, particularly following the landing of British troops in the country. Under Article XVI of the Treaty of Capitulation, all antiquities were to be ceded to the British, but Menou claimed that the stone was his own property in an attempt to prevent its removal. However, in October, a team of artillerymen were ultimately sent to take possession, and the stone was embarked in HMS *L'Égyptienne* (also an ex-French prize), and arrived at Portsmouth in February 1802. Moved to the Society of Antiquaries in London on 11 March, it then underwent intensive study. Within a month, a translation of the Greek text had been read to the Society, and in July casts were sent to Oxford, Cambridge, Edinburgh and Dublin Universities, with complete facsimiles being distributed around Europe. Towards the end of the year, the stone was moved once more, to its permanent home in British Museum.

YOUNG AND CHAMPOLLION

Real progress only came from the work of two individuals, the British physicist Thomas Young (1773–1829), and Jean-François Champollion (1790–1832) in France. Young was a polymath of the kind that no longer seems to exist today, a child prodigy who allegedly could read at the age of two, and

by 14 had a knowledge of a dozen languages. Initially trained as a doctor, he became an optical specialist who was elected a Fellow of the Royal Society at the age of 20. Two years later, he went to Göttingen to study physics, returning to England after being awarded his doctorate to study at Cambridge University. In 1799 he set up a medical practice in London .

Above: The town of Rashid (Rosetta), near the mouth of western branch of the Nile Delta. The all-important stone was discovered here.

Although a distinguished physician, Young's interests in physics and linguistics continued to develop. On the linguistic front, he was drawn to the problem of the Rosetta Stone, and in 1814 managed to divide large portions of the two Egyptian texts into specific words, with their Greek equivalents, and in November produced a conjectural translation of them. By the following year, he had prepared a demotic alphabet and a list of 86 demotic words, with their Greek equivalents. Importantly, he also recognized that the demotic, hieratic and hieroglyphic scripts were merely variants of the same writing system. This was based on his study of various manuscripts of the Book of the Dead, the religious text that accompanied many Egyptians to the grave from the New Kingdom onwards. The Book of the Dead has a very standardized formulation, and is found written in all three scripts; indeed, some are display signs that are half-way between hieroglyphic and hieratic. Careful study made it possible to see which hieroglyphic, hieratic and demotic signs were equivalent to one another, and to see differences between the ways that equivalent signs were used within different scripts.

Below: Napoleonic fortifications at Rosetta. It was here, in Fort Julien, that an inscribed slab was found in 1799.

In 1819, Young published a digest of his researches to date in a supplement to *Encyclopedia Britannica*. He had concluded that the hieroglyphic script used for writing foreign royal names was largely phonetic, rather than pictorial; he had determined the value of certain individual signs; and he had identified the cartouches of Ptolemy, Berinike and 'Tuthmosis' (= Thutmose). The latter was essentially a guess based on the appearance of an ibis within his cartouche: from Greek sources, it was known that this bird was sacred to the god Thoth. Unfortunately, having got so far, Young was unable to convince himself

THE ROSETTA STONE

THE ROSETTA STONE, as it is known, was once part of a stela, originally about 250 cm (98.4 inches) high and 80 cm (31.5 inches) wide, of which the top 30 cm (11.8 inches) or so is now missing, taking with it a considerable proportion of the Hieroglyphic text. The Demotic and Greek portions are, however, largely complete, and the latter was read immediately after the discovery as being a decree recounting the temple benefactions of King Ptolemy V, and dated to his ninth regnal year (196 BC). The key part from the point of view of the decipherment of ancient Egyptian scripts, however, was that the decree should be reproduced on a series of stelae, all

bearing the hieroglyphic, demotic and greek scripts, the first two writing the ancient Egyptian language, the last the Greek. Comparison of the three texts should thus, in theory at least, make the decipherment of the Egyptian texts fairly straightforward. Unfortunately, this was not to be the case.

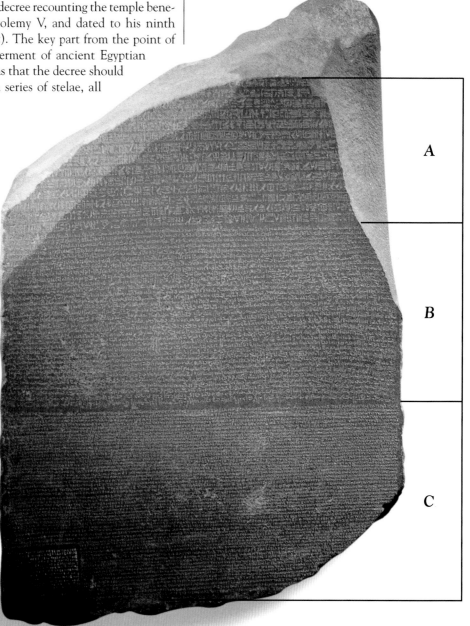

A

B

C

At first, scholars studying the Rosetta Stone concentrated on the demotic text in view of the amount of the hieroglyphic section that was missing. The fact that the script had been developed as simplified hand-written letters hid from most observers the direct relationship between it and the hieroglyphs. The general feeling was still that while the latter were an esoteric, 'symbolic' confection, demotic was likely to be 'real' writing. Nevertheless, Jean-Joseph Marcel (1776–1854) and Remi Raige, both members of the scientific commission that had accompanied the French army to Egypt, had recognized demotic as cursive hieroglyphs while the stone was still in Egypt.

The incompleteness of the hieroglyphic text may also have contributed to the delay in decoding the text. The first breakthrough came in 1802, with the work of the French orientalist Baron Antoine-Silvestre de Sacy (1758–1838) on the demotic text. He managed to isolate some of the proper names, but failed to explain them correctly. De Sacy's work was continued by the Swedish diplomat Johan David Åkerblad (1763–1819), who managed to establish the demotic groups for all proper names on the stone, as well for 'temples', 'Greeks' and 'him/his'. Unfortunately, Åkerblad was unable to go further, as he had assumed demotic to be a wholly alphabetic script. He had made important insights, however, unlike a number of other putative decipherers.

At one extreme, Tandeau de St Nicholas claimed that hieroglyphs were no more than decorative patterns, and not writing at all. Count Palin (*see page 227*) continued to advance his 'Chinese' theories, compounded with allegory. One of his suggestions was that the Psalms of David were Hebrew translations of Egyptian texts; this could be proved by translating the Hebrew text into Chinese(!), thus providing a key to the decipherment. Joseph von Hammer Purgstall (1774–1856) based his ideas on an Arabic treatise on certain enigmatic alphabets although they did not actually include hieroglyphs; on the other hand, he was one of the first adherents of the true decipherment when it came. Alexandre Lenoir (1762–1839) applied astronomical approaches to the hieroglyphs with less than happy results. Pierre Lacour (1779–1858) suggested that hieroglyphs were versions of Hebrew letters, and in turn the ancestors of the Greek alphabet.

These are but a few examples of the various strands of argument that ran in parallel with rather more productive researches.

A

Above: The hieroglyphic section of the Rosetta Stone is the most severely damaged part, having lost more than half of its 29 lines, together with the images that would have been placed above the text.

B

Above: The demotic section of the Stone was that first addressed by would-be decipherers. Not only was it almost complete, but its cursive nature led some to suspect that it might be a more 'rational' script than the 'symbolic' hieroglyphic.

C

The Greek text at the bottom of the Stone was easily readable. It thus provided the key that allowed the decipherment of the other two scripts.

Right: The Mammisi, or Birth House of Isis, at Philae. Ptolemy V issued a number of decrees in more than one script. He covered the east side of the Birth House with two inscriptions in hieroglyphic and demotic, (but not greek.) The texts were subsequently over-cut with scenes of Ptolemy XII Neos Dionysos and the gods.

Above: Ptolemy III's multilingual Decree of Canopus. A number survive; this one was found re-used as the threshold of a Cairene mosque, but was too badly damaged to play a role in hieroglyphic decipherment.

that alphabetic signs were used as such in ordinary narrative hieroglyphic script, despite the fact that a number of his existing transliterations pointed in this very direction.

The final resolution of the problem was therefore to be to the credit of Champollion, who had been working in parallel with Young. Like his British counterpart, Champollion had also been a child prodigy, who was learning both Hebrew and Arabic by the time he was 11 years old. Subsequently he learned Coptic at Grenoble, and obtained a university teaching post there at the tender age of 18. His formal career was much disrupted by his Republican political views, both under the late First Empire, and the Restoration of the monarchy in France after 1815. He obtained a Chair at Grenoble in 1818, but it was only in 1824 that he received official forgiveness from Louis XVIII, and the reward of a scientific mission to Italy to study Egyptian material there.

Champollion's first published contribution to the decipherment debate came in 1814, when he stated his view that Demotic and Coptic were the same language, differing only in the alphabets used. This conclusion was crucial, since it is a common (but not wholly true) axiom that an unknown language in an unknown script is undecipherable. Like Young, he also worked through many Book of the Dead manuscripts to establish equivalences between hieroglyphic and hieratic signs, but until 1820 was still tied to the idea that hieroglyphs were an entirely symbolic system, rather than having an alphabetic basis. Soon afterwards, however, he recanted, and embraced the theory that, for foreign names at least, hieroglyphs could be phonetic. Whether this was a result of having read Young's work, or arrived at independently, is still a hotly debated issue. Champollion certainly always claimed the latter; at this distance we shall never know.

Regardless of why he took the step, Champollion's recognition of the hieroglyphs' basic phonetic nature opened the way for rapid further progress. One useful experiment was to test Young's premise as to the relationship between the hieroglyphic, demotic, and hieratic scripts. Champollion experimentally worked backwards from the now long-established demotic group for 'Ptolemy', and ultimately arrived at a group of hieroglyphs identical with that on the Rosetta Stone supposed to be that of Ptolemy. He tried this again with

Left: The Rosetta Stone on display at the British Museum. The Museum took charge of the Rosetta Stone in June 1802, after its formal presentation by King George III. It has remained there on display ever since, except for a visit to Paris to mark the 150th anniversary of the decipherment.

Kleopatra, but was unable to check his result until a definite hieroglyphic writing of that queenly name was forthcoming.

THE STRONGMAN AND THE QUEEN

This was provided in 1821, with the arrival in England of an obelisk, removed from Philae by Giovanni Belzoni (1778–1823). A former circus strongman, he had first gone to Egypt as a hydraulic engineer. He subsequently undertook a series of commissions for Henry Salt (1780–1827), the British Consul in Egypt who, like his counterparts from the other European powers, was busy collecting antiquities on behalf of both his country and himself. Belzoni obtained a number of major monuments and opened a series of tombs, including the renowned sepulchre of Sethy I in the Valley of the Kings and the Second Pyramid at Giza. He also cleared a way into the Great Temple at Abu Simbel. Although often condemned as a plunderer, he took more care of his finds than most contemporaries, and published a comprehensive account of his work that was in many ways far ahead of its time. After leaving Egypt, he mounted an exhibition of his finds in Britain, and then went to explore west Africa; he died in Benin, en route to Timbuktu.

Following pages:
The gods Re-Harakhty and Osiris enthroned on a wall painting from Rameses I's tomb in the Valley of Kings. The splendour and mystery of Egyptian tombs and temples inspired generations of scholars to search for the meaning behind the fascinating enigma of hieroglyphic writing.

Left: Lunette of bilingual decree from Kom el-Hisn. The upper part of the Rosetta Stone is now lost; however, it most probably resembled that of this slightly earlier decree.

Above: *Thomas Young (1773–1829), one of the great polymaths of his age, made fundamental discoveries in the fields of medicine, physics and language. Although soon overtaken by Champollion, his work on papyri and the Rosetta Stone marked a quantum leap forward in the process leading to the final decipherment.*

In 1816, William John Bankes (1786–1855) had discovered an obelisk outside the temple of the goddess Isis on the island of Philae. As usual, the obelisk itself bore texts in hieroglyphs, but its pedestal had a text in Greek. Belzoni was commissioned to bring the monument back to England, and it was ultimately erected in 1839 on Bankes' estate at Kingston Lacy, Dorset.

Bankes was a land-owner and Member of Parliament who travelled extensively in the Near East in 1815–19. He took a deep interest in Egyptian antiquities and followed the hieroglyphic debate. He took the view that the cartouches on the obelisk bore the same royal names (Ptolemy and Kleopatra) that appeared in Greek on the base, and made a similar observation regarding greek and hieroglyphic texts on the pylon of a now destroyed temple at Hu in Middle Egypt. However, he also believed (wrongly) that the hieroglyphic and greek texts on the obelisk were translations of each other, something also believed by Young and Consul Salt who, without much justification, fancied himself to be a hieroglyphic scholar.

With the availability of the Philae text, Champollion now had his two known cartouches. Both of them could be checked against their demotic versions, as well as against each other, since they belonged to individuals whose Greek names (Ptolemaios and Kleopatra) shared a number of letters. If hieroglyphs were indeed phonetic, their cartouches, and , should also share hieroglyphic signs. It was immediately apparent that the letters P, O and L were in their expected places: P⌒OL⌐ ¶¶...; ⊿L¶OP⬧⌐⌐⬧⌐○. With this taken as read, it was possible to identify most of the remaining signs: PTOLMEES; KLEOPA⌐RA⌐○. Given that the rest of the name was clearly that of Kleopatra, it was inevitable that ⌐ had to be something akin to 't' (it is actually a 'd'). The remaining ⌐○ had been observed by Young as following the signs which, by context, had to be feminine names. It was thus clear that it was a feminine ending, not meant to be read.

EXIT YOUNG

Champollion's basic approach had been very similar to that used by Young, working from greek and demotic names back to the hieroglyphic royal names, and thence to the values of the alphabetic signs, but with the important difference that most of his equivalences were correct. Nevertheless, Young had made important progress, which continued until he dropped active Egyptological work in 1823, following the publication of his *Account of some recent Discoveries in the Hieroglyphical Literature*. In doing so, he remarked that 'Champollion is doing so much that he will not suffer anything of material consequence to be lost'. Taking a sample of 14 signs, Young got five correct, and four partly correct; in contrast, 11 of Champollion's readings were right, and the remaining three partly so.

At the end of his initial work on the cartouches of Ptolemy and Kleopatra, Champollion had 13 alphabetic signs to work with. The cartouches of 'Alexander' and 'Berenike', together with certain early Roman emperors were rapidly identified, thus further adding to the number of known signs.

Above: *Jean-François Champollion (1790–1832). The principal decipherer of hieroglyphs and the holder of the world's first university Chair of Egyptology.*

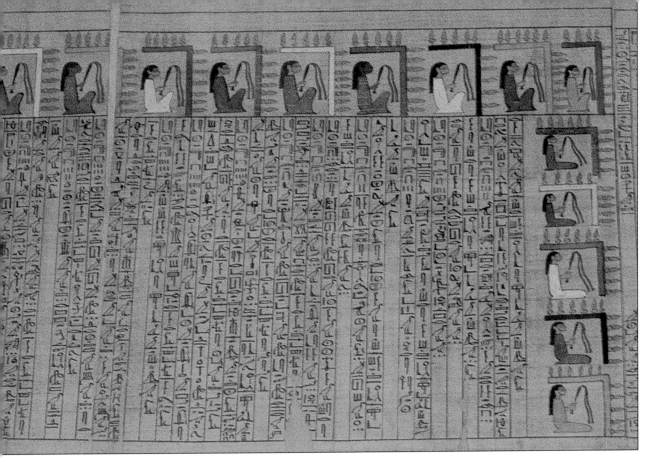

Having reached this point, Champollion was able to present his preliminary results in a famous communication to the French Académie des Inscriptions et Belles-Lettres ('the Academy') on 29 September 1822, the *Lettre à M. Dacier, relative à l'alphabet des hieroglyphes phonétiques* ('Letter to M. Dacier, regarding the phonetic hieroglyphic alphabet'). He still remained doubtful, however, as to whether all hieroglyphic texts were phonetic. It seemed possible that signs could have been adapted to write foreign names alphabetically in the Graeco-Roman Period, but were more normally employed in a symbolic fashion, which would mean that narratives and non-Greek names would still be a closed book. This was the same concern that had ultimately blocked Young from moving any further forward in his studies.

THE BREAKTHROUGH

It was therefore vital to test the theory against earlier, native, royal names. This was successfully carried out when, using the Coptic 're' for the sun sign in the cartouche ⟨hieroglyphs⟩, Champollion arrived at RE-?-SS (⟨hieroglyph⟩ had already been recognized as an epithet, meaning 'beloved of the god Amun', and not part of the actual name); there was also the cartouche ⟨hieroglyphs⟩, which Young had guessed might conceal the Greek 'Tuthmosis', which might be read as 'THOTH-?-S'. The king list written by the third-century BC Egyptian priest, Manetho strongly suggested that '?' should be '*m*' or '*ms*'. The Coptic link could once more be invoked, since the Greek word for 'to bear' apparently corresponded with ⟨hieroglyph⟩ in the hieroglyphic text of the Rosetta Stone, and the Coptic for 'to bear' is '*mosi*'. Champollion was thus able to read the purely

Egyptian names 'Rameses' and 'Thutmose', showing that the phonetic use of hieroglyphs was Egyptian practice, not simply that of later foreign conquerors.

Progress was then rapid. In 1824, Champollion published his *Précis du système hiéroglyphique* ('Summary of the hieroglyphic system'), and two years later was made Conservator of the Egyptian collection in the Louvre Museum in Paris. He undertook an expedition to Egypt in 1828–9, which built on the Napoleonic Commission's work to further enhance the documentation of the Egyptian monuments. His triumph was then capped by his appointment to the world's first full Professorship of Egyptology in March 1831. However, Champollion's constitution had been undermined by earlier experiences, and he died of a stroke only a year later.

While in Egypt, Champollion had met the Englishman John Gardner Wilkinson (1797–1875), who lived at Thebes from 1821 to 1833, studying the monuments and making a mass of notes and illustrations (now kept in Oxford University's Bodleian Library). With the vast amount of material of the Theban tombs and temples before him, Wilkinson was able to develop and correct a number of aspects of Champollion's work, in particular some of the latter's historical views. Knighted in 1839, he distilled his conclusions in a number of books, his great *Manners and Customs of the Ancient Egyptians* (1837) being the standard work for many decades; indeed, an abridged edition is still in print.

CHAMPOLLION'S LEGACY

At the time of Champollion's death, the manuscript of his *Grammaire Égyptienne* was complete, and was published in 1838. However, his remaining work was far from ready for publication and, worse, a number of items could not be found, including a large proportion of his projected dictionary. Luckily for Egyptology, Champollion's elder brother, Jacques-Joseph Champollion-Figeac (1778–1867) was zealous in placing his sibling's work before the world at large, following the government's purchase of his manuscripts in 1833. Thus, he piloted the *Grammaire* through the press, and began the publication of Jean-François' Egyptian expedition in 1835.

Champollion-Figeac's biggest problem, however, was the dictionary, of which about half the manuscript material had disappeared. He publicized the loss widely, in the hope that Jean-François had merely lent the papers to a colleague prior to his demise. Champollion-Figeac's suspicions were raised a year later, when he was sent a prospectus that described a three-volume work on the Rosetta Stone and Book of the Dead, to be published by one François

Above: *The island of Philae, as drawn by the French expedition, as it appears in* Commission des Monuments d'Egypte, *1809–22.*

Above: *Giovanni Battista Belzoni (1778–1823), adventurer, explorer and excavator.*

Opposite: *The First Pylon of the Temple of Isis, Philae. Two obelisks flanking the approach were erected by Ptolemy VIII Euergetes II and Kleopatra III.*

Above: *The Bankes Obelisk, now in the grounds of Kingston Lacy House, Dorset. It had been found by the Temple of Isis at Philae, by William John Bankes and taken to England some 20 years after its discovery.*

Above: *Gustavus Seyffarth (1796–1885), the longest lived of Champollion's opponents. His 'system' embraced various bizarre concepts, which produced 'translations' that bore little resemblance to the true meaning of texts. Nevertheless, he did useful work, most importantly making the first reconstruction of the Canon of Kings in Turin.*

Salvolini, a 22-year-old former student of the younger Champollion, who had been studying Egyptology for only a year.

At meeting of the Academy in August 1833, Silvestre de Sacy, who had also been Champollion's mentor, appealed for information on the lost manuscripts' whereabouts – to which Salvolini added his own tearful appeal; nothing was then heard for seven years. Then, Charles Lenormant (1802–59), one of Champollion's former collaborators, was approached by Luigi Verardi, who was attempting to wind up the affairs of Salvolini, who had died tragically young in 1838. Verardi had been trying, with very little success, to sell a series of manuscripts bearing Salvolini's name, and was seeking advice on how to proceed. As soon as Lenormant saw these manuscripts, it was clear to him that the lost writings of Champollion had been found. Confronted by this fact, Verardi agreed to sell Salvolini's archive to Lenormant for 600 French francs, the Champollion material joining the rest of his material under Champollion-Figeac's editorial pen.

The *Dictionnaire* was published in 1841, but suffered from its words being arranged by the kind of thing represented by their initial sign, rather than alphabetically. The decision to do so had been taken by Champollion-Figeac, since his brother had not had time to undertake any kind of arrangement before his death. In addition, the hieroglyphs had been transcribed into coptic letters, with an underlying assumption that all words written in hieroglyphs would correspond to ones in Coptic – which was not the case (*see pages 160–181*). There was a more fundamental problem in that Champollion had never grasped the difference between uniliteral, biliteral and triliteral signs, believing, for example, that 𓈙 (m), 𓌒 (mr), 𓏶 (mi), 𓏞 (mn), 𓄿 (ms), were all simply 'm'; this multiplication of signs with allegedly the same reading had been a major cause for disquiet amongst those opposing Champollion's system. Finally, many of Champollion's conclusions were presented only in provisional form; there remained many gaps and inconsistencies, and clearly very much more work was required before it would be possible to read a connected ancient Egyptian narrative without recourse to a bilingual text such as the Rosetta Stone.

THE PRETENDERS

Considerable time elapsed before the whole of the orientalist world was able to accept that Champollion had indeed identified the correct system for deciphering the hieroglyphs. During the 13 years that followed the first appearance of the 1824 *Précis*, opponents of Champollion's conclusions included I.A. Goulianov (1784–1841), Heinrich Klaproth (1783–1835), Cataldi Janelli (*fl.* 1830), Francesco Ricardi (*fl.* 1821–43) and Friedrich Spohn (1792–1824). A number of these presented more-or-less misguided alternative approaches, one of the longest lived being that developed by Spohn and Gustavus Seyffarth (1796–1885).

In 1830, Seyffarth received the first Professorship in Archaeology at Leipzig University, but the hieroglyphic system he embraced suffered from a fundamental problem: no two users seemed able to produce the same translation of a given text – not surprisingly, given that a single sign could apparently have a up to a dozen different values, depending on context!

Ultimately, he emigrated to America in 1854 against the background of the wholesale rejection of his philological theories in his native Germany. Nevertheless, his researches had important practical results, including in 1826 the first reconstruction of the the great King List from the myriad papyrus fragments in Turin. Seyffarth's misfortune was to cling to his erroneous hypotheses long beyond the point at which Champollion's correct one had started to prove itself, even into the phase during which it had received universal acceptance. By the early 1860s, he had only one disciple left, Max Uhlemann, who himself died in 1862; however, Seyffarth still felt sufficiently sure of himself that year to engage in vitriolic exchange in print with the British Egyptologist, Sir Peter Le Page Renouf (1822–97), who had had the temerity to point out the main flaws in Seyffarth's theories. Seyffarth maintained his position until his death, aged 91, in 1885, a tragic loss to the true study of Egyptian.

THE END OF THE MYSTERY

The death-knell to these alternate theories of decipherment had already come in 1837, when the Prussian Egyptologist Carl Richard Lepsius (1810–84) produced his *Lettre à M. le Professeur H. Rosellini sur l'Alphabet Hiéroglyphique* (Letter to Professor H. Rossellini about the Hieroglyohic Alphabet). Having undertaken a systematic comparison of all the various proposed methods of

Above: *Carl Richard Lepsius (1810–84). In addition to his great contribution to the study of the Egyptian language, Lepsius led the Prussian expedition to Egypt in 1842–5, whose discoveries and records remain fundamental. From 1864 he was Professor of Egyptology at Berlin and in 1866 discovered a complete copy of the Decree of Canopus at Tanis.*

Left: *The Great Temple of Rameses II at Abu Simbel in Nubia, which provided the cartouche of Rameses II that so helped Champollion. The area south of Aswan also contains some of the very last hieroglyphic inscriptions ever made in Egypt.*

Tableau des Signes Phonétiques
des Écritures hiéroglyphique et Démotique des anciens Égyptiens

decipherment, he was able to show that Champollion's was certainly the correct one, although not without its problems. These he undertook to correct, for example those regarding the existence of signs that represented more than one letter, and the true relationship between Coptic and the more ancient versions of the language. Thirty years later, Lepsius discovered a copy of another trilingual text, the Decree of Canopus, that allowed scholars to verify the conclusions of Champollion and his successors.

In England, Samuel Birch (1813–85), from 1836 of the British Museum, was also involved in widening and deepening Champollion's system. He had previously studied Chinese and, unlike earlier writers such as de Guignes and Palin who had misused the similarities between the Chinese and Egyptian scripts (*see previous chapter*), made good use of his knowledge in the classification of Egyptian words. The dictionary which he began to prepare was based on Chinese phonetic classification principles, and drew on all Egyptian material in the museum, together with all the words in the texts published by James Burton (1788–1862), John Gardiner Wilkinson (1797–1875), Ippolito Rosellini (1800–43), Champollion and Salvolini. In 1838, Birch published a sampler for the proposed dictionary, containing 12 pages with 93 words; unfortunately, there was insufficient interest to allow the publication of the whole book to go ahead. It was not until nearly 30 years later that Birch's dictionary would finally appear.

Meanwhile, in Ireland, Edward Hincks (1792–1866) was engaged in important work on both hieroglyphs and the Mesopotamian cuneiform script, being both dubbed the 'founder of Assyrian grammar', and described as the first person to correctly transliterate Egyptian texts, and to fully recognize the language's Semitic characteristics. In France, Champollion's mantle had now been picked up by Emmanuel de Rougé (1811–72), and by the 1850s he was able to read running texts, something no previous worker had been able to do. He was a key figure in the recognition of the earlier phases of the language, in particular Old Egyptian, through his production of the first translation of the Sixth Dynasty inscription of Uni. This important work had hitherto been regarded as too difficult. De Rougé's career culminated in his assumption of Champollion's Chair at the Collège de France in Paris in 1860, where he taught many of the next generation of Egyptologists. His pupil, Gaston Maspero (1846–1916) summarized the relative achievements of Champollion and de Rougé as follows: 'Champollion deciphered the texts .... De Rougé gave us the method which allowed us to utilize and bring to perfection the discovery of Champollion'.

THE END OF THE BEGINNING

De Rougé's work marked the end of the formative phase of the study of Egyptian. Although texts could now be read for the first time since the Roman Period,

Below: Champollion's Dictionnaire *was arranged by his brother according to the items that the first sign of a word represented. Thus,* ♀ (ḥr) *and* ⬭ (tp) *are together; in a modern dictionary, the words shown here are placed far apart, under their initial letters. Like many dictionaries of ancient Egyptian, the text was handwritten and lithographed, owing to the problems with typesetting hieroglyphs.*

Above: *Samuel Birch (1813–85) worked in the Public Records Office before moving to the British Museum in 1836. The pivotal British figure in establishing the correctness of Champollion's decipherment, he was much in demand as a lecturer, as well as writing for both the academic and popular audience.*

many areas of obscurity remained, some of which have still not been properly resolved. Throughout the middle years of the nineteenth century, scholars such as de Rougé, Birch, Lepsius, Heinrich Brugsch (1827–94), Charles Goodwin (1817–78) and François Chabas (1817–82) laboured to resolve problems. Birch's long-planned *Dictionary* was finally published in 1867, although unfortunately 'hidden' as the fifth volume of a multi-volume history of Egypt. Even more unfortunately, it rapidly went out of print, and in the 1870s, the budding Egyptologist Wallis Budge (1857–1934) was forced to trace his own copy of it – all 612 pages! The same year (1867), Brugsch brought out his hieroglyphic-demotic dictionary, a vast work of 759 pages and some 5,000 words, plus a supplement of similar length.

The production of these great volumes was the culmination of what has been termed the 'lexicographical' phase of the study of ancient Egyptian. Since Young and Champollion's day, the focus of studies had been on the decipherment and collection of words. Although there had, of course, been work on the grammar that glued them all together, quite rightly the priority was to find out the basic meanings of the signs and groups of signs. However, from the 1870s onwards, the focus began to switch, particularly through the work of a group of young German scholars based in Berlin – the so-called 'Berlin School'. The leading member of this grouping was Adolf Erman (1854–1937), whose works, together with those of his students and associates, revolutionized the whole study of the language.

THE BERLIN SCHOOL

Erman was the first worker to fully understand the differences between the different phases of Egyptian – Old, Middle and Late – and also the way it fitted into its family of languages. His volume on Late Egyptian grammar was issued in 1880, the same year as his fellow Berliner, Ludwig Stern (1846–1911), produced his important Coptic grammar. Stern, however, abandoned the subject in 1884 on Erman's appointment as head of the Egyptian Department at the Berlin Museum, the Coptic mantle in Berlin being picked up by Georg Steindorff (1861–1951), who had been Erman's first student. The 'Berlin School' triumvirate was completed by Kurt Sethe (1869–1934), another student of Erman's, who later was to become Professor at Göttingen University.

The Berlin School was especially concerned with the way that Egyptian grammar operated, particularly with reference to the verb. They attempted to put linguistic study on a fully systematic basis, one example being their promotion of the method of transliteration that is largely still being used today. In the latter part of the nineteenth century, a wide range of methods was used to transcribe Egyptian scripts into roman letters. A long drawn out discussion of transliteration methods was to be found in the various Egyptological and archaeological journals, from which the 'Berlin method' ultimately emerged victorious. Nevertheless, some scholars refused to accept the 'new' method, and some of the old approaches were still to be found down to the 1930s, particularly in the works of French Egyptologists and in the writings of the British scholar Wallis Budge.

The other legacy of the Berlin school is the greatest of all hieroglyphic dictionaries, the *Wörterbuch der ägyptischen Sprache* ('Dictionary of the Egyptian Language'), begun in 1897 and edited by Erman and Hermann Grapow (1885–1967). The latter was yet another student of Erman and Steindorff, upon whom almost all the work gradually devolved after World War I. Comprising 11 folio volumes, the material was compiled by a commission on which many of the leading Egyptologists of the day served. As with most such enterprises, the words and their references were collected on slips of paper, known as '*Zettel*', and aimed to include all known inscriptions and manuscripts. In the end, over 1,500,000 slips were compiled. The published text was handwritten and lithographed, six volumes being written out by the Danish Egyptologist, Wolja Erichsen (1890–1966). The *Wörterbuch* remains the fundamental reference work of its kind, although supplemented by various one-volume dictionaries, the most widely used one into the English language being *A Concise Dictionary of Middle Egyptian* (1962), by Raymond Faulkner (1894–1982) of University College London.

One of those who accepted many of the Berlin findings was Francis Llewellyn Griffith (1862–1934), the first great British philologist since the death of Birch. As the first Professor of Egyptology at Oxford University he laid the foundations for that institution's own 'school', of whom the key figures were Sir Alan Gardiner (1879–1963) and Battiscombe Gunn (1883–1950). Gardiner had studied under Erman, and did a vast amount of work on the translation and publication of texts, testing out the syntax lying behind them while doing so. A major fruit of this work is his *Egyptian Grammar*, first published in 1927, and still in print three-quarters of a century later. Intended as a teaching tool, the vast majority of today's English speaking Egyptologists first learned their hieroglyphs from it and, although new teaching grammars are now appearing, modern students are still experiencing its 31 lessons.

Gunn, Griffith's successor in the Oxford Chair, published relatively little, a situation to which his extremely high standards contributed much. Nevertheless, his *Studies in the Egyptian Syntax* (1924) broke new ground in the study

Right: A column from Samuel Birch's dictionary, published in 1867. It was the first to use a hieroglyphic font, made especially for his work, and was the first complete Egyptian dictionary to be issued, and listed some 9,270 words.

ME

mâkhi. Balance 8 8. c B. M.

makh i t Balance P 8 127; L. T 125. 9

mâkhà Go E R 6655

mâkhà Balance 8 S. c B M.

mâkhà Balance P. Br , L. T 1 16.

mâkhà. Ba lance P Br. 217, L. T 1. 1

mâkha. Balance Ch 1 d M. d'Or p. 34.

mâkhà. Strangle. 8 P cxi. 17.

mâkhâu. Despoil, strangle, kidnap. Goodwin, R. A 1861, p. 133.

mâkhâi. Balance G. 75

mâkhen. Vessel, boat. L. T. xxxviii. 106. 3

mâsh. Archer E S 866

mâshà. Walk. D. O. xiii. 1.

mâsht. Battle, slaughter L. D. iv. 90. a.

mâa. Come (?). M. d. C xxi. hor. 2.

mâti. Neck. D. 140.

mâshau. (Uncer- tain.) S. P. cliv. 7.

mefka. Copper. D. 140.

mehbi (?). Humble. M. ccxx. See *hbi.*

I. Alphabet phonétique général

II. Signes devenus phonétiques au commencement de certains groupes.

of the verb, and compressed a vast amount of material into a compact form. Another key British figure was Walter Crum (1865–1944), a Berlin-trained Copticist, assessed as the equal of only Steindorff in modern studies of the last phase of the Egyptian language. His greatest monument is his *Coptic Dictionary* (1929–39), a 1,000-page tome that was published in spite of the author having to abandon many of his materials in Vienna, when caught there by the outbreak of World War I.

MODERN TIMES

The work of the Berlin School and its immediate successors brought Egyptian philological studies to a level at which they remained until after World War II. It was then that the work of Hans Jakob Polotsky (1905–91) came under consideration. Yet another product of Berlin, as well as Göttingen, Polotsky's work on aspects of the Coptic and Egyptian syntax led to a revolutionary reconsideration of key aspects of the underlying structure of the language.

His work has been a point of departure for many of the more recent scholars of the language, concerned not so much with the words and grammar, but with the fundamentals of *why* meanings are as they are, rather than simply *what* a given passage means. Some of Polotsky's conclusions, such as the nature of Egyptian verbal forms, are now being challenged by such scholars as Mark Collier of the University of Liverpool, but his standing is without question.

The ongoing debate on this and many other issues is an indication both of the health of Egyptian philology as a subject, and the fact that, much as we now know about the ancient language of Egypt, that knowledge is still incomplete. As new texts are discovered, areas of uncertainty can be resolved, but it is certain that some obscure texts will remain so, particularly those dealing with religious concepts that may have been somewhat opaque to the majority of the ancients themselves! As well as this refinement of our knowledge of the mature language, important research is revealing evidence for the very earliest years of the hieroglyphic script's life. While the 'mystery' of the

Above: *Francis Llewellyn Griffith (1862–1934), the first Professor of Egyptology at Oxford University. For years Britain's foremost Egyptian philologist, he did much important work in publishing texts.*

In addition, he performed the feat of deciphering the Sudanese Meroitic script, although the actual language written still remains largely obscure. Meroitic is written in a script ultimately derived from hieroglyphs, but is unrelated linguistically to ancient Egyptian.

---

107 — **ḥm**

ḥnw — belegt seit M.R. (Gr. nicht belegt). Kopt. ϨΝΑΑΥ, ϨΝΟ.

I. Topf für Flüssiges 1, für Korn 2, zum Kochen 3 u. dgl; aus Stein 4, Ton 5, Metall 6. Oft im Plural als allgemeine Bez. für Gefässe 7.

auch in Verbindungen wie:
Nä. 8.
D.18 9.
die Gefässe für den Schenktisch 10.

II. Sachen, Hausrat u. ä. 11.

ḥnwt — belegt seit Pyr. Herrin, Herrscherin.

A. mit folg. Genetiv: Gebieterin über ····
Gewöhnlich mit direktem Genetiv; seit M.R. auch mit nt des Genetivs, aber selten und ungewöhnlich 12.

Herrin von ····, Gebieterin über ····

I. Personen (Götter 13, Göttinnen 14, Menschen 15).

II. eines Landes 16, einer Stadt 17; insbesondere:
Herrin des Landes
a) Seit M.R. von der Königin 18.
b) Seit D.18 auch von Göttinnen 19.

Herrin der beiden Länder
a) Seit D.18 als Titel der Königin 20, auch selbständig wie ein Wort für Königin gebraucht 21.
b) Seit M.R. sehr oft von einer Göttin 22.

Left: *A page from the great Berlin Wörterbuch, showing its inclusion of meanings, together with variant writings. It was the culmination of Egyptian lexicography.*

THE TANIS STELA

On 15th April 1866, four researchers – Carl Lepsius, Maximilian Weidenbach, Leo Reinisch and Robert Roessler – were visiting the site of ancient Tanis when they stumbled across the corner of a stone projecting from the debris near some fallen obelisks. This had been spotted earlier, but ignored, by an engineer working on the nearby Suez Canal. It was a stela inscribed with a decree containing almost perfect hieroglyphic and greek versions of the same text. It was not until two years after its discovery that Heinrich Brugsch realized that some 'scratches' on the left-hand edge of the stela were actually the demotic version of the text! The Tanis Decree offered confirmation of the theories put forward on the basis of the Rosetta Stone.

FALLEN OBELISKS AT SAN EL-HAGAR, ANCIENT TANIS   THE FACE OF THE TANIS DECREE

hieroglyphs is no more, there will long be material to keep researchers occupied just as intensively as were the founding fathers of hiero-glyphic studies.

Knowledge of the ancient script is also now more widespread than at any time since the Greco-Roman times. Universities all over the world teach the language, while adult education classes in the subject remain extremely popular. As recently as 1998, a self-teaching guide (Collier and Manley's *How to Read Egyptian Hieroglyphs*) became an unexpected best-seller in the United Kingdom, an eloquent testimony to the attractions of an Egyptian culture that has been dead for nearly two millennia.

The study of hieroglyphs and the language they enshrine has moved from the first fumbling attempts to isolate the significance of individual signs, to the situation today where the minutiae of the language are being investigated to the same degree as any other language. Ancient Egyptian texts are no longer 'deciphered' – they are simply 'read', but this position has only been reached as the result of the labours of many individuals over nearly four centuries. Without such scholars as Kircher, Young, Champollion, de Rougé and Erman, the hieroglyphs might still hold their mystery.

Opposite: King Sethy I before the god Anubis, in the king's temple at Abydos.

Left: Sir Alan Gardiner whose Egyptian Grammar was for over 50 years the text book most commonly used by students of ancient Egyptian.

DYNASTIES AND CHRONOLOGIES

ROYAL NAMES ARE TO BE FOUND on a wide variety of ancient Egyptian monuments, from tombs and temples to obelisks. As we have seen, a monarch had up to five 'great names', but they were seldom all found used together. While the preferred name(s) varied with time, it is the cartouche-names – the nomen and prenomen – which are most frequently seen.

While the spellings seen in them were fairly standard down to the New Kingdom, from the Nineteenth Dynasty onwards, there was an increasing variety of ways in which a given king's name could be written. At worst, there can be 20 or more ways of writing a given cartouche, although normally there are only two or three regularly found variants. In some cases this reflected the

fact that a given king used a number of different epithets to add to his basic names (*see pages 150–1*). In other cases, it was simply that a range of spellings or arrangements of signs were used to write the same name.

The latter often explains the differences between cartouches when written vertically, as against horizontally. The Egyptian scribe was usually keen to ensure that the most aesthetic arrangement of signs was used, even if this meant placing them out of their logical order. Thus it is frequently almost impossible to decipher such a royal name from first principles, without fairly extensive background knowledge.

In the following tables, the most common or characteristic forms are given, although it should be noted that in the Roman Period the variety of spellings increases to such an extent that it is difficult to pin down a single writing. Readers interested in a comprehensive listing of known royal names should consult the *Handbuch der ägyptische Königsnamen* (*The Handbook of Egyptian King-Names*), von Beckerath, 1984/1999.

THE HIEROGLYPHIC NAMES OF THE KINGS OF EGYPT

The lists below give the hieroglyphic forms of the principal names of some of the more important kings. Some rulers used a wide variety of spellings; this list attempts to give the most characteristic or straightforward version.

DYNASTY I

Aha · Djer · Djet · Den · Adjib · Semerkhet · Qaa

DYNASTY II

Hotepsekhemwy · Reneb · Ninetjer · Sened · Peribsen · Khasekhemwy

DYNASTY III

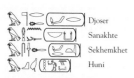

Djoser · Sanakhte · Sekhemkhet · Huni

DYNASTY IV

Seneferu · Khufu · Djedefre · Khaefre · Menkaure · Shepseskaf

DYNASTY V

Userkaf · Sahure · Neferirkare · Niuserre · Isesi · Unas

DYNASTY VI

Teti · Pepy I · Merenre · Pepy II

DYNASTY XI

Inyotef II · Montjuhotpe II · Montjuhotpe III

DYNASTY XII

Amenemhat I · Senwosret I · Amenemhat II · Senwosret II · Senwosret III · Amenemhat III · Amenemhat IV · Sobkneferu

DYNASTY XIII

Sobkhotpe I · Amenemhat V · Qemau · Amenemhat VI · Sinedjhiryotef

Sobkhotpe II · Hor · Amenemhat VII · Wegaf · Khendjer · Imyromesho · Inyotef IV · Seth (y) · Sobkhotpe III · Neferhotpe I · Sobkhotpe IV · Sobkhotpe V · Sobkhotpe VI · Iaib · Iy

DYNASTY XV

Khyan · Apopi

DYNASTY XVI

Djehuty · Nebiriau I

DYNASTY XVII

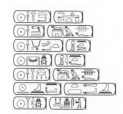

Rahotpe · Sobkemsaf I · Inyotef V · Inyotef VI · Sobkemsaf II · Taa II · Kamose

DYNASTY XVIII

Ahmose · Amenhotep I · Thutmose I · Thutmose II · Thutmose III · Hatshepsut · Amenhotep II · Thutmose IV · Amenhotep III · Akhenaten · Neferneferuaten · Tutankhamun · Ay · Horemheb

DYNASTY XIX

	Rameses I
	Sethy I
	Rameses II
	Merenptah
	Sethy II
	Amenmesse
	Siptah
	Tawosret

DYNASTY XX

	Sethnakhte
	Rameses III
	Rameses IV
	Rameses V Amenhirkopshef I
	Rameses VI Amenhirkopshef II
	Rameses VII Itamun
	Rameses VIII Sethhirkopshef
	Rameses IX Khaemwaset I
	Rameses X Amenhirkopshef III
	Rameses XI Khaemwaset II

DYNASTY XXI

	Nesibanebdjed
	Pinudjem I
	Pasebkhanu I
	Amenemopet
	Osorkon the Elder
	Siamun
	Pasebkhanu II

DYNASTY XXII

	Shoshenq I
	Osorkon I
	Takelot I
	Osorkon II
	Shoshenq III
	Shoshenq IV
	Pimay
	Shoshenq V
	Pedubast II
	Osorkon IV

DYNASTY XXIII

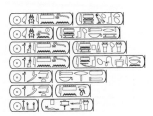

	Harsiese
	Takelot II
	Pedubast I
	Osorkon III
	Takelot III
	Rudamun
	Peftjauawybast

DYNASTY XXIV

	Tefnakhte
	Bakenrenef

DYNASTY XXV

	Pi(ankh)y
	Shabaka
	Shabataka
	Taharqa
	Tanutamun

DYNASTY XXVI

	Psametik I
	Nekau II
	Psametik II
	Wahibre
	Ahmose II
	Psametik III

DYNASTY XXVII

	Kambyses
	Darios I
	Xerxes I
	Artaxerxes I

DYNASTY XXVIII

	Amenirdis

DYNASTY XXIX

	Nayfarud I
	Pashhermut
	Hakar

DYNASTY XXX

	Nakhtnebef
	Djedhor
	Nakhthorheb

DYNASTY OF MACEDONIA

	Alexander III
	Philippos Arrhidaeos
	Alexander IV

DYNASTY OF PTOLEMY

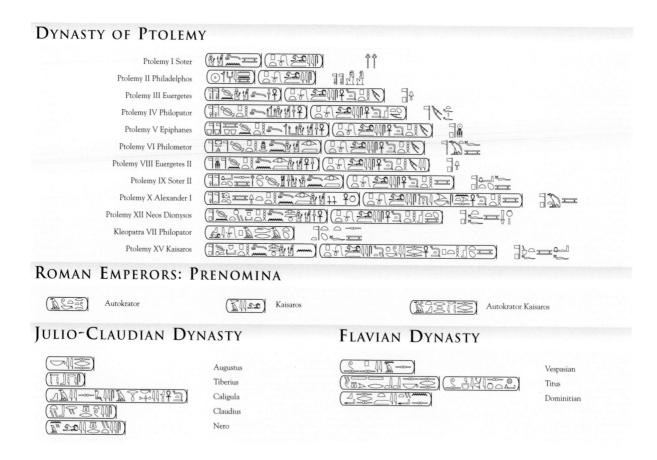

Ptolemy I Soter	
Ptolemy II Philadelphos	
Ptolemy III Euergetes	
Ptolemy IV Philopator	
Ptolemy V Epiphanes	
Ptolemy VI Philometor	
Ptolemy VIII Euergetes II	
Ptolemy IX Soter II	
Ptolemy X Alexander I	
Ptolemy XII Neos Dionysos	
Kleopatra VII Philopator	
Ptolemy XV Kaisaros	

ROMAN EMPERORS: PRENOMINA

Autokrator   Kaisaros   Autokrator Kaisaros

JULIO-CLAUDIAN DYNASTY

Augustus
Tiberius
Caligula
Claudius
Nero

FLAVIAN DYNASTY

Vespasian
Titus
Dominitian

CHRONOLOGY AND THE KINGS OF ANCIENT EGYPT

A Note on Egyptian Chronology

The scheme used by modern scholars for structuring the chronology of historic ancient Egypt is based upon one drawn up by the Egyptian priest, Manetho, around 300 BC. He divided the succession of kings into a series of numbered 'dynasties', corresponding to our idea of royal 'houses' (e.g. Plantagenet, Windsor, Bourbon, Hapsburg, Hohenzollern). These broadly fit in with our knowledge of changes in the ruling family, but in some cases the reason for a shift is unclear.

Historians of ancient Egypt have refined this structure by grouping dynasties into 'Kingdoms' and 'Periods', during which constant socio-political themes can be identified.

Ancient dating was by means of regnal years, rather than the kind of 'era' dating used today (e.g. BC, AD and AH). Thus, absolute dates, in terms of years BC, have to be established through various indirect methods. Some reigns can be fixed by relation to events linked to better-dated cultures, while others can be placed by reference to mentions of various astronomical phenomena. These allow other reigns' extent to be calculated by dead-reckoning. Nevertheless, there remain many areas of uncertainty and, while dating is solid back to 663 BC, margins of error before then may run in excess of century.

Another area of uncertainty is caused by the fact that a number of kings were crowned in advance of their fathers' deaths, to serve as their co-regents; in some cases they died before the elder king. In most, but not all cases, the younger king employed his own regnal years in parallel with those of the senior monarch. During the Middle Kingdom we have a few double-dates, which allow us to work out how the two dating systems relate to one another. However, the majority of co-regencies lack such guides, and in at least one case debate still rages over whether a co-regency lasted one or twelve years. As much of Egyptian chronology is based on the counting back of known regnal years from a fixed point, such uncertainties magnify the existing problems.

NB. Parentheses indicate co-ruler only

PREDYNASTIC PERIOD

Badarian Culture 5000–4000 BC
Naqada I (Amratian) Culture 4000–3500 BC
Naqada II (Gerzian) Culture 3500–3150 BC

PROTODYNASTIC PERIOD

Naqada III Culture 3150–3000 BC

HORUS OR THRONE NAME	PERSONAL NAME	CONJECTURAL DATES (YRS BC)	REGNAL YEARS	LOCATION OF TOMB	TOMB DESIGNATION
ARCHAIC (OR EARLY DYNASTIC) PERIOD					
Dynasty I					
Horus Narmer		3050–		Umm el-Qaab	B17/18
Horus Aha		:		Umm el-Qaab	B10/15/19
Horus Djer	Itit	:		Umm el-Qaab	O
Horus Djet	Iti	:		Umm el-Qaab	Z
Horus Den	Semti	:		Umm el-Qaab	T
Horus Adjib	Merpibia	:		Umm el-Qaab	X
Horus Semerkhet	Irinetjer	:		Umm el-Qaab	U
Horus Qaa	Qebh	–2813		Umm el-Qaab	Q
Dynasty II					
Horus Hotepsekhemwy	Baunetjer	2813–		Saqqara	A
Horus Nebre	Kakau	:		?Saqqara	
Horus Ninetjer	Ninetjer	:		Saqqara	B
?	Weneg	:		?	
?	Sened	:		?Saqqara	
Horus Sekhemib/ Seth Peribsen	Peribsen	:		Umm el-Qaab	P
?	Neferkare	–2709			
?	Neferkasokar	2709–2701	8		
?	?	2701–2690	11		
Horus and Seth Khasekhemwy	Nebwyhetepimyef	2690–2663	27	Umm el-Qaab	V
OLD KINGDOM					
Dynasty III					
Horus Netjerkhet	Djoser	2663–2643	19	Saqqara	L.XXXII; Step Pyramid
Horus Sanakht	Nebka	2643–2633	9	?Abu Rowash	El-Deir
Horus Sekhemkhet	Djoser-ti	2633–2626	6	Saqqara	Unfinished Pyramid
Horus Khaba	Teti?	2626–2621	6	Zaiwiyet el-Aryan	L.XIV; Layer Pyramid
Horus Qahedjet?	Huni	2621–2597	24	?Abu Rowash	L.I; Brick Pyramid
Dynasty IV					
Horus Nebmaet	Seneferu	2597–2547	50	Dahshur	L.XLI; Red Pyramid
Horus Medjedu	Khufu	2547–2524	23	Giza	L.IV; Great Pyramid
Horus Kheper	Djedefre	2524–2516	8	Abu Rowash	L.II
?	Seth?ka	2516–2515		Zawiyet el-Aryan	L.XIII; Unfinished Pyramid
Horus Userib	Khaefre	2515–2493	23	Giza	L.VIII; Second Pyramid
Horus Kakhet	Menkaure	2493–2475	18	Giza	L.IX; Third Pyramid
Horus Shepseskhet	Shepseskaf	2475–2471	4	Saqqara-South	L.XLIII; Mastabat Faraun
Dynasty V					
Horus Irimaet	Userkaf	2471–2464	7	Saqqara	L.XXXI
Horus Nebkhau	Sahure	2464–2452	12	Abusir	L.XLVIII
Neferirkare	Kakai	2452–2442	10	Abusir	L.XXI
Shepseskare	Isi	2442–2435	7	Abusir	–
Horus Neferkhau	Neferefre	2435–2432	3	Abusir	L.XXVI; Unfinished Pyramid
Niuserre	Ini	2432–2421	11	Abusir	L.XX
Menkauhor	Ikauhor	2421–2413	8	Saqqara	L.XXIX
Djedkare	Isesi	2413–2385	28	Saqqara-South	L.XXXVII
Horus Wadjtawy	Unas	2385–2355	30		
Dynasty VI					
Horus Seheteptawy	Teti	2355–2343	12	Saqqara	L.XXX
Nefersahor/Meryre	Pepy I	2343–2297	46	Saqqara-South	L.XXXVI
Merenre	Nemtyemsaf I	2297–2290	7	Saqqara-South	L.XXXIX
Neferkare	Pepy II	2290–2196	94	Saqqara-South	L.XLI
Merenre?	Nemtyemsaf II	2196–2195	1		

HORUS OR THRONE NAME	PERSONAL NAME	CONJECTURAL DATES	REGNAL YEARS	LOCATION OF TOMB	TOMB DESIGNATION
FIRST INTERMEDIATE PERIOD					
Dynasty VII/VIII					
Netjerkare	?	2195–			
Menkare?	Nitokris	:			
Neferkare	?	:			
Neferkare	Neby	:			
Djedkare	Shemay	:			
Neferkare	Khendu	:			
Merenhor	?	:			
Nikare	?	:			
Neferkare	Tereru	:			
Neferkahor	?	:			
Neferkare	Pepysonbe	:			
Neferkamin	Anu	:			
Qakare	Ibi	:	4	Saqqara-South	L.XL
Wadjkare	?	:			
Neferkauhor	Khuihapy	:			
Neferirkare	?	–2160			
Dynasties IX/X					
Meryibre	Akhtoy I	2160–			
Neferkare	?	:			
Wahkare	Akhtoy II	:			
?	Senenen ...	:			
Neferkare	Akhtoy III	:			
Mery...	Akhtoy IV	:			
(Various)	(Various)	:			
?	Meryhathor	:			
Nebkaure	Akhtoy V	:			
Merykare	?	:		?Saqqara	
?	?	–2040			
Dynasty XIa					
Horus Tepya	Montjuhotpe I	2160–			
Horus Sehertawy	Inyotef I	–2123		El-Tarif	Saff el-Dawaba
Horus Wahankh	Inyotef II	2123–2074	49	El-Tarif	Saff el-Qisasiya
Horus Nakhtnebtepnefer	Inyotef III	2074–2066	8	El-Tarif	Saff el-Baqar
MIDDLE KINGDOM					
Dynasty XIb					
Nebhepetre	Montjuhotpe II	2066–2014	52	Deir el-Bahari	XIth Dynasty Temple
Sankhkare	Montjuhotpe III	2014–2001	13	?Sheikh Abd el-Qurna West	TT280
Nebtawyre	Montjuhotpe IV	2001–1994	7		
Dynasty XII					
Sehetepibre	Amenemhat I	1994–1964	30	Lisht	L.LX
Kheperkare	Senwosret I	1974–1929	45	Lisht	L.LXI
Nubkhaure	Amenemhat II	1932–1896	36	Dahshur	L.LI; White Pyramid
Khakheperre	Senwosret II	1900–1880	20	Lahun	L.LXVI
Khakaure	Senwosret III	1881–1840	41	Dahshur	L.XLVII
Nimaetre	Amenemhat III	1842–1794	48	Hawara	L.LXVII; Black Pyramid
Maekherure	Amenemhat IV	1798–1785	13	?Dahshur	L.LIV
Sobkkare	Sobkneferu	1785–1781	4	?Dahshur	L.LIV
Dynasty XIII					
Sekhemre–khutawi	Sobkhotpe I	1781–	3		
Sekhemkare	Sonbef	:	3		
Nerikare	?	:	1		
Sekhemkare	Amenemhat V	:	3	?Dahshurq	L.LIV
Sehetepibre	Qemau	:	2	Dahshur-South	–
Sankhibre	Amenemhat VI	:		?Dahshur	L.LIV
Smenkare	Nebnuni	:			
?	Iufeni	:			
Hotepibre	Sihornedjhiryotef	:			
Swadjkare	?	:			
Nedjemibre	?	:			
Khaankhre	Sobkhotpe II	:			
Sekhemre-khutawi	Renisonbe	:			
Auibre	Hor	:		Dahshur	L.LVIII/1
Sedjefakare	Amenemhat VII	:			
Khutawire	Wegaf	:			
Userkare/ Nikhanimaetre	Khendjer			Saqqara-South	L.XLIV

HORUS OR THRONE NAME	PERSONAL NAME	CONJECTURAL DATES	REGNAL YEARS	LOCATION OF TOMB	TOMB DESIGNATION
Smenkhkare	Imyromesha	:			
Sehotepkare	Inyotef IV	:			
Meryibre	Seth(y)	:			
Sekhemre-swadjtawi	Sobkhotpe III	:	3		
Khasekhemre	Neferhotpe I	:	11		
Menwadjre	Sihathor	:			
Khaneferre	Sobkhotpe IV	:			
Merhotepre	Sobkhotpe V	:			
Khahetepre	Sobkhotpe VI	:	4		
Wahibre	Iaib	:	10		
Merneferre	Iy	:	23		
Merhetepre	Ini	:	2		
Sankhenre	Sewadjtu	:			
Mersekhemre	Ined	:			
Sewadjkare	Hori	:			
Merkaure	Sobkhotpe VII	:			
Mershepsesre	Ini	:			
Mersekhemre	Neferhotpe II	:			
[5 unknown kings]		:			
Mer[...]re	?	:			
Merkheperre	?	:			
Merkare	?	:			
?		:			
Sewadjare	Montjuhotpe V	:			
[...]mesre	?	:			
[...]maetre	Ibi	:			
[...]webenre	Hor[..]	:			
Se[...]kare	?	:			
Seheqaenre	Sankhptahi	:			
Sekhaenre	[...]s	:			
Sewahenre	Senebmiu	−1650			

SECOND INTERMEDIATE PERIOD

Dynasty XV

	Semqen?	1650–			
˴	Sakirhar	:			
Seuserenre	Khyan	:			
Nebkhepeshre/ Aqenenre/Auserre	Apopi	1585–1545	40		
?	Khamudy	1545–1535			

Dynasty XVI

?	?	1650–			
Sekhemre-smentawi	Djehuty	:			
Sekhemre-sewosertawi	Sobkhotpe VIII	:			
Sekhemre-seankhtawi	Neferhotpe III	:			
Sankhenre	Montjuhotepi	:			
Swadjenre	Nebiriau I	:			
Neferkare?	Nebiriau II	:			
Semenre	?	:			
Seuserenre	Bebiankh	:			
Sekhemreshedwaset	?	:			
Djedhotepre	Dedumose I	:			
Djedneferre	Dedumose II	:			
Djedankhre	Montjuemsaf	:			
Merankhre	Montjuhotpe VI	:			
Seneferibre	Senwosret IV	1590			

Dynasty XVII

Sekhemre-wahkhau	Rehotpe	1585–			
Sekhemre-shedtawi	Sobkemsaf I	:			
Sekhemre-wepmaet	Inyotef V	:		Dira Abu'l-Naga	
Nubkheperre	Inyotef VI	:		Dira Abu'l-Naga	
Sekhemre-heruhirmaet	Inyotef VII	:			
Sekhemre-wadjkhau	Sobkemsaf II	:		Dira Abu'l-Naga	
Senakhtenre	Taa I	1558–		Dira Abu'l-Naga	
Seqenenre	Taa II	1558–1553	5	Dira Abu'l-Naga	
Wadjkheperre	Kamose	1553–1549	4	Dira Abu'l-Naga	

HORUS OR THRONE NAME	PERSONAL NAME	CONJECTURAL DATES	REGNAL YEARS	LOCATION OF TOMB	TOMB DESIGNATION
NEW KINGDOM					
Dynasty XVIII					
Nebpehtire	Ahmose I	1549–1524	25	Abydos	
Djeserkare	Amenhotep I	1524–1503	21	?Dira Abu'l-Naga	K93.11
Akheperkare	Thutmose I	1503–1491	12	Valley of Kings	KV20 & KV38
Akheperenre	Thutmose II	1491–1479	12	Valley of Kings	KV42
Menkheper(en)re	Thutmose III	1479–1424	54	Valley of Kings	KV34
(Maetkare	Hatshepsut	1472–1457		Valley of Kings	KV20
Akheperure	Amenhotep II	1424–1398	26	Valley of Kings	KV35
Menkheperure	Thutmose IV	1398–1388	10	Valley of Kings	KV43
Nebmaetre	Amenhotep III	1388–1348	40	Valley of Kings	WV22
Neferkheperure-waenre	Amenhotep IV/ Akhenaten	1360–1343	17	Tell el-Amarna	TA26
Ankhkheperure	Smenkhkare	1346		Valley of Kings	KV55
Ankhkheperure-merwaenre	Neferneferuaten	1346–1343	3		
Nebkheperre	Tutankhamun	1343–1333	10	Valley of Kings	KV62
Kheperkheperure	Ay	1333–1328	5	Valley of Kings	WV23
Djeserkheperure-setpenre	Horemheb	1328–1298	30	Valley of Kings	KV57
Dynasty XIX					
Menpehtire	Rameses I	1298–1296	2	Valley of Kings	KV16
Menmaetre	Sethy I	1296–1279	17	Valley of Kings	KV17
Usermaetre-setpenre	Rameses II	1279–1212	67	Valley of Kings	KV7
Banenre	Merenptah	1212–1201	11	Valley of Kings	KV8
Userkheperure	Sethy II	1201–1195	6	Valley of Kings	KV15
(Menmire-setpenre	Amenmesse	1200–1196	4)	Valley of Kings	KV10
Sekhaenre/Akheperre	Siptah	1195–1189	6	Valley of Kings	KV47
Sitre-merenamun	Tawosret	1189–1187	2	Valley of Kings	KV14
Dynasty XX					
Userkhaure	Sethnakhte	1187–1185	2	Valley of Kings	KV14
Usermaetre-meryamun	Rameses III	1185–1153	32	Valley of Kings	KV11
User/Heqamaetre-setpenamun	Rameses IV	1153–1146	7	Valley of Kings	KV2
Usermaetre-sekheperenre	Rameses V Amenhirkopshef I	1146–1141	5	Valley of Kings	KV9
Nebmaetre-meryamun	Rameses VI Amenhirkopshef II	1141–1133	8	Valley of Kings	KV9
Usermaetre-setpenre-meryamun	Rameses VII Itamun	1133–1125	8	Valley of Kings	KV1
Usermaetre-akhenamun	Rameses VIII Sethhirkopshef	1125–1123	2		
Neferkare-setpenre	Rameses IX Khaemwaset I	1123–1104	19	Valley of Kings	KV6
Khepermaetre-setpenre	Rameses X Amenhirkopshef III	1104–1094	10	Valley of Kings	KV18
Menmaetre-setpenptah	Rameses XI Khaemwaset II	1094–1064	30	Valley of Kings	KV4
(Hemnetjertepyenamun	Hrihor	1075–1069	6)		
THIRD INTERMEDIATE PERIOD					
Dynasty XXI					
Hedjkheperre-setpenre	Nesibanebdjed	1064–1038	26	?Tanis	NRT-I
Neferkare-heqawaset	Amenemnesu	1038–1034	4		
(Kheperkhare-setpenamun	Pinudjem I	1049–1026	23)		
Akheperre-setpenamun	Pasebkhanu I	1034–981	53	Tanis	NRT-III
Usermaetre-setpenamun	Amenemopet	984–974	10	Tanis	NRT-IV
Akheperre-setpenre	Osorkon the Elder	974–968	6		
Netjerkheperre-meryamun	Siamun	968–948	20	Tanis	NRT-III
(Tyetkheperure-setpenre	Pasebkhanu II	945–940)		Tanis	NRT-III
Dynasty XXII					
Hedjkheperre-setpenre	Shoshenq I	948–927	21		
Sekhemkheperre-setpenre	Osorkon I	927–892	35	Tanis	NRT-I
(Heqakheperre-setpenre	Shoshenq II	895–895)			
Hedjkheprre-setpenre	Takelot I	892–877	15		
Usermaetre-setpenamun	Osorkon II	877–838	39		
Usermaetre-setpenre	Shoshenq III	838–798	40	Tanis	NRT-V
Hedjkheperre-setpenre	Shoshenq IV	798–786	12	Tanis	NRT-V

HORUS OR THRONE NAME	PERSONAL NAME	CONJECTURAL DATES	REGNAL YEARS	LOCATION OF TOMB	TOMB DESIGNATION
Usermaetre-setpenamun	Pimay	786–780	6	Tanis	NRT-II
Akheperre	Shoshenq V	780–743	37	Tanis	NRT-I
Sehetepibenre	Pedubast II	743–733	10		
Akheperre-setpenamun	Osorkon IV	733–715	18		
Dynasty XXIII					
Hedjkheperre-setpenamun	Harsiese	867–857	10	Medinet Habu	MH1
Hedjkheperre-setpenre	Takelot II	841–815	26		
Usermaetre-setpenamun	Pedubast I	830–799	30		
(?	Iuput I	815–813)			
Usermaetre-setpenamun	Osorkon III	799–769	30		
Usermaetre	Takelot III	774–759	15		
Usermaetre-setpenamun	Rudamun	759–739	20		
	Iny	739–734	5		
Neferkare	Peftjauawybast	734–724	10		
Dynasty XXIV					
Shepsesre	Tefnakhte	731–723	8		
Wahkare	Bakenrenef	723–717	6		
Dynasty XXV					
Seneferre	Pi(ankh)y	752–717	35	El-Kurru	Ku17
Neferkare	Shabaka	717–703	14	El-Kurru	Ku15
Djedkare	Shabataka	703–690	13	El-Kurru	Ku18
Khunefertumre	Taharqa	690–664	26	Nuri	Nu1
Bakare	Tanutamun	664–656	8	El-Kurru	Ku16

SAITE PERIOD

				Sais (according to Herodotus)	
Dynasty XXVI					
Wahibre	Psametik I	664–610	54		
Wehemibre	Nekau II	610–595	15		
Neferibre	Psametik II	595–589	6		
Haaibre	Wahibre	589–570	19		
Khnemibre	Ahmose II	570–526	44		
Ankhka(en)re	Psametik III	526–525	1		

LATE PERIOD

Dynasty XXVII					
Mesutire	Kambyses (Kembitjet)	525–522	3	?	
Setutre	Darios I (Intiryosh)	521–486	35	Nashq-i Rastam, Iran	
?	Xerxes I (Khashyarsha)	486–465	21	Nashq-i Rastam, Iran	
?	Artaxerxes I (Artakheshes)	465–424	41	Nashq-i Rastam, Iran	
?	Xerxes II	424	1	Nashq-i Rastam, Iran	
?	Darios II	423–405	18	Nashq-i Rastam, Iran	
Dynasty XXVIII					
?	Amenirdis	404–399	5		
Dynasty XXIX					
Baenre-merynetjeru	Nayfarud I	399–393	6	Mendes	
Userre-setpenptah	Pashermut	393	1		
Khnemmaetre	Hakar	393–380	13		
?	Nayfarud II	380	1		
Dynasty XXX					
Kheperkare	Nakhtnebef	380–362	18		
Irimaetenre	Teos	362–360	2		
Senedjemibre-setpenanhur	Nakhthorheb	360–342	18		
Dynasty XXXI					
	Artaxerxes III Okhos	342–338	5	Perseopolis, Iran	
	Arses	338–336	2	?	
	Darios III	335–332	3		

HORUS OR THRONE NAME	PERSONAL NAME	CONJECTURAL DATES	REGNAL YEARS	LOCATION OF TOMB	TOMB DESIGNATION
HELLENISTIC PERIOD					
Dynasty of Macedonia					
Setpenre-meryamun	Alexander III	332–323	9		
Setepkaenre-meryamun	Philippos Arrhidaeos	323–317	5		
Haaibre	Alexander IV	317–310	7		
Dynasty of Ptolemy					
Setpenre-meryamun	Ptolemy I Soter	310–282	28		
Userka(en)re-meryamun	Ptolemy II Philadelphos	285–246	36		
Iwaennetjerwysenwy-setpenre-sekhemankhen-amun	Ptolemy III Euergetes I	246–222	24		
Iwaennetjerwymenek-hwysetpenptah-userkare-sekhemankhenamun	Ptolemy IV Philopator	222–205	17		
Iwaennetjerwy-merwyyot-setpenptah-userkare-sekhemankhenamun	Ptolemy V Epiphanes	205–180	25		
Iwaennetjerwyperwy-setpenptahkhepri-irimaetamunre	Ptolemy VI Philometor	180–164	16		
Iwaennetjerwyperwy-setpenptah-irimaetre-sekhemankenamun	Ptolemy VIII Euergetes II	170–163	7		
	Ptolemy VI (again)	163–145	18		
?	Ptolemy VII Neos Philopator	145	1		
	Ptolemy VIII (again)	145–116	29		
Iwaennetjermenekhnet-jeretmerymutesnedjet-sepenptah-merymaetre-sekhemankhamun	Ptolemy IX Soter II	116–110	6		
Iwaennetjermenekh-netjeretmenekhsatre-setpenptah-irimaetre-senenankhenamun	Ptolemy X Alexander I	110–109	1		
	Ptolemy IX (again)	109–107	2		
	Ptolemy X (again)	107–88	19		
	Ptolemy IX (again)	88–80	8		
(?	Ptolemy XI	80	1)		
Iwaenpanetjerentine-hem-setpenptah-mery maetenresekhemankh amun	Ptolemy XII Neos Dionysos	80–58	22		
	Ptolemy XII (again)	55–51	4		
	Kleopatra VII Philopator	51–30	21		
(?	Ptolemy XIII	51–57	4)		
(?	Ptolemy XIV	47–44	3)		
(Iwaenpanetjerentinehem-setpenptah-irimeryre-sekhemankhamun	Ptolemy XV Kaisaros	41–30	11)		

Alternate forms of Pharaoh's names

As mentioned in Chapter I, there are various ways of transcribing royal names, both based on the original Egyptian, and using the Greek forms used by Classical authors. Some of the most common equivalences are given below:

Horus Narmer	Menes	Nesibanebdjed	Smendes
Khufu	Kheops	Pasebkhanu	Psusennes
Khaefre	Khephren, Rekhaef	Bakenrenef	Bokkhoris
Menkaure	Mycerinus	Wahibre	Apries
Amenemhat	Ammenemes	Nayfarud	Nepherites
Senwosret	Sesostris, Senusert	Pashermut	Teos
Ahmose	Amosis, Amasis	Hakar	Akhoris
Amenhotep	Amenophis	Nakhtnebef	Nektanebo I
Thutmose	Tuthmosis	Nakhthorheb	Nektanebo II
Sethy	Sethos, Seti		

ROMAN PERIOD	BC 30–395 AD
BYZANTINE PERIOD	395–640
ARAB PERIOD	640–1517
OTTOMAN PERIOD	1517–1805
KHEDEVAL PERIOD	1805–1914
BRITISH PROTECTORATE	1914–1922
MONARCHY	1922–1953
REPUBLIC	1953–

WHERE TO SEE HIEROGLYPHS

Egyptian collections are to be found all around the world. This list gives a selection of some of the more important collections, particularly those rich in inscribed items.

AUSTRIA
VIENNA Kunsthistorisches Museum

BELGIUM
BRUSSELS Musées Royaux d'Art et d'Histoire

CANADA
TORONTO Royal Ontario Museum

DENMARK
COPENHAGEN Nationalmuseet
COPENHAGEN Ny Carlsberg Glyptotek

EGYPT
ALEXANDRIA Greco-Roman Museum
ASWAN Nubian Museum
CAIRO Egyptian Museum
LUXOR Luxor Museum
PORT SAID Port Said Museum

ENGLAND
BIRMINGHAM City Museums and Art Gallery
BOLTON Museum and Art Gallery
BRISTOL City Museum and Art Gallery
CAMBRIDGE Fitzwilliam Museum

THE SECOND PYRAMID AT GIZA

DURHAM Oriental Museum
ETON Myers Collection, Eton College
EXETER Royal Albert Museum
LIVERPOOL Liverpool Museum
LONDON British Museum
LONDON Petrie Museum of Egyptian Archaeology,
  University College
MANCHESTER Manchester Museum
NORWICH Castle Museum
OXFORD Ashmolean Museum
TRURO Royal Cornwall Museum

FRANCE
MARSEILLE Musée d'Archéologie Mediterranéenne
PARIS Musée du Louvre

GERMANY
BERLIN Ägyptisches Museum und Papyrussammlung
HANOVER Kestner-Museum
HEIDELBERG Sammlung des Ägyptologischen Instituts
  der Universität
HILDESHEIM Pelizaeus-Museum
LEIPZIG Ägyptischen Museum der Universität
MUNICH Staatliche Sammlung Ägyptischer Kunst
TUBINGEN Ägyptische Sammlung der Universität

HUNGARY
BUDAPEST Szépmüvészeti Múzeum

IRELAND
DUBLIN National Museum

ITALY
BOLOGNA Museo Civico Archeologico
FLORENCE Museo Egizio
MILAN Civiche Raccolte Archeologiche e
  Numismatiche
PISA Collezioni Egittologiche di Ateneo
TURIN Museo Egizio

NETHERLANDS
AMSTERDAM Allard Pierson Museum
LEIDEN Rijksmuseum van Oedheden

POLAND
WARSAW Museum Narodowe

THE VALLEY OF THE KINGS

RUSSIA
MOSCOW State Pushkin Museum of Fine Arts
ST PETERSBURG Hermitage Museum

SCOTLAND
ABERDEEN Marischel Museum
EDINBURGH Royal Museum
GLASGOW Burrell Collection
GLASGOW Hunterian Museum

SPAIN
BARCELONA Museu Egyipci de Barcleona
MADRID Museo Arqueológico Nacional

SWEDEN
STOCKHOLM Medelhavsmuseet
UPPSALA Victoriamuseet

SWITZERLAND
BASEL Antikenmuseum Basel und Sammlung Ludwig
GENEVA Musée d'art et d'histoire

THUTMOSE III ON THE VII PYLON AT KARNAK

'FECUNDITY FIGURE' IN THE TEMPLE OF RAMESES II AT ABYDOS

UNITED STATES OF AMERICA
ANN ARBOR, MI Kelsey Museum of Ancient and
   Medieval Archaeology
ATLANTA, GA Michael C. Carlos Museum, Emory
   University
BALTIMORE, MD Walters Art Gallery
BOSTON, MA Museum of Fine Arts
BROOKLYN, NY Brooklyn Museum of Art
CHICAGO, IL Art Institute
CHICAGO, IL Field Museum of Natural History
CHICAGO, IL Oriental Institute Museum
CLEVELAND, OH Cleveland Museum of Art
DETROIT, MI Detroit Institute of Arts
LOS ANGELES, CA County Museum of Art
MEMPHIS, TN Institute of Egyptian Art and
   Archaeology, Memphis University
NEWARK, NJ Newark Museum
NEW HAVEN, CT Peabody Museum, Yale University
NEW YORK, NY Metropolitan Museum of Art
PHILADELPHIA, PA University Museum of Archaeology
   & Anthropology
SAN JOSE, CA Rosicrucian Egyptian Museum

VATICAN
VATICAN CITY Museo Gregoriano Egizio

WALES
SWANSEA Egypt Centre, University of Wales Swansea

GLOSSARY

Amun(-Re) Chief god of Thebes and paramount god of Egypt from the New Kingdom onward.

Anubis God of embalming, represented with a jackal's head.

Apis Sacred bull of Memphis, a form of Ptah.

biliteral Hieroglyphic sign representing combination of two consonants.

Book of the Dead Compilation of texts and images intended to facilitate the movement of the dead person's spirit to the next world.

Books of the Underworld Compositions dating to the New Kingdom that are mainly concerned with the nocturnal journey of the Sun God through the Underworld. They include the Books of the Gates, Amduat and the Earth.

canopic Of or pertaining to the preservation of the viscera removed from the body in the course of embalming.

cartouche Oval enclosure with flat bar at one end, enclosing the king's prenomen and nomen; sometimes used for queens and royal children, and also for gods in the Greco-Roman Period.

coffin A container for a body of a type usually intended to lie within a sarcophagus. It may be rectangular or anthropoid, of stone or wood, but will always have a separate lid and box/trough.

Coffin Texts Set of religious texts originally inscribed on the interior of coffins of the Middle Kingdom.

consonant Letter other than a vowel.

Coptic Final variant of the ancient Egyptian language, written in a script largely composed of greek

letters, with admixture of some demotic, known as coptic.

corbel-roofing Arrangement for spanning a space by setting each successive course of the walls slightly further out than the one below until they meet at the apex.

cursive Writing done without lifting the pen between letters.

demotic Cursive script derived from hieratic, introduced during Dynasty XXV.

Demotic The variant of the ancient Egyptian language written in the demotic script.

determinative Hieroglyphic sign that usually has no phonetic value, but indicates the general meaning of group of signs that precede it.

epithet Word or collection of words that describes or characterizes a noun or a name.

faience Glazed blue vitreous material made from quartz sand, soda and a copper-ore based colourant.

false door A vertical slab of stone carved in imitation of a door, usually bearing texts referring to the provision of offerings. It normally stood in the sanctuary and was the focus of the cult of the deceased. Symbolically, it was the place where the dead and the living came together, through which the dead could

emerge and partake of offerings.

'Golden falcon' name Third name of the royal five-fold titulary, of obscure significance.

Heb-sed The jubilee festival celebrated by the Egyptian king, usually after 30 years on the throne, and then repeated every three years.

hieratic Cursive script derived from hieroglyphs, introduced during the Old Kingdom.

hieroglyph Figure of object standing for sound or word.

Horus name First name of the royal five-fold titulary, written in a serekh and associating the ruler with the falcon-god, Horus.

hypostyle hall Chamber with its room supported by a number of columns.

Late Egyptian The version of the ancient Egyptian language first used for written documents in the New Kingdom.

lexicography The making of dictionaries.

mastaba A tomb-type, common from the Archaic Period onward. The name, mastaba, derives from the Arabic word for mudbrick bench, which the tombs resemble.

Middle Egyptian The version of the ancient Egyptian language in general use during the Middle Kingdom and retained as a literary form, especially for religious texts, until the Roman Period.

mummy Artificially preserved human or animal corpse. The word is derived from the Persian 'mum', meaning wax or bitumen.

natron Combination of sodium carbonate and sodium bicarbonate, used for dessication and purification purposes in mummification. Occurs naturally in the Wadi Natrun, some 65 kilometres north-west of Cairo, as well as in certain other locations.

Nebty name Second name of the royal five-fold titulary, associating the ruler with the two goddesses, Edjo and Nekhbet.

nomen Fifth name of the royal five-fold titulary, written in a cartouche, and often preceded by the title 'son of the sun-god'.

Old Egyptian The version of the ancient Egyptian language used during the Old Kingdom.

Opening of the Mouth Ceremony which served to reanimate the corpse.

ordinal Roman numeral placed after the name of a monarch to distinguish them from earlier bearers of the same name; e.g. George V, George VI.

Osiris God of the Dead and resurrection, brother-husband of Isis, murdered by his brother Seth and who consequently became the first mummy.

papyrus Paper manufactured from the pith of the papyrus plant.

peristyle court Courtyard with a row of columns round its edges.

Pharaoh Biblical version of the Egyptian phrase pr-ʿ3, 'great house'; originally referred to the palace, but from the New Kingdom was used as a title for the king; occasionally found written in a cartouche in the Greco-Roman Period.

philology The science of the study of language.

phonetic Of or representing vocal sound.

prenomen Fourth name of the royal five-fold titulary, written in a cartouche, and preceded by a title that emphasizes the kingships dual aspect.

pronoun Word serving as substitute for a noun.

Pyramid Texts Set of religious texts originally inscribed on the walls of the passages and chambers of the pyramids of the Old Kingdom.

pyramidion Cap-stone of a pyramid, often made of hardstone and bearing inscriptions; some examples may have been gilded.

rock-cut tomb A sepulchre whose chapel is carved out of the living rock, with minimal, if any, built structure.

sarcophagus Rectangular/quasi-rectangular outermost container, intended to hold coffins of a different form or material. It may be composed of stone or wood.

serdab Closed chamber containingstatue(s), normally with a narrow slit or other opening leading into the offering chapel to allow the statue(s) to 'see' out and for incense to drift in.

serekh Rectangular frame with panelled lower part, usually surmounted by an image of the falcon-god Horus, and enclosing the king's Horus-name.

shabti Magical servant figure found in tombs mid-Middle Kingdom onward. From the middle of the Eighteenth Dynasty, large numbers of shabti are to be found in a single burial, ultimately exceeding 400 in certain interments.

step pyramid Pyramid rising in a series of deep steps to the summit, perhaps symbolic of a stairway to heaven.

titulary Combination of titles used by kings and officials.

transliteration The direct conversion of hieroglyphic, hieratic or demotic texts into the roman (western) alphabet.

triliteral Hieroglyphic sign representing combination of three consonants.

true pyramid Pyramid intended to have a uniform, smooth slope to the summit, perhaps representative of the sun's descending rays and a ramp to aid the kings ascension.

uniliteral Hieroglyphic sign representing single consonants.

verb Part of speech expressing action, occurence or being.

vernacular Speech in common use.

ABBREVIATIONS

AJSLL *American Journal of Semitic Languages and Literatures* (Chicago)

ASAE *Annales du Service des Antiquités de l'Égypte* (Cairo)

AS2000 *Abusir and Saqqara in the Year 2000*, ed M. Bárta and J. Krejcí (Prague: Academy of Sciences of the Czech Republic, 2000)

AUC American University in Cairo

BIFAO *Bulletin de l'Institut Français d'Archéologie Orientale du Caire* (Cairo)

BioAnth *Biological Anthropology and the Study of Ancient Egypt* (ed. W.V.Davies and R. Walker) (London: British Museum Press, 1993)

BM British Museum, London.

BMA Brooklyn Museum of Art

BMFA *Bulletin of the Museum of Fine Arts* (Boston)

BMMA *Bulletin of the Metropolitan Museum of Art* (New York)

BMP British Museum Press

BSAA *Bulletin Societé archéologique d'Alexandrie* (Alexandria)

BSAE British School of Archaeology in Egypt

BSFE *Buletin de la Societé Français d'Egyptologie* (Paris)

CdE *Chronique d'Egypte* (Brussels)

CM Egyptian Museum, Cairo

DE *Discussions in Egyptology* (Oxford)

EAE *Encyclopedia of the Archaeology of Ancient Egypt*, ed. by K.A. Bard (London: Routledge, 1999)

EEF/S Egypt Exploration Fund/Society

EgArch *Egyptian Archaeology: Bulletin of the Egypt Exploration Society* (London)

ERA Egyptian Research Account

Études Lauer *Études sur l'Ancien Empire et la nécropole de Saqqâra dédiées à Jean-Phillipe Lauer* (ed. C. Berger and B. Mathieu) (Montpellier: Université Paiul Valéry, 1997)

GI Griffith Institute, Ashmolean Museum, University of Oxford

GM *Göttinger Miszellen* (Göttingen)

Hommages Leclant C. Berger, G. Clerc and N. Grimal (eds.), *Hommages à Jean Leclant*, I (Cairo: IFAO)

IFAO Institut Français d'Archéologie Orientale

ILN *Illustrated London News* (London)

JARCE *Journal of the American Research Center in Egypt* (New York, &c)

JE Journal d'Entrée (CM)

JEA *Journal of Egyptian Archaeology* (London)

JNES *Journal of Near Eastern Studies* (Chicago)

KMT: *A Modern Journal of Ancient Egypt* (San Francisco/Sebastopol)

KV Prefix for tombs in Valley of the Kings

L. Prefix for pyramids numbered by Lepsius

LÄ *Lexikon der Ägyptologie* (Weisbaden)

LG Prefix for tombs at Giza numbered by Lepsius

LS Prefix for tombs at Saqqara numbered by Lepsius

MDAIK *Mitteilungen des Deutschen Archäologischen Instituts, Kairo* (Mainz)

MFA Museum of Fine Arts, Boston

MMA Metropolitan Museum of Art, New York

NRT Prefix for royal tombs at Tanis

OMD Oriental Museum Durham

OMRO *Oudheidkundige*

Mededelingen uit het Rijksmuseum van Oudheden te Leiden (Leiden)

P7ICE *Proceedings of the Seventh International Congress of Egyptologists*, ed. C.J. Eyre (Leuven: Peeters, 1997)

P8ICE *Egyptology at the Dawn of the Twenty-First Century: Proceedings of the Eighth International Congress of Egyptologists, Cairo, 2000*, ed. Z.Hawass & L.P. Brock (Cairo: AUC Press 2001)

RdE *Revue d'Egyptologie* (Leuven)

RMS Royal Museum of Scotland

SAK *Studien zur altägyptschen Kultur* (Hamburg)

SR Special Register (CM)

Stud. Smith A. Leahy and J. Tait (eds.), *Studies on Ancient Egypt in Honour of H.S. Smith* (London: EES, 1999)

TA Prefix for tombs at Tell el-Amarna

TAE B.E. Schafer (ed.), *Temples in Ancient Egypt* (London: I.B. Tauris, 1998)

TR Temporary Register (CM)

TSBA *Transactions of the Society of Biblical Archaeology* (London)

TT Theban Tomb (the numbering system used for important tombs outside the Valley of the Kings and Queens)

UC Petrie Museum, University College London

U. Reed C. Eyre, A. Leahy and L.M. Leahy (eds.), *The Unbroken Reed: Studies in the Culture and Heritage of Ancient Egypt In Honour of A.F. Shore* (London: Egypt Exploration Society, 1994)

VA *Varia Ægyptiaca* (San Antonio, TX)

ZÄS *Zeitschrift für Ägyptische Sprache und Altertumskunde* (Leipzig, Berlin)

FURTHER READING: THE PYRAMIDS

The published literature on the pyramids is massive, and potentially bewildering, in its volume and complexity. Comprehensive lists of primary publications of *all* ancient Egyptian monuments are to be found in Porter and Moss 1933–99 (and continuing), although many volumes are now of course out of date. An indispensable large-scale compilation of technical data and plans concerning the pyramids themselves is provided in Maragioglio and Rinaldi 1964–77 (its text in Italian and English), continued until the end of the Old Kingdom in Labrousse 1996–2000. As far as general treatments are concerned, two long-lived classics are Edwards 1947–85 and Fakhry 1961–72. Each takes a rather different approach, Edwards dealing in detail with only certain pyramids, but going into some depth regarding theoretical issues to do with the pyramid complex. Fakhry's is a more straightforward monument-based work, reflecting its author's status as a distinguished field archaeologist. However, although still key texts, both are now are becoming increasingly out of date, as is Grinsell 1947. Interestingly, both this and Edwards' book were written while their authors were on war service in Egypt. Lehner 1997 and Silotti 1997 include much more recent work, but both have notable omissions, while Silotti dilutes his book with a seemingly random set of Old Kingdom private tombs. Another recent work is Verner 2001, a worthy successor to Edwards' volume, which is particularly good on the significance of the pyramid.

The same author is also responsible for a masterly account of the Abusir cemetery, where he has excavated for many years (Verner 1994). A similar

ABOVE: FUNERARY STELA OF HOR
OPPOSITE: HATSHEPSUT'S OBELISK AT KARNAK

work on Saqqara is provided by Lauer (1976), while substantial volumes focus of the Sudanese pyramids (Dunham 1950, 1955, 1958 and 1963; Dunham and Chapman 1952), but the remaining pyramid necropoleis currently lack equivalents, although a volume on Giza is promised by Hawass, and an elaborate technical study of the Old Kingdom private tombs of Giza was provided by Reisner (1942). Otherwise, one is forced to fall back on the general pyramid books already mentioned, or search out the original excavation reports. These are in a range of languages, and also vary widely in readability: at the positive extreme are the works of Winlock; at the other are numerous other volumes and articles!

Queenly pyramids are generally little treated, receiving only passing mention in most books, apart from Maragioglio and Rinaldi's work, and specific excavation reports. The exception is Janosi 1996, which is a dedicated study of queen's tombs during the Old and Middle Kingdoms. Details of the queens themselves are to be found in Dodson and Hilton 2003.

For royal tombs subsequent to the demise of the pyramid, the New Kingdom sepulchres of the Valley of the Kings have been covered by a range of books, for example Hornung 1990 and Reeves and Wilkinson 1996, but few books also cover later burial places, with the exception of Dodson 2000a.

It is important to note the large number of excavations that are only accessible via journal articles, it being an uncomfortable fact that few archaeological excavations, no matter how well run, are followed up with appropriate publication within a reasonable period. The great exceptions are the works of Petrie, who would generally write up the season on the ship back to Europe, a complete manuscript being handed over to the publishers within weeks. Of course this often led to published conclusions that would have benefited from further digestion of the evidence, but certainly made that evidence available to scholarship in the shortest possible time. In more recent times, the gap between excavation and definitive (or even preliminary!) publication has stretched to years, if not decades. The latest regulations issued by the Supreme Council for Antiquities threaten to deny a new site to any archaeologist who has not yet published his or her previous one: it remains to be seen how effective this may be ….

The history of the study of ancient Egypt has been treated by various works, but key for the early years is Greener 1966. For the earlier Arab explorers, works from the ninth through sixteenth centuries are abstracted in Vyse 1840–42, II: 181–318, with some summarised (not necessarily accurately) in Cottrell 1956. The latter is a most readable account of pyramid exploration up to the 1930s, but lacking in detail, except for early work at Giza. Such detail concerning work at Saqqara is, however, provided in Lauer 1976, as it is for Abusir by Verner (1994). For the pyramid explorers themselves, biographies are given for most in Dawson, Uphill and Bierbrier 1995; some have left memoirs, for example Jéquier 1940, and the posthumous De Morgan 1997.

Ongoing work can be traced through the annual summaries published by Jean Leclant and others in the journal *Orientalia*, and more regularly by Patricia Spencer in *Egyptian Archaeology* and Salima Ikram in *KMT*. The printed and online press also sometimes picks up snippets of Egyptological news, unfortunately often badly transmogrified in the transmission, with names and places mangled or wholly wrong! For reliable online news, one cannot easily beat *Egyptology Resources* (http://www.newton.cam.ac.uk/egypt/), run by Nigel Strudwick, and providing links to most reputable Egyptological websites. It goes without saying that cyberspace hosts many sites whose engagement with Egyptological reality is tangential!

BIBLIOGRAPHY

PYRAMIDS

ALDRED, C. 1949. *Old Kingdom Art in Egypt* (London: Tirani).

ARNOLD, Di. 1974–81. *Der Tempel des Königs Montjuhotpe von Deir el-Bahari*, 3vv (Mainz: Philipp von Zabern).

- 1976. *Gräber des Alten und Mittleren Reiches in El-Tarif* (Mainz: Philipp von Zabern).

- 1979a. *The Temple of Mentuhotep at Deir el-Bahri* (New York: MMA).

- 1979b. 'Das Labyrinth und seine Vorbilder'. *MDAIK* 35: 1–9.

- 1987. *Der Pyramidbezirk des Königs Amenemhet III in Dahschur I: Die Pyramide* (Mainz: Philipp von Zabern).

- 1988. *The Pyramid of Senwosret I* (New York: Metropolitan Museum of Art).

- 1991. *Building in Egypt: Pharaonic Stone Masonry* (New York: Oxford University Press).

- 1992. *The Pyramid Complex of Senwosret I* (New York: MMA).

- 1998. 'Royal Cult Complexes of the Old and Middle Kingdoms', *TAE*: 86–126.

- 2002. *The Encyclopedia of Ancient Egyptian Architecture* (London: I.B. Tauris).

ARNOLD, Di. and A. OPPENHEIM 1995. 'Reexcavating the Senwosret III Pyramid Complex at Dahshur', *KMT* 6/2: 44–56.

ARNOLD, Di. and R. STADELMANN 1975. 'Dahschur: Grabungsberichte', *DAIK* 31: 169–174.

ARNOLD, Do. 1991. 'Amenemhat I and the early Twelfth Dynasty at Thebes', *MMJ* 26: 5–48.

AYRTON, E., C.T. CURRELLY and A.E.P. WEIGALL 1904. *Abydos III* (London: EEF).

BADAWY, A. 1954–68. *A History of Egyptian Architecture*, 3vv. (Cairo; Berkeley: University of California Press).

BAINES, J. and J. MÁLEK 1980. *Atlas of Ancient Egypt* (New York and Oxford: Facts on File).

BARSANTI, A. 1902–12. 'Fouilles de Zaouiét el-Aryân', *ASAE* 7: 257–86; 8: 201–10; 12: 57–63.

BAUD, M. 1997. 'Aux pieds de Djoser: les mastabas entre fosse et enceinte de la partie nord du complexe funéraire', *Études Lauer*: 69–87.

BELZONI, G. 1820. *Narrative of the Operations and Recent Discoveries in Egypt and Nubia* (London: John Murray).

BERLANDINI, J. 1979. 'La pyramide "ruinée" de Sakkara-nord et le roi Ikaouhor-Menkaouhor', *RdE* 31: 3–28.

BORCHARDT, L. 1907. *Das Grabdenkmal des Königs Ne-user-re'* (Leipzig: Heinrichs').

- 1909. *Das Grabdenkmal des Königs Nefer-ir-ka-re'* (Leipzig: Heinrichs').

- 1910–13. *Das Grabdenkmal des Königs S'a3hu-re'*, 2vv (Leipzig: Heinrichs').

BOURRIAU, J.D. 1988. *Pharaohs and Mortals: Egyptian art in the Middle Kingdom* (Cambridge: University Press).

BRUNTON, G. 1920. *Lahun I: The Treasure* (London: BSAE).

CARTER, H. 1901. 'Report on the tomb of Mentuhotep Ist at Deir el-Bahari, known as Bab el-Hoçan', *ASAE* 2: 201–205.

COTTRELL, L. 1956. *The Mountains of Pharaoh* (London: Robert Hale).

DAVID, R. 1986. *The Pyramid Builders of Ancient Egypt* (London: Routledge & Kegan Paul).

DAWSON, W.R., E.P. UPHILL and M.L. BIERBRIER 1995. *Who Was Who in Egyptology*, 3rd edition (London: EES).

DE MORGAN, J. 1895, 1903. *Fouilles à Dahchour* I, II (Vienna: Adolphe Holzhausen).

- 1997. *Mémoirs de Jacques de Morgan* (Paris and Montreal: L'Harmattan).

DODSON, A.M. 1987. 'The Tombs of the Kings of the Thirteenth Dynasty in the Memphite Necropolis', *ZÄS* 114: 36–45.

- 1988a. 'The Tombs of the Queens of the Middle Kingdom', *ZÄS* 115: 123–36.

- 1988b. 'Egypt's first antiquarians?'. *Antiquity* 62/236: 513–17.

- 1994. *The Canopic Equipment of the Kings of Egypt* (London: Kegan Paul International).

- 1996. 'Mysterious Second Dynasty', *KMT* 7/2: 19–31.

- 1997. 'The Strange Affair of Dr Muses', *KMT* 8/3: 60–63.

- 1998. 'On The Threshold of Glory: The Third Dynasty', *KMT* 9/2: 26–40.

- 2000a. *After the Pyramids* (London: Rubicon).

- 2000b. 'The Layer Pyramid at Zawiyet el-Aryan: Its Layout and Context', *JARCE* 38: 81–90.

DODSON, A.M. and D.L. HILTON 2004. *The Royal Family in Ancient Egypt: a genealogical sourcebook* (London: Thames and Hudson).

DODSON, A.M. and S. IKRAM 2007. *The Tomb in*

Ancient Egypt (London: Thames and Hudson).

DONADONI ROVERI, A.M. 1969. *I sarcophagi egizi dalle origini alla fine dell' Antico Regno* (Rome: Università degli Studi di Roma).

DREYER, G. and N. SWELIM 1982. 'Die kleine Stufen-pyramide von Abydos-Süd (Sinki)', *MDAIK* 38: 83–95.

DUNHAM, D. 1950. *El-Kurru* (Boston: MFA).

- 1955. *Nuri* (Boston: MFA).

- 1958. *Royal Tombs at Meroe and Barkal* (Boston: MFA).

- 1963. *The West and South Cemeteries at Meroe* (Boston: MFA).

DUNHAM, D. and S.E. CHAPMAN 1952. *Decorated Chapels of the Meroitic Pyramids at Meroe and Barkal* (Boston: MFA).

EDWARDS, I.E.S. 1947/85. *The Pyramids of Egypt* (3rd edition) (Harmondsworth: Penguin).

- 1965. 'Lord Dufferin's Excavations at Deir el-Bahri and the Clandeboye Collection', *JEA* 51: 16–28.

- 1994. 'Do the Pyramid Texts suggest an explanation for the abandonment of the subterranean chamber of the Great Pyramid?', *Hommages Leclant*, I: 161–7.

- 1997. 'The Pyramid of Seila and its Place in the Succession of Snofru's Pyramids', in E. Goring, N. Reeves and J. Ruffle (eds.), *Chief of Seers: Egyptian Studies in Memory of Cyril Aldred* (London: Kegan Paul International): 88–96.

EL-KHOULI, A. 1991. *Meidum* (Sydney: Australian Centre for Egyptology).

EMERY, W.B. 1961. *Archaic Egypt* (Harmondsworth: Penguin).

FAKHRY, A. 1959–61. *The*

Monuments of Snefru at Dahshur, 2vv (Cairo: General Organisation for Government Printing Offices).

- 1961/72. The Pyramids, 2nd edition (Chicago: University Press).

FARAG, N. and Z. ISKANDER 1971. The Discovery of Neferwptah (Cairo: General Organization for Government Printing Offices).

FAULKNER, R.O. 1969. The Ancient Egyptian Pyramid Texts (Oxford: Griffith Institute).

FIRTH, C.M. and J.E. QUIBELL 1935. The Step Pyramid (Cairo: IFAO).

GASM EL SEED, A. 1985. 'La Tombe de Tanoutamon à El Kurru (KU. 16)', RdE 36: 67–72.

GAUTIER, J.E. and G. JÉQUIER 1902. Memoire sur les fouilles de Licht (Cairo: IFAO).

GONEIM, M.Z. 1956. The Buried Pyramid (London: Longman, Green)/The Lost Pyramid (New York: Rinehart).

- 1957. Horus Sekhemkhet: The Unfinished Step Pyramid at Saqqara, I (Cairo: IFAO).

GREENER, L. 1966. The Discovery of Egypt (London: Cassell).

GRINSELL, L. 1947. Egyptian Pyramids (Gloucester: John Bellows).

HARPUR, Y. 2001. The Tombs of Nefermaat and Rahotep at Maidum: Discovery, Destruction and Reconstruction (Oxford: Oxford Expedition to Egypt).

HARVEY, S.P 1994. 'Monuments of Ahmose at Abydos', EgArch 4: 3–5.

- 2001. 'Tribute To A Conquering King', Archaeology 54/4.

HASSAN, S. 1932–60.

Excavations at Gîza, 10vv (Cairo:

HAWASS, Z. 2000. 'Recent discoveries in the pyramid complex of Teti at Saqqara', in AS2000: 413–444.

HAYES, W.C. 1953, 1959. Scepter of Egypt, I, II (Cambridge, MA: Harvard University Press).

HÖLSCHER, U. 1912. Das Grabdenkmal des Königs Chephren (Leipzig: Heinrichs').

HORNUNG, H. 1990. Valley of the Kings: Horizon of Eternity (New York: Timken).

IKRAM, S. and A.M. DODSON, 1998. The Mummy in Ancient Egypt: Equipment for Eternity (London and New York: Thames and Hudson; Cairo: American University in Cairo Press).

JANOSI, P. 1996. Die Pyramidenanlagen der Königinnen: Untersuchungen zu einem Grabtyp des Alten und Mittleren Reiches (Vienna: Akademie der Wissenschaften).

JÉQUIER, G. 1928a. Le MastabatFaraoun (Cairo: IFAO).

- 1928b. Le Pyramide d'Oudjebten (Cairo: IFAO).

- 1929. Tombeaux de particuliers contemporains de Pepi II (Cairo: IFAO).

- 1933. Les Pyramides des Reines Neit et Apouit (Cairo: IFAO).

- 1935. La Pyramide d'Aba (Cairo: IFAO).

- 1936–8. Le monument funéraire de Pepi II, 2vv (Cairo: IFAO).

- 1938. Deux pyramides du Moyen Empire (Cairo: IFAO).

- 1940. Douze ans de fouilles dans la Nécropole Memphite (Neuchâtel: Secrétariat de l'université).

KAISER, W. and G. DREYER 1979. 'Zu den kleinen

Stufenpyramiden Ober- und Mittelägyptens', MDAIK 36: 43–59.

KAMAL, A. 1912. 'Fouilles à Dara et à Qoçéir el-Amarna', ASAE 12: 128–42.

KEMP, B.J. 1966. 'Abydos and the Royal Tombs of the First Dynasty', JEA 52: 13–22.

- 1967. 'The Egyptian First Dynasty Royal Cemetery', Antiquity 41: 22–32.

LABROUSSE, A. 1994. 'Les reines de Teti, Khouit et Ipout I, recherches architecturales', Hommages Leclant, I: 231–44.

- 1996–2000. L'architecture des pyramides à textes, 2vv (Cairo: IFAO).

- 1999. Les pyramides des reines. Une nouvelle nécropole à Saqqâra (Paris: Hazen).

LABROUSSE, A. and J.-Ph. LAUER 2000. Les complexes funéraires d'Ouserkaf et de Néferhétepes (Cairo: IFAO).

LABROUSSE, A, J.-P. LAUER and J. LECLANT 1977, Le Temple haut du complexe funéraire du roi Ounas (Cairo: IFAO).

LABROUSSE, A. and A.M. MOUSSA 1996, Le temple d'accueil du complexe funéraire du roi Ounas (Cairo: IFAO).

- 2002. La chaussée du complexe funéraire du roi Ounas (Cairo: IFAO).

LANDUA-MACCORMACK, D. 2002. 'Evidence for XIII Dynasty Royal Mortuary Activity at South Abydos', in 53rd Annual Meeting of the American Research Center in Egypt (Baltimore: Johns Hopkins University): 62–3.

LAUER, J.-Ph. 1936–9. La pyramide à degrés, I-III (Cairo: IFAO).

- 1976. Saqqara, Royal Necropolis of Memphis (London: Thames and Hudson).

LAUER, J.-Ph. and J. LECLANT 1972. Le temple

haut du complexe funéraire du roi Téti (Cairo: IFAO).

LAWTON, I. and C. OGILVIE-HERALD 1999. Giza: the Truth (London: Virgin).

LEHNER, M. 1985. The Pyramid Tomb of Hetepheres and the Satellite Pyramid of Khufu (Mainz: Philipp von Zabern).

- 1996. 'Z500 and the Layer Pyramid of Zaiyet el-Aryan', in P. Der Manuelian (ed.), Studies in Honor of William Kelly Simpson (Boston: MFA).

- 1997. The Complete Pyramids (London and New York: Thames and Hudson).

LEPSIUS, C.R. 1849–59. Denkmaeler aus Aegypten und Aethiopien, 6vv (Berlin/Leipzig: Nicolaische Buchandlung).

- 1897. Denkmaeler aus Aegypten und Aethiopien, Text (ed. E. Naville, L. Borchardt and K. Sethe) (Leipzig: J.C. Heinrichs').

LYTHGOE, A.M. 1907–8. 'Egyptian Expedition', BMMA 2: 163–69; 3: 183–4.

MACE, A.C. 1914. 'Excavations at the North Pyramid of Lisht', BMMA 9: 207-22.

- 1921-2. 'Excavations at Lisht', BMMA 16 Part II: 5–19; 17 Part II: 4–18.

MALEK, J. 1994. 'King Merykare and his Pyramid', in Hommages Leclant, I: 203–14.

MARAGIOGLIO, V. and C.A. RINALDI 1962. Notizie sulle piramidi di Zedefrâ, Zedkarâ Isesi, Teti (Turin: Tip. Artale).

- 1964–77, L'architettura delle Piramidi Menfite, II–VIII (Rapallo: Officine Grafiche Canessa).

- 1968. 'Nota sulla piramide di Ameny 'Aamu', Orientalia NS 37: 325–38.

MOND, R. 1905. 'Report of work in the necropolis of

Thebes during the winter of 1903–04', *ASAE* 6: 78–80.

MUNRO, P. 1993. *Der Unas-Friedhof Nord-West, I* (Mainz: Philipp von Zabern).

MURNANE, W.J. 1996. *The Penguin Guide to Ancient Egypt* (2nd edition) (London: Penguin).

NAVILLE, E. and H.R. HALL 1907–13. *The XIth Dynasty Temple at Deir el-Bahari*, 3vv (London: EEF).

OPPENHEIM, A, 1995. 'A First Look at Recently Discovered 12th Dynasty Royal Jewelry from Dahshur', *KMT* 6/1: 10–11.

PETRIE, W.M.F. 1883. *The Pyramids and Temples of Gizeh* (London: Field and Tuer).

- 1889. *Hawara, Biahmu and Arsinoe* (London: Field and Tuer).

- 1891. *Illahun, Kahun and Gorub. 1889–1890.* (London: David Nutt).

- 1892. *Medum* (London: D. Nutt).

- 1896. *Naqada and Ballas 1895* (London: B. Quaritch).

- 1900. *Dendereh* (London: EEF).

- 1901a. *The Royal Tombs of the Earliest Dynasties*, 2vv (London: EEF).

PETRIE, W.M.F, E. MACKAY and G. WAINWRIGHT, 1910. *Meydum and Memphis III* (London: ERA).

PETRIE, W.M.F. et al. 1912. *The Labyrinth, Gerzeh and Mazghuneh* (London: BSAE).

PETRIE, W.M.F. et al. 1923. *Lahun II* (London: BSAE).

PETRIE, W.M.F. et al. 1925. *The Tombs of the Courtiers and Oxyrhynkhos* (London: BSAE).

PIANKOFF, A. 1968. *The Pyramid of Unas* (New York: Bollingen).

PICKAVANCE, K.M. 1981. 'The Pyramids of Snofru at Dahshur: Three

Seventeenth-Century Travellers', *JEA* 67: 136–42.

POCOCKE, R. 1743–5. A *Description of the East, and some other countries* (London: J. and P. Knapton, W. Innys, W. Meadows, G. Hawkins, S. Birt, T. Longman, C. Hitch, R. Dodsley, J. Nourse, and J. Rivington).

POLZ, D. and A. SEILER 2003. *Die Pyramidenanlage des Königs Nub-Cheper-Re Intef in Dra' Abu el-Naga* (Mainz: Philipp von Zabern).

- 2003a. 'Die Grabanlage des Konigs Nub-Cheper-Re Intef in Dra' Abu el-Naga - Ein Vorbericht', *MDAIK* 59.

- 2003b. 'The pyramid complex of king Nubkheperre Intef', *EgArch* 22: 12–15.

PORTER, B. and R.B. MOSS 1933–99. *Topographical Bibliography of Ancient Egyptian Hieroglyphic Texts, Reliefs and Paintings*, 8vv, VIII by J. Malek, D. Magee and E. Miles. (Oxford: Griffith Institute).

RANDALL-MACIVER, D. and A.C. MACE 1902. *El Amrah and Abydos* (London: EES).

REEVES, N. & R. WILKINSON 1996. *The Complete Valley of the Kings* (London & New York: Thames & Hudson).

REISNER, G.A. 1931. *Mycerinus: the temples of the Third Pyramid at Giza* (Cambridge MA: Harvard UP).

- 1936. *The Development of the Egyptian Tomb Down to the Accession of Cheops.* (Oxford: University Press/Cambridge, MA: Harvard University Press).

- 1942. *A History of the Giza Necropolis, I* (Cambridge, MA: Harvard University Press).

REISNER, G.A. and W.S. SMITH 1955. *A History of*

the Giza Necropolis, II (Cambridge, MA: Harvard University Press).

RIDLEY, R.T. 1983. 'The Discovery of the Pyramid Texts', *ZÄS* 110: 74–80.

ROWE, A. 1931. 'Excavations of the Eckley B. Cox, Jr. Expedition at Meydum, Egypt, 1929–30, *Pannsylvania University Museum Journal* 22 (1931): 3–46.

RYHOLT, K.S.B. 1997. *The Political Situation in Egypt During the Second Intermediate Period, c. 1800–1550 B.C.* (Copenhagen: Museum Tusculanum Press).

SALEH, M. and H. SOUROUZIAN 1987. *The Egyptian Museum Cairo: Official Catalogue* (Mainz/Cairo: Philipp von Zabern).

SANDYS, G. 1673. *The relation of a Journey begun in An. Dom. 1610*, 7th ed. (London: John Williams Junior, at the Crown in Little-Britain).

SHARP, D. 2001. 'German Excavators Find a Royal Tomb of the 17th Dynasty at Dra Abu el Naga', *KMT* 12/3: 8.

SILOTTI, A. 1996. *Guide to the Valley of the Kings* (London: Wiedenfield and Nicholson).

- 1997. *The Pyramids* (London: Weidenfeld and Nicholson).

SMITH, W.S. 1949. *History of Egyptian Sculpture and Painting in the Old Kingdom2* (Oxford: University Press).

- 1981. *The Art and Architecture of Ancient Egypt*, rev. W.K. Simpson Harmondsworth: Penguin)

SPENCER, A.J. 1979. *Brick Architecture in Ancient Egypt* (Warminster: Aris and Phillips).

- 1982. *Death in Ancient Egypt* (Harmondsworth: Penguin).

- 1993. *Early Egypt: the Rise of Civilisation in the Nile Valley*

(London: BMP).

STADELMANN, R. 1991. *Die ägyptischen Pyramiden* (Mainz: Philipp von Zabern).

STADELMANN, R. et al. 1982–3. 'Die Pyramiden des Snofru in Dahshur', *MDAIK* 38: 379–93; 39: 228–9.

- 1993. 'Pyramiden und nekropole des Snofru in Dahshur', *MDAIK* 49: 259–94.

STIÉNON, J. 1950. 'El Kôlah: Mission de la Fondation Égyptologique Reine Élisabeth, 1949', *CdE* 49: 43–5.

STROUHAL, E., V. ČERNY and L. VYHNÁNEK 2000. 'An X-ray examination of the mummy found in pyramid Lepsius No. XXIV' *AS2000*: 543–50.

STROUHAL, E. and M.F. GABALLAH 1993. 'King Djedkare Isesi and his Daughters', in W.V. Davis and R. Walker (eds.), *Biological Anthropology and the Study of Ancient Egypt* (London: BMP): 104–18.

STROUHAL, E. and L. VYHNÁNEK 2000. 'The identification of the remains of King Neferefra found in his pyramid at Abusir' *AS2000*: 551–60.

SWELIM, N. 1983. *Some Problems on the History of the Third Dynasty* (Alexandria: The Archaeological Society of Alexandria).

- 1987. *The Brick Pyramid at Abu Rowash, Number '1' by Lepsius: a preliminary study* (Alexandria: The Archaeological Society of Alexandria).

- 1994. 'Pyramid Research from the Archaic to the Second Intermediate Period: Lists, catalogues and Objectives', in *Hommages Leclant*, I: 337–49

SWELIM, N. and A. DODSON 1998. 'On the Pyramid of Ameny-Qemau and its Canopic Equipment', *MDAIK* 54: 319–34.

TAYLOR, J.H. 1989. *Egyptian Coffins* (Princes Risborough: Shire Publications).

THOMAS, E. 1966. *The Royal Necropoleis of Thebes* (Princeton: privately printed).

UPHILL, E.P. 2000. *Pharaoh's Gateway to Eternity: The Hawara Labyrinth of King Amenemhat III* (London & New York: Kegan Paul International).

VALERIANI, D. 1837. *Atlante del basso ed alto Egitto* (Florence).

VALLOGGIA, M. 2001. *Au cœur d'une pyramide. Une mission archéologique en Egypte* (Lausanne: Musée romain de Lausanne-Vidy).

VERNER, M. 1982. 'Excavations at Abusir. Season 1980/1 – Preliminary Report', ZÄS 109: 75–8.

- 1994a. *Forgotten Pharaohs, Lost Pyramids* (Prague: Akademia/Skodaexport).

- 1994b. 'Abusir Pyramids 'Lepsius no. XXIV and no. XXV', in *Hommages Leclant*: 371–8.

- 1995. *The Pyramid Complex of the Royal Mother Khentkaus* (Prague: Universitas Carolina Pragensis/Academia).

- 2000. 'Who was Shepsekara, and when did he reign?', *AS2000*: 581–602.

- 2001. *The Pyramids: The Mystery, Culture and Science of Egypt's Great Monuments* (New York: Grove Press).

- 2002. *Abusir: The Realm of Osiris* (Cairo & New York: AUC Press).

VYSE, R.W.H. 1840–42. *Operations carried on at the Pyramids of Gizeh in 1837*, 3vv (London: James Fraser/John Weale/G.W. Nickisson).

WEGNER, J. 1996. *The Mortuary Complex of Senwosret III: A Study of Middle Kingdom State Activity and the Cult of Osiris at Abydos* (Ann Arbor: UMI).

WEILL, R., Mme TONY-REVILLON and M. PILLET 1958. *Dara: campaignes de 1946–1948* (Cairo: Organisme Générale des Imprimeries Gouvernmentales).

WILKINSON, R.H. 2000. *The Complete Temples of Ancient Egypt* (London: Thames and Hudson).

WINLOCK, H.E. 1915. 'The Theban Necropolis in the Middle Kingdom', *AJSLL* 32: 1–37.

- 1924a. 'The Tombs of the Kings of the Seventeenth Dynasty at Thebes', *JEA* 10: 217–77.

- 1942. *Excavations at Deir el Bahri* (New York: Macmillan).

- 1947 *The Rise and Fall of the Middle Kingdom in Thebes* (New York: Macmillan).

HIEROGLYPHS
GENERAL

ALDRED, C. 1998. *The Egyptians*, 3rd edition, revised by A. Dodson (London: Thames and Hudson)

DAVIS, W.V. 1987. *Egyptian Hieroglyphs* (London: British Museum Press)

DODSON, A. 1996/2001. *Monarchs of the Nile* (London: Rubicon Press/Cairo: American University in Cairo Press)

KEMP, B.J. 1989. *Ancient Egypt: Anatomy of a Civilisation* (London: Routledge)

MANLEY, B. 1996. *The Penguin Historical Atlas of Ancient Egypt* (London: Penguin, 1996)

REDFORD, D.B. 2001 (ed.) *The Oxford Encyclopedia of Ancient Egypt* (New York: Oxford University Press)

SHAW, I. (Ed) 2000. *The Oxford History of Ancient Egypt* (Oxford: Oxford University Press)

THE ORIGINS OF EGYPTIAN LANGUAGE

BAINES, J. & J. MALEK 1980. *Atlas of Ancient Egypt* (New York and Oxford: Facts on File)

MOST ANCIENT EGYPT

ADAMS, B. 1995. *Ancient Nekhen: Garstang in the City of Hierakonpolis* (New Malden: Sia Publishing)

HOFFMAN, M.A. 1980. *Egypt Before the Pharaohs* (London: Routledge and Kegan Paul)

MIDANT-REYNES, B. 2000. *The Prehistory of Egypt* (Oxford: Blackwell)

THE DAWN OF WRITING

BAINES, J. 1989. 'Commununication and display: the integration of early Egyptian art and writing', *Antiquity* 63: 471–82

BAINES, J. 1999. 'Writing, invention and early development', *EAE*, 882–5

DAVIS, W. V. 1992. *Masking the Blow: The Scene of Representation in Late Prehistoric Egyptian Art* (Berkeley: University of Californian Press)

DREYER, G. 1998. *Umm el-Qaab I. Das prädynastiche Königsgrab U-j und seine frühen Schriftzeugnisse* (Mainz: Philipp von Zabern)

DREYER, G. 1999. 'Abydos Umm el-Qa'ab', *EAE*: 109–14

RAY, J.D. 1986. 'The Emergence of Writing in Egypt', *World Archaeology* 17/3: 307–16

EGYPTIAN NAMES AND TITLES

BECKERATH, J. von 1984/1999. *Handbuch der ägyptischen Königsnamen* (Munich: Deutscher Kunstverlag/ Mainz: Philipp von Zabern)

QUIRKE, S. 1990. *Who were the Pharaohs?* (London: British Museum Press)

THE ANCIENT EGYPTIAN LANGUAGE

ALLEN, J.P. 2000. *Middle Egyptian: An Introduction to the Language and Culture of Hieroglyphs* (Cambridge: Cambridge University Press)

COLLIER, M. and B. MANLEY 1998. *How to Read Egyptian Hieroglyphs* (London: British Museum Press)

DEPUYOT, L. 1999. *Fundamentals of Egyptian Grammar (Part I: Elements)* (Norton/Merken: Frog Publishing)

ERMAN, A. and H. GRAPOW 1926–31. *Wörterbuch der ägyptischen Sprache*, 5vv (Leipzig: Heinrichs')

GARDINER, Sir A. 1957. *Egyptian Grammar: being an introduction to the study of hieroglyphs*, 3rd edition (Oxford: Griffith Institute)

FAULKNER, R.O. 1962. *A Concise Dictionary of Middle Egyptian* (Oxford: Griffith Institute)

GELB, I.J. 1963. *A Study of Writing*, rev. edn. (Chicago: Chicago University Press)

LOPRIENO, A. 1995. *Ancient Egyptian: A Linguistic Introduction* (Cambridge: Cambridge University Press).

MÖLLER, G. 1909–12. *Hieratische Paläographie* (Leipzig: Heinrichs)

THOMPSON, S.E. 1999. 'Egyptian language and writing', *EAE*: 274–7

THREE MILLENNIA OF WRITING

BAINES, J.R. 1983. 'Literacy and Ancient Egyptian Society', *Man* 18: 572-99

CERNY, J. 1952. *Paper and books in Ancient Egypt* (London: H.K. Lewis, reprinted Chicago: Ares Press)

DAVIES, N.M. 1958. *Picture Writing in Ancient Egypt*

(Oxford: Oxford University Press)

GOEDICKE, H. 1972. 'Hieroglyphic Inscriptions of the Old Kingdom', in *Textes et languages de'Égypte pharaonique. Cent cinqante ans de recherches (1822-1972). Hommage à J.-F. Champollion* (Cairo: IFAO): 16–24.

HARRIS, J.R. (ed.) 1971. *The Legacy of Egypt* (Oxford: Clarendon Press).

JAMES, T.G.H., 1984. *Pharaoh's People* (London: Bodley Head; New York: Oxford University Press)

LICHTHEIM, M. 1975–80. *Ancient Egyptian Literature*, 3vv (Berkeley: University of California Press)

MERTZ, B. 1978. *Red Land, Black Land* (New York: Dodd, Mead & Co.)

PARKINSON, R.B., 1991. *Voices from Ancient Egypt* (London: British Museum Press)

SCHÄFER, H. 1974. *Principles of Egyptian Art* (Oxford: Oxford University Press)

SIMPSON, W.K. (ed.) 1972. *The Literature of Ancient Egypt* (New Haven and London: Yale University Press)

SMITH, W.S., 1998. *The Art and Architecture of Ancient Egypt*, rev by W.K. Simpson (New Haven: Yale University Press)

WILKINSON, R.H. 1994. *Symbol and Magic in Egyptian Art* (London: Thames and Hudson)

INSCRIPTIONS FOR THE GODS

SCHAFER, B.E. (ed.) 1997. *Temples of Ancient Egypt* (London: I.B. Tauris)

SCHWALLER DE LUBCZ, R.A. 1999. *The Temples of Karnak* (London: Thames and Hudson)

THE TEXTS OF BURIAL

DODSON, A. and S. IKRAM 2004. *The Tomb in Ancient Egypt* (London: Thames & Hudson)

FAULKNER, R.O. 1969. *The Ancient Egyptian Pyramid Texts* (Oxford: University Press)

FAULKNER, R.O. 1994. *The Egyptian Book of the Dead* (San Francisco: Chronicle Books)

HORNUNG, E. 1990. *The Valley of the Kings: Horizon of Eternity* (New York: Timken Publishers)

HORNUNG, E., 1999. *The Ancient Egyptian Books of the Afterlife* (Ithaca & London: Cornell University Press)

IKRAM, S. and A. DODSON 1998. *The Mummy in Ancient Egypt* (London: Thames and Hudson)

SPENCER, J. 1982. *Death in Ancient Egypt* (Harmondsworth: Penguin)

HISTORICAL INSCRIPTIONS

BREASTED, J.H. 1905. *Ancient Records of Egypt*, 5vv (Chicago: Chicago University Press; reprinted London: Histories and Mysteries of Man, 1988)

CHRONICLES

REDFORD, D.B. l986. *Pharaonic King-Lists, Annals and Day-Books* (Mississauga: Benben)

EXPEDITION RECORDS

ALBRIGHT, W.F. 1966. *The Proto-Sinaitic Inscriptions and their Decipherment* (Cambridge MA: Harvard University Press)

GARDINER, A.H. 1916. 'The Egyptian Origin of the Semitic Alphabet', *JEA* 3: 1–16

TEXTS OF MAGIC AND MEDICINE

NUNN, J.F. 1996. *Ancient Egyptian Medicine* (London: British Museum Press)

THE MYSTERY OF THE HIEROGLYPHS

HORAPOLLO 1993. The *Hieroglyphics of Horapollo*, translated and introduced by G. Boas (Princeton: University Press)

IVERSEN, E. 1961/1993. *The Myth of Egypt and Its Hieroglyphs in European Tradition* (Copenhagen: Gadd/Princeton: University Press)

DECIPHERMENT OF HIEROGLYPHS

ADKINS, L. and R. 2000. *The Keys of Egypt: The Race to Read the Hieroglyphs*. (London: HarperCollins)

ANDREWS, C. 1981. *The Rosetta Stone* (London: British Museum Press)

BUDGE, E.A.W. 1893. 'Memoir of Samuel Birch', *TSBA* 9: 1–43

BUDGE, E.A.W. 1904. *The Decrees of Mamphis and Canopus*, 3vv (London: Kegan Paul, Trench, Trübner)

BUDGE, E.A.W. 1920. An *Egyptian Hieroglyphic Dictionary*, I (London: John Murray): v–lxxiv

BUDGE, E.A.W. 1925. 'The Decipherment of the Egyptian Hieroglyphs', in *The Mummy* (Cambridge: University Press): 123–64

COMMISSION DES MONUMENTS D'ÉGYPTE 1809–22. *Description de l'Égypte, ou Recueil des observations et des recherches qui ont été faites en Égypte pendent l'expédition de l'armée français: Antiquités* (Planches), 9 + 10vv (Paris: Imprimerie impériale)

DAWSON, W.R. 1958. 'The Discoverer of the Rosetta Stone: a Correction', *JEA* 44: 123

DAWSON, W.R. and E.P. UPHILL 1995. *Who Was Who in Egyptology*, 3rd edition by M.L. Bierbrier

(London: Egypt Exploration Society)

DEPUYOT, L. 1999. 'Egyptian (language), deciperment of', *EAE*: 271–4

GRIFFITH, F.Ll. 1951. 'The Decipherment of the Hieroglyphs', *JEA* 37: 38–46

HALL, H.R. 1916. 'Letters of Champollion le Jeune and of Seyffarth to Sir William Gell', *JEA* 2: 76–87

IVERSEN, E. 1972. 'The Bankes Obelisk', in *Obelisks in Exile*, II (Copenhagen: Gadd): 62–85

KAMAL, A. 1904–5. *Stèles ptolémaiques et romaines* (Cairo: Institut français d'archéologie orientale)

MAYES, S. 1959. *The Great Belzoni* (London)

PARKINSON, R. 1999. *Cracking Codes: the Rosetta Stone and Decipherment* (London: British Museum Press)

POPE, M. 1999. *The Story of Decipherment, from Egyptian Hieroglyyphs to Maya Script*, revised edition (London: Thames & Hudson)

RENOUF, Sir P. Le Page 1859. 'Seyffarth and Uhleman on Egyptian Hieroglyphics', *Atlantis* 1859, II/3: 74–97, reprinted in G. Maspero and W.H Rylands (eds), *The Life Work of Sir Peter Le Page Renouf I* (Paris: Ernest Leroux, 1902): 1–31

RENOUF, Sir P. 1862. 'Dr Seyffarth and the Atlantis on Egyptology' *Atlantis* III/6: 306–38, reprinted in *Life Work*: 33–80

SIMPSON, R.S. 1996. *Demotic Grammar in the Ptolemaic Sacerdotal Decrees* (Oxford: Griffith Institute)

VERCOUTTER, J. 1992. *The Search for Ancient Egypt* (London: Thames & Hudson)

INDEX

PICTURE ACKNOWLEDGEMENTS

Where appropriate, the photographer/artist is followed by the owner of the object and the object's museum number; for museum abbreviations see page 267:
t = top; c = centre; b = bottom; l =left; r =right

AMD Aidan Dodson
A Axiom Photographic Agency Ltd

Front cover: AMD/Louvre N3292; Back cover (l): E. Simanor/A, (c): James Morris/A, (r): Pictures Colour Library Ltd; Spine: James Morris/A; Author image: Dyan Hilton

3 Pictures Colour Library Ltd; 4: AMD/CM CG14; 5: AMD; 8–17: AMD; 18: V. Denon, *Voyage dans la Basse et la Haute Egypte*, II (Paris, 1802), pl. 20bis[1]; 19: *Illustrated London News* 1895; 20–23: AMD; 24: Sandys 1673: 106; 25 (t): Pococke 1743–35: pl. XVIII, (b): AMD; 26 (t): Vyse 1840–42, (b): AMD; 27 (l): AMD collection, (b): *Illustrated London News* 1895, (r): G. Brunton, *ASAE* 48 (1948); 28 (l): AMD collection, (r): AMD/Louvre; 29: AMD collection; p.30: Pictures Colour Library Ltd; 32: Pictures Colour Library Ltd; 33: The Ancient Egypt Picture Library; 34 (t): David Moyer/BM EA32751, (bl): AMD/BM EA58522, (bc): AMD/BM EA36327, (br): AMD/ Ashmolean Museum E 3632; 35 (t): AMD, (bl): AMD/Louvre E11007, (bc): AMD/BM EA32650, (br): AMD/BM EA35597; 36–7: AMD; 38 (t): AMD, (b) Leslie Grinsell Collection, courtesy of Bristol's City Museum & Art Gallery; 39: AMD/BM EA35597; 40 (t): Pictures Colour Library Ltd., (bl): AMD, (bcl): AMD/CM JE36143, (bcr): AMD/CM CG14, (br): AMD/CM JE–79195; 41 (t): AMD, (bl): AMD/Louvre E3023, (br): AMD/CM JE65908; 42: AMD; 43: Girolamo Segato, from Valeriani 1837: pl.37D; 44–5: AMD; 46: Royal Air Force, from Leslie Grinsell Collection, courtesy of Bristol's City Museum & Art Gallery; 47: Lepsius 1859: I, pl. 12; 48: Tarek Swelim, courtesy of Nabil Swelim; 49–51: AMD; 52: AMD/CM JE98943; 53: Dyan Hilton; 54: AMD; 55: Dennis C. Forbes; 56: AMD; 57 (t): AMD, (b): Leslie Grinsell, courtesy of Department of Archaeology & Anthropology, University of Bristol; 58–9: AMD; 60 (t): Leslie Grinsell Collection, courtesy of Bristol's City Museum & Art Gallery, (b): AMD; 61: AMD; 62: AMD/CM CG15; 63–6: AMD; 67: AMD/CM JE39532; 68–70: AMD; 71 (t): AMD/Louvre E3028, (b): AMD; 72–9: AMD; 80: AMD (t): , (bl): AMD/BM EA720. (bcl): AMD/Louvre A23, (bcr): MMA 26.7.1394, (br): AMD/CM CG392; 81 (br): AMD/CM CG259, (bcl): Leslie Grinsell, courtesy of Department of Archaeology & Anthropology, University of Bristol/CM JE53668, (bcr): AMD/ CM CG42027, (br): AMD/Louvre E.3020 and E.3019; 82: Leslie Grinsell, courtesy of Bristol's City Museum & Art Gallery; 84–6: AMD; 87: AMD/CM JE58909+58910+58914; 88: AMD; 90 (t): Petrie et al. 1923; 91: AMD/CM CG23043; 92: Adela Oppenheim, courtesy of the Egyptian Expedition of The Metropolitan Museum of Art, New York; 93: Josef Wegner; 94: AMD; 96: AMD/CM CG42022; 97–101: AMD; 102 (t): AMD/CM JE53045, (b): Leslie Grinsell, courtesy of Bristol's City Museum & Art Gallery; 104: AMD/CM TR 5/1/15/12; 105: AMD; 106: AMD/Brussels Royal Museum of Art & History E.6857; 107 (t): AMD/BM EA478, (b): AMD/Louvre E3020, E3019; 108: AMD; 109: G. Elliot Smith, *The Royal Mummies* (Cairo, 1912); 110: AMD; 111: Laura Foos, courtesy of Stephen P. Harvey; 112–13: AMD; 114–17: Jacke Phillips; 118–128: AMD; 129 (t): AMD, (b): Leslie Grinsell, courtesy of Bristol's City Museum & Art Gallery/CM 47397; 130–32: AMD; 132: Petrie et al. 1923; 133: AMD; 134: AMD/CM JE90199, 90201/2;

136–7 Chris Caldicott/A; 138(t) AMD, (bl) AMD/BM EA 58522, (bc) AMD/BM EA 36327, (br) AMD/Louvre E11255; 139(t) AMD, (bc) Peter Wilson/A, (br) Chris Caldicott/A; 140 Chris Coe/A; 141(t) AMD, (b) AMD; 142–3 Chris Caldicott/A; 144(t) AMD/BM EA 32571, (b) AMD/CM; 145(t) AMD/Louvre E11255, (b) AMD/CM CG 14716; 147(t) AMD/ Ashmolean Museum E 3632, (b) AMD; 148 AMD/Louvre E 11007; 149(t) AMD/BM EA 32650,55586, (b) AMD/Louvre AO29562; 150 AMD/CM JE 79195; 151 AMD/CM JE 40678; 152(t) James Morris/A, (c) James Morris/A; 153 James Morris/A; 154 AMD/Munich GL.WAF 38; 155 AMD/OMD N 511; 156(l) James Morris/A, (r) James Morris/A; 157(l) James Morris/A, (r) James Morris/A; 158–9 James Morris/A 160(t) AMD, (bl) AMD/Louvre E11007, (bc) AMD Louvre A 23; 161(t) James Morris/A, (b) AMD/Louvre E12982; 164 AMD/Möller 1909–12; 165 AMD/Möller 1909–12; 166 AMD/RMS; 167 James Morris/A; 168 AMD/BM EA 5603; 169(tl) AMD/Louvre N328; 170 James Morris/A; 171(t) AMD/BM EA 884, (b) AMD/Louvre E12982; 172 AMD/Bristol H.4586; 173 AMD/BM EA 495; 174 James Morris/A ; 175 James Morris/A; 176(t) AMD/Louvre c 166; 176–7 James Morris/A; 178(t); 178–9 James Morris/A; 180 background AMD; 182 AMD/CM CG14; 183(t) James Morris/A, (bl) AMD/MFA 03.1631, (br) AMD/Manchester Museum; 184 AMD; 185(t) James Morris/A, (b) AMD/Louvre A23; 186(tl) Heidi Grassley/A, (tr) AMD, (b) AMD; 187(t) AMD, (b) AMD/CM JE 46993; 188(t) AMD, (b) AMD/BM 6666A; 189(t) James Morris/A, (b) AMD/ Louvre N3292; 190–1 AMD; 192 AMD/Luxor Museum J2; 193(t) AMD, (b) AMD; 194 James Morris/A; 195(t) James Morris/A, (b) James Morris/A; 196(t) James Morris/A, (b) AMD; 197(t) AMD, (b) AMD/CM CG 34010; 198(t) AMD/CM JE 65908, (bl) AMD/Turin N 1874, (br) AMD; 199(tl) James Morris/A, (br) AMD, (b) AMD; 200(t) AMD, (b) AMD; 201(t) James Morris/A, (c) AMD/RMS 1956.319, (b) AMD; 202(tl) AMD, (bl) AMD, (br) AMD/CM JE 57102; 203(t) AMD, (b) Sara Orel; 204(t) AMD/CM JE 36143; (b) AMD/Louvre E3023; 205 James Morris/A; 206–7 James Morris/A; 208 James Morris/A; 209(t) AMD/MMA, (b) AMD; 210 James Morris/A; 211 James H. Morris/A; 212 AMD/OMD; 213 James Morris/A; 214 Dyan Hilton; 215(t) AMD, (b) AMD; 216(t) AMD, (c) AMD, (b) E. Simanor/A; 217(tc) AMD, (r) AMD, (b) AMD; 218(c) AMD, (bl) AMD, (br) AMD/BM EA 1606; 219(t) AMD, (c) AMD, (bl) AMD/BM OA 10845, (br) Vanessa Fletcher; 220(t) Linda Pike, (b) James Morris/A; 221 (tl) AMD/BM EA 10, (tr) AMD, (b) AMD; 222(tl) E. Simanor/A, (tr) Chris Coe/A, (b) James Morris/A; 223(t) James Morris/A, (b) James Morris/A; 224(tl) Peter Clayton, (tc) Peter Clayton, (r) AMD; 225 AMD; 226(tl) AMD, (tc) AMD; 227(tl) Peter Clayton, (tr) AMD; 228(t) AMD, (bl) AMD, (br) AMD; 229(t) James Morris/A, (bl) AMD/BM EA 24, (br) AMD/Louvre; 230 AMD; 231(t) AMD/Commission des Monuments d'Egypte 1809–22 E.M.I. pl 81, (b) AMD/Commission des Monuments d'Egypte 1809–22 E.M.I. pl. 81; 232 AMD/BM EA 24; 233(t) AMD/Commission des Monuments d'Egypte 1809–22 A.V. pl. 52, (c) AMD Commission des Monuments d'Egypte 1809–22 A.V. pl. 53, (b) AMD/Commission des Monuments d'Egypte 1809–22 A.V. pl. 54; 234(t) AMD, (c) AMD/Louvre C 122, 235(t) AMD/*Illustrated London News*, 1874, (b) AMD/CM CG 22186; 236–7 James Morris/A; 238(t) AMD, (b) AMD/ Louvre; 239 AMD/Louvre N3073; 240 Heidi Grassley/A; 241(t) AMD/ Commission des Monuments d'Egypte 1809–22 A.I. pl. 17, (c) AMD; 242(t) AMD, (b) AMD; 243(t) AMD, (b) AMD; 244 AMD; 245 AMD; 246 AMD/ Budge 1893, facing p.1; 247 AMD; 249(tl) AMD, (br) AMD/Erman & Grapow 1926–31; 250 James Morris/A; 251(tl) AMD, (br) AMD, (b) AMD; 252–3 Chris Caldicott/A; 263 AMD; 264(tl) Chris Caldicott/A, (tr) James Morris/A, (b) AMD; 265 James Morris/A. 268 James Morris/A. 269 James Morris/A.

AUTHOR'S ACKNOWLEDGEMENTS

To my wife Dyan Hilton for continuing a relationship that began against the backdrop of pyramids and hieroglyphs; to both her and Sheila Hilton for their painstaking reading of the manuscript; to Salima Ikram for many years of companionship in and around pyramids; to Nabil Swelim, Josef Wegner, Adela Oppenheim and Dennis Forbes for the provision of photographs, and also to Nabil for many discussions regarding the pyramids and various offprints and advance copies of articles; to Miroslav Verner, Miroslav Bárta and Ladislav Bareš for many kindnesses over the years at 'their' site of Abusir, including the opportunity to climb the pyramid of Neferirkare – and get down again alive! Last but not least, to Professor John R. Harris and Dr Chris Eyre for first initiating me into the language of the hieroglyphs at the Universities of Durham and Liverpool.